RAPTURE:

A Transformation of Christ in You

Archbishop Audrey Drummonds, Ph.D.

authorHOUSE®

AuthorHouse™
1663 Liberty Drive
Bloomington, IN 47403
www.authorhouse.com
Phone: 833-262-8899

Published by AuthorHouse 09/28/2021

ISBN: 978-1-5462-1228-7 (sc)
ISBN: 978-1-5462-1227-0 (e)

Library of Congress Control Number: 2017916929

Print information available on the last page.

Other Books by Bishop Audrey Drummonds, PH.D.

Bringing Forth the Sons of God; Walking Spiritual Maturity

God's Redemption For All; Being One in Christ

The Book of Revelation (Vol 1); Christ in You, the Hope of Glory

The Book of Revelation (Vol. 2) Chapters 8-13

Living in the Inheritance of God

Rising to Royalty

CONTENTS

INTRODUCTION

*T*he phone rings… "Hello?"

"Is this Audrey Drummonds?"

"Yes, who's calling?"

"This is the doctor's office where you had your biopsy. I'm sorry Mrs. Drummonds, but the report came back positive. You have CANCER!"

What does one do with that information? How does one process those words?

Scream, yell, cry, deny, laugh and call the test wrong?

When people go through major trials of sudden negative information, a variety of emotions take place trying to categorize what to do with that knowledge. For me, it took me spiritually, mentally, and physically to the edge of confronting death in the face. My relationship with God was challenged daily with one minute praising Him, and then next falling apart, questioning if He was even real. Were all those promises in the Bible really for me NOW, or was I just entrapped by wanting to feel joyful, knowing I was confronted with death?

I knew how to quote Scriptures, teach doctrines, tell Bible stories all about Jesus, and lead people to the Lord in a prayer that gave them peace of knowing they were going to heaven someday, but what about NOW?

I had been passionate in my Christian faith before I had cancer for 50 + years, spending hours daily in Bible study and meditation. I had earned college and seminary degrees on the highest level, yet here I was at death's door questioning all that I knew.

Where was the RESURRECTION of Jesus today who heals the blind, restores the deaf ears, and raises the dead? This was the Jesus I needed to know NOW, not someday when I knew I would be with Him in Heaven. I needed to experience those words He shared for us to pray as my spirit, mind, and body were at its lowest, ready to give up.

> *"Our Father in heaven, Hallowed be Your name.*
> *Your kingdom come.*
> *Your will be done*
> *On earth as it is in heaven." (Luke 11:2)*

I would get angry with God, screaming for Him to show me these words NOW...Your Heavenly Kingdom Now on earth, not when I crossed over.

The amazing TRUTH in my journey is to testify His faithfulness, bringing the universe of Heaven's glory into my world one day at a time. Each chapter in this book has been part of the process of being transformed as I was being translated into His image called Christ – the glory of God. Each chapter stands alone with nuggets of Christ being unveiled in my earthen vessel to share with the world.

Today around the world there is a company of people that are preparing themselves as a bride for her beloved to come to rule and reign together in the earth. It's not just about going to Heaven someday when you leave your natural body, but while you are still alive in your natural body. It's about bringing what has already been completed in Heaven into the earth through you as a living letter of the CHRIST – the WORD made flesh and dwelling among men (John 1:14).

Before the fall of man in Genesis chapter three, the glory of God was in both Heaven and earth together as one glory. The glory of God departed from the earth after mankind ate the fruit from the Tree of Knowledge that brought death into the earth and separation of the relationship man had with God. After the death, burial, and resurrection of Jesus, the glory of God was restored back into the earth as Christ in You (Colossians 1:27). Jesus ascended into Heaven, but Christ remained in the earth in a people.

Today we have the potential of being raptured with the LOVE of the bridegroom, Jesus Christ, to be transformed by the renewing of our mind into one new man called Christ. We qualify today to share in the inheritance of the saints in light (Col. 1:12). We have been redeemed, forgiven, delivered, and translated from darkness and ignorance into the Kingdom of Christ (Col. 1:13).

When we were translated, we were removed from one dimension of minimal wisdom and understanding called darkness into a higher realm called Heaven. This higher realm was more than just the logic and reason of enlightment, but the LIGHT of God that is found in the Tree of Life. This is all taking place while we are in our natural body in the earth. What is sad is humanity leaving their natural body only to found out they had all the glorification of Christ already with them.

This unveiling of truth is One New Man – Christ all and in all with Jesus Christ the head, and humanity created in the image of God, the body and feet – the many members of one man.

"Blessed are the feet of them that bring the good news" (Romans 10:15).

Jesus Christ is the first-born, the head of the body (Col. 1:18). When a newborn baby is born, the head comes first into the world. The baby is not complete until the entire body is birthed. The Kingdom of God is the Kingdom of His Son whom we have been translated into called Christ (Col. 1:18). Christ is our life (Col. 3:4). It is Christ in you the image of God (Col. 1:15). It is Christ in you the power of God and wisdom of God (1 Corinthians 1:24).

It is this body called Christ we find the glory of God in Heaven and earth now. *"Now you are Christ body, and individually members of it"* (1 Corinthians 12:27).

Let us begin our transformation with the renewing of the spirit of our mind, putting on the new man – Christ, the likeness of God, you have already been created in as righteousness, and holiness of the Truth (Ephesians 4:23-24).

God saves us and calls us with a holy calling according to His own purpose and grace granted in Jesus Christ from all eternity. As the Holy Spirit moves upon the face of our ignorance, this grace and calling is unveiled through the resurrection of Christ Jesus who abolished death and brought us into Christ Life and Light through the gospel (1 Timothy 1:9-10).

As we are clothed from perishable to imperishable, and mortal to immortal being the feet of Christ Jesus, our voices will shout as many waters, *"Death is swallowed up in victory, O death where is your victory? O death where is your sting?"* (1 Corinthians 15:53-55).

Are you a chosen one that Paul talked about in his letters to the Ephesians (Ephesians 1:4)? Do you have a passion to know Him and the power of His resurrection and the fellowship of His sufferings, being conformed to His death in order that you attain to the resurrection from the dead while in your natural body? (Philippians 3:10-11).

Are you one desiring to call forth the blessings of Heaven into the earth, prophesying to the dead and dying dry bones of humanity? Are you willing to BE the breath of Christ in you to breathe LIFE into those dead bones because this is what God commanded (Ezekiel 37)?

If you're looking for this pathway, this journey and desire for ALL of God in your life today to bring transformation of Heaven into the world, you must be prepared to be naked before God, stripped of everything you thought was the pathway to Eternal Life, and hear the words of Jesus Christ in a fresh way as he converses with Papa…

"This is eternal life, that they may know You, the only true God, and Jesus Christ whom You have sent. I have glorified You on the earth. I have finished the work which You have given Me to do." (John 17:3-4).

What did Jesus finish while hanging on the cross and shouting, "It is finished!" (John 19:30)? The cross was symbolic of the Tree of Knowledge of Good and Evil. He destroyed everything identified with this tree in the garden of God, our mind and heart where Christ resides. This is the beginning of wisdom when we realize that we carry our cross, the Tree of Knowledge, outside the temple and outside the city gates. Judgment begins in the house of God. Is the Tree of Knowledge trying to take root again? The only judgment that should be within us is Christ, the Tree of Life that releases the fruit of Love, joy, peace, patience, kindness, gentleness, goodness, faithfulness, and self-control upon the world for the Kingdom of God is in our hands (Galatians 5:22-23).

Be blessed as you are being raptured with the love of the Father into transformation as a new creation in Christ Jesus today. Hear Him say, "You are bone of My bone, and flesh of My flesh. Call Me husband."

"It shall be, in that day," Says the LORD, "That you will call Me 'My Husband,' And no longer call Me 'My Master'" (Hosea 2:16).

CHAPTER 1

THE RESURRECTION LIFE OF CHRIST JESUS MANIFESTED TODAY

Today we live in a world that is suddenly changing. What occurs in one country on the earth suddenly has an impact on another country on the other side of the world. An earthquake occurs in Japan, but it can be measured by instruments in central Florida located in the United States. Nuclear reactors are destroyed in one area, but the fallout consequence is felt around the world through the economic system.

Though we see things in the natural realm which seem to be a dominating kingdom, everything about our lives is ruled from an invisible domain called God's kingdom. The invisible place that He resides is within each of our hearts. The condition of our heart determines the power of the words we release in the atmosphere giving power to either the Kingdom of Light or the kingdom of darkness. *"For as he thinks in his heart, so is he"* (Proverbs 23:7).

Around the world most people live their lives within the control and manipulation of being governed by systems and kingdoms of this world. These include: cultures, religions, genders, life styles, age, education, economics, and family values. Their hearts may say one thing, but their minds are being overruled by the outward reflection of their feelings and senses governed by the kingdoms of the world around them.

When we look at a person, we can evaluate their outer covering; their gender, age, possibly culture, life style, and economics by the way they live and the way they clothe themselves. As a person speaks, we may learn more about their education and religion. This information allows us to compartmentalize an individual in our world, and will be helpful someday when their obituaries are to be written, but may or may not be of any real significance to connect with.

However, when we allow this information to draw us to asking the real question of where is Jesus Christ in this person's life, we are offered the opportunity to connect with the heart of God. Is there a testimony of the mystery of God - Christ in them, the hope of glory? Is there an unveiling in their life that says, "As He is, so am I in this world? When you see me, you see the Father?"

People tend to focus their thoughts on the past, and/or the potential of what the future holds. It is only when we subject our thoughts to the present moment that we engage our heart in the matter that is taking place now. It is at this moment that the Kingdom of God is energized within us challenging us to come up higher in our thoughts than what our senses are acknowledging and dictating in our lives.

"Then said he, unto what is the kingdom of God like? And whereunto shall I resemble it? It is like a grain of mustard seed, which a man took, and cast into his garden; and it grew, and waxed a great tree; and the fowls of the air lodged in the branches of it." (Luke 13:18-19).

The Kingdom of God has never changed. We may hear words of doctrines and traditions that may be considered vital that have carried us through seasons of change throughout history, but the Kingdom of God is the same yesterday, today, and tomorrow. We may find ourselves comfortable fellowshipping with certain groups of people that have similar knowledge of God's testimony allowing us to lift and edify one another in that knowledge, but this is not the fullness of His Kingdom. We must be cautious not to judge the difference, but to unite the foundation of God's

Kingdom—The resurrected LIFE of Jesus Christ who is the head of the body of Christ (Colossians 1:18).

The life of Daniel in the Old Testament shows us that the Kingdom of God is a counter kingdom to the kingdoms of this world. It comes, interrupts, and invades the kingdoms of this world very slowly, undiscerning as a small mustard seed, but ultimately, everything in the heavens, where God resides, will be ruled by it.

We read in Daniel 2:21-23, *"God changes the times and the seasons: he removes kings, and sets up kings: he gives wisdom unto the wise, and knowledge to them that know understanding: He reveals the deep and secret things: he knows what is in the darkness, and the light dwells with him. I thank thee, and praise thee, O thou God of my fathers, who hast given me wisdom and might, and hast made known unto me now what we desired of thee: for thou hast now made known unto us the King's matter."*

Proverbs 25:2 says, *"It is the glory of God to conceal a thing: but the honor of kings is to search out a matter."* God gives wisdom unto the wise and His knowledge to those that know understanding. These come from Isaiah 11:1-3, *"There shall come forth a rod* (Jesus Christ) *out of the stem of Jesse, and a Branch* (body of Christ) *shall grow out of his roots: And the spirit of the LORD shall rest upon him, the spirit of wisdom and understanding, the spirit of counsel and might, the spirit of knowledge and of the fear of the LORD; And shall make him of quick understanding in the fear of the LORD: and he shall not judge after the sight of his eyes, neither reprove after the hearing of his ears."*

The patriarchs of the Old Testament unveiled to us that the Kingdom of God is a counter kingdom to the kingdom of this world. It sets up and interrupts the systems, governments, and kingdoms of this world by a system that rules from the invisible, heavenly realm, yet is so powerful, it penetrates to the heart of man without any surgical incision made to the

God's Kingdom moves into the world's kingdom like a mustard seed penetrating to the heart of man.

flesh. It moves with minute invisible force like a mustard seed planted from God, but in His timing, everything in heaven, earth, and under the earth will be ruled by the Kingdom of God (Philippians 2:10).

This kingdom is a position of royalty that will be an atmosphere of righteousness, peace, and joy released by the Spirit of Christ within man (Romans 14:17). Those whom God has given wisdom and understanding will receive more as God changes the times and seasons for His kingdom to be manifested in the earth through man. God's kingdom has nothing to do with economics, gender, race, cultures, education, or governments that dictate our natural world. It is spiritual.

Every spiritual influence or presence is looking for one thing—it must manifest itself to express itself. The Kingdom of God, being the most influential and powerful, invades, violates, and conquers all other spiritual kingdoms. God looks to the overcomers, those that have gone through trials and tribulations in their lives that have the testimony of God's goodness, mercy, and grace giving glory to Him of their position as an overcomer. *"For everyone to whom much is given, of him shall much be required"* (Luke 12:48).

We read in Genesis 1:28 AMP, *"God blessed them and said to them, be fruitful, multiply, and fill the earth, and subdue it [using all its vast resources in the service of God and man]; and have dominion over the fish of the sea, the birds of the air, and over every living creature that moves upon the earth."*

The position of mankind before the fall was to fill the earth with "God kind" or the Spirit of God while subduing and taking dominion over all other creatures or other spiritual beings.

Scripture refers to these other spiritual beings as familiar, demonic, or antichrist spirits. When we look to fight the "demons" around every corner, we often miss the real battle that is taking place. *"For we wrestle not against flesh and blood, but against principalities, against powers, against the rulers of the darkness of this world, against spiritual wickedness in high places"* (Ephesians 6:12).

When we acknowledge Jesus Christ as our Lord, we become a part of His diverse membered body called Christ (Romans 12:5). His body only has the Holy Spirit. Any other spirit that rules in His body grieves the Spirit of God in us. *"Know you not that you are the temple of God, and that the Spirit of God dwells in you? If any man defiles the temple of God, him shall God destroy; for the temple of God is holy, which temple you are."* (1 Corinthians 3:16-17). God is a jealous God and will not share His Temple, His throne, His Kingdom with any other spirit. So what are the names of some of these "other spirits" that will try to take over the body of Christ Jesus?

The spirit of: depression, anxiety, low-self-esteem, loneliness, insecurity, hopeless, unhappy, disgraced, humiliated, worried, bitter, impatient, outraged, furious, repulsed, vengeful, vindictive, envious, jealous, intimidated, manipulated, disrespected, and on and on and on. These are words that express "feelings" of what we may be going through in particular circumstances. Often, the medical profession tries to get patients to express their feelings to help with the diagnosis of what their body is troubled with. Unfortunately, the quick fix is to give a medication which usually carries with it side effects. The big picture is that the Spirit of God is not leading and guiding, and the house of God is being shared by other spirits. Ask yourself, would you allow a thief or child molester to come into your home, take up residence, and fellowship with your family, especially if they were unwilling to respect and change according to your family values?

A logical thing to do in our everyday lives is to lock the door to your house and car to protect against easy access for thieves to steal from you, yet most of us have been allowing thieves in the house of God whenever we speak the words "I am" that are contrary to who God is. *"Nadab and Abihu,* (sons of the high priest Aaron), *died when they offered strange fire before the LORD"* (Numbers 26:61). They had allowed other familiar spirits within themselves to come into the holy place of God's house.

The Kingdom of God is a counter kingdom, a counter culture. It comes and interrupts the kingdoms that have been established. If the words that believers in Christ Jesus are releasing from their thoughts and mouth are things like, "I am anxious, I am depressed, I am insecure, I am lonely, I am ugly, I am scared, I am fearful, etc." there will be a battle of Armageddon going on between their ears; between their "I" and who God says "I AM" in them.

The Kingdom of God is so powerful among other kingdoms that it is always looking to invade, violate, and conquer. Again, it comes as a small mustard seed, but will grow as the largest tree. It will transform the atmosphere of fear and darkness into glory and light by the faithfulness of His presence.

"We know that all things work together for good to them that love God, to them who are the called according to his purpose" (Romans 8:28). God uses the overcomers in life to bring in the Kingdom of God. Some things to remember are:

- The Kingdom of God is appointed (Luke 22:29)
- It is a Divine calling (1 Thessalonians 2:12)
- It is entered into through tribulation or pressure (Acts. 14:22)
- It requires a change in thinking (Matthew 3:2)
- It requires a new birth to see it (John 3:3)
- It is eternal in its power (2 Peter 1:11)
- It is all spiritual (Romans 14:17)
- It belongs to the Father and His Son (Ephesians 5:5)
- It belongs to the Father and Christ (Matthew 6:29)
- Seek it first and He will add everything to you (Matthew 6:33)
- It becomes the largest Kingdom (Matthew 2:32)
- It consumes and is unstoppable (Daniel 2:44)
- What it opens, no man can shut, and what it shuts, no man can open (Revelation 3:7)
- It does not come by observation, and it eternally abides in you (Luke 17:21)

The Kingdom of God is the way in God – Christ Jesus - that once it has entered in, it cannot be stopped. It works as a spontaneous reflex. When we listen to the stories of the patriarchs, apostles, and Jesus Christ, we see the conversion that comes in times and seasons that cannot be stopped. There is a certain place, dominion, plain, and atmosphere that when the Kingdom of God abides in you, even though it may begin as a small mustard seed, it will cause transformation out of you that will affect everything and everyone around you. The omnipresence of God goes with you wherever you go. He will never leave you nor forsake you. There is NOT a little bit of the kingdom on this side of life and then we get the rest after we leave the body. Our body is the residence of His Holy Spirit. This is where God is. He gives us the ability and wisdom to rule and reign on this earth with His Kingdom authority. Christ is in you!

"Verily, verily, I say unto you, He that believeth on me, the works that I do shall he do also; and greater works than these shall he do; because I go unto my Father" (John 14:12).

"Beloved, believe not every spirit, but try the spirits whether they are of God: because many false prophets are gone out into the world. Hereby know you the Spirit of God: Every spirit that confesses that Jesus Christ is come in the flesh is of God: And every spirit that confesses not that Jesus Christ is come in the flesh is not of God: and this is that spirit of antichrist, whereof ye have heard that it should come; and even now already is it in the world." (1 John 4:1-3).

There are many in the world today that refer to themselves as Christians, but they do not consider that Jesus Christ is THE WAY, THE TRUTH, and THE LIFE. The play on words here is they will consider He is a "way maker," an example to be followed on having a relationship with the Divine. There is "truth" in this belief, but there is not power as an overcomer in this world. This concept may get you into heaven after you die, but it does not equip you

"Therefore, You delivered them into the hand of their enemies, who oppressed them; And in the time of their trouble,

When they cried to You, You heard from heaven; And according to Your abundant mercies You gave them deliverers who saved them from the hand of their enemies."Nehemiah 9:27

to be an overcomer filled with the anointing to BE the deliverer/savior in the lives of others.

It was the belief and eye-witness experience of the resurrected Jesus Christ from death, hell, and the grave that gave the first church in the Book of Acts the ability to receive the power of the Holy Spirit and to do greater works than Jesus Christ; healing the sick, and raising the dead. This is the works of the body of Jesus Christ, the church and bride of Christ should be manifesting in the earth today. *"Therefore, leaving the discussion of the elementary principles of Christ, let us go on to perfection, not laying again the foundation of repentance from dead works and of faith toward God, of the doctrine of baptisms, of laying on of hands, of resurrection of the dead, and of eternal judgment. And this we will do if God permits"* (Hebrews 6:1-3).

Jesus Christ is THE WAY, THE TRUTH, and THE LIFE to know God in a personal intimacy as Father. All other religions, doctrines, and theologies will show you God, but only by knowing Jesus Christ personally as the only begotten SON of God is the Holy Spirit able to release in us the words to call God ABBA, FATHER. *"And because you are sons, God hath sent forth the Spirit of his Son into your hearts, crying, Abba, Father"* (Galatians 4:6).

It is this identity of "I AM" that is unveiled in us by the Holy Spirit which allows the releasing of His authority through us that decrees, *"As He is, so are we in this world today"* (1 John 4:17).

CHAPTER 2

I AM THE RESURRECTION AND THE LIFE

*E*very year there is a celebration of a major spring holiday calledPassover. For the Jews it is a celebration of a historical time when they were released by God to come out of bondage and slavery for over 400 years into freedom. The blood of the lamb was placed on their doorpost to signify to the death angel to pass over their home not killing the first born child. For Christians, this holiday is also celebrated in remembrance of Jesus as the lamb of God dying on the cross for the sins of all mankind, and then being raised from death, hell, and the grave three days later as the Resurrection Life of Christ. The correlation of these two events in history are considered to be overlaid with Jesus fulfilling the Passover as the LAMB.

The intriguing issue about this is that the dates of celebration each year with Passover for the Jews and Resurrection season for the Christians are not always on the same dates. So, do we celebrate the truth or what man creates in their calendars? Which dates do we celebrate so that we are truly honoring Passover? Then what about resurrection? The moment in history that Jesus Christ redeemed man from death, hell, and the grave? Have we missed the Lord's feast of celebration if we honor this day on separate occasions as most churches do apart from the Jews honoring Passover?

When I presented these questions before the Lord, the Father said, "Both and all according to your hearts understand is correct? Then the Lord said for me to come up higher beyond the seasons and calendars of time. "I AM the Resurrection and the LIFE. I AM ETERNAL LOVE and LIGHT."

In the Old Testament, man was required to go to Mt. Zion in Jerusalem three times a year to honor and celebrate the Lord's Feast unto HIM. These feasts are Passover, Pentecost, and Tabernacles. For over 2000 years, believers in Christ have celebrated Passover putting Jesus on the cross each year and then raising Him up on Easter with a salvation message for mankind that when we die a natural death we can have eternal life on the other side.

At the same time, we take the old man, the no good sinner, and crucify him when we receive Jesus as our personal Savior, but then quickly do CPR since we're not really dead to ourselves. So we live the Christian life of someday I'll have eternal life, but while I'm in this natural body I can never be good enough, so I'll do good works to identify as righteous. This tends to be the best the church has done with the GOOD NEWS that Jesus commanded us to take to the world in sharing the Gospel.

Within the past couple hundred years we have become aware of the presence of the Holy Spirit and the fulfillment of Pentecost which, in reality, was complete during the time of Jesus. We have allowed our customs and traditions to dictate God's actions, placing limits and boundaries on the body of Christ. Yet, as we went through the season of Pentecost we still did not recognize the pattern of the Lord's feast to move into the fall feasts and Tabernacles. Most of the church is still justifying this season is to come, but what if it is already completed and we have simply been looking in the wrong direction?

While on the cross, Jesus said "It is finished." What did He finish? Passover, Pentecost and/or Tabernacles? I asked these questions to the Father and He showed me a vision...

I AM the Resurrection and the Life! Most of the body of Christ, the bride of Christ, is trying to determine if they are a Martha or a Mary. When death is at their door with the brother they loved, they still didn't get it. Martha was the voice of the thief on the cross that we often mimic—when the resurrection comes someday, and Mary speaks out of the thief of our past, "If only." Both women loved Jesus, saw the miracles He released, listened to His messages, and followed Him, yet at death's door, they were missing something that could not bring LIFE to the one they loved. They didn't know Jesus as I AM.

The curtain entering into the Holy of Holies was torn from top to bottom on resurrection morning. God does not change. He is the same yesterday, today, and tomorrow. The torn curtain allowed man to boldly enter into the Father's presence, yet, the Father didn't lower the Holiness of His presence. Instead, He raised man up through the blood of Jesus Christ to BE Holy as He is in oneness in Christ. A mystery of Passover/Resurrection is that the High Priest did not enter into the Holy of Holies in this season. He only entered once a year on Yom Kippur in the fall season, not spring. Selah!

God is eternal. He is not bound by time or space or calendars. Tabernacles is coming into the presence of God in oneness, looking up for our redemption is here now. The finished work of Jesus Christ begins in Tabernacles, the new creation in Christ. The old man is dead and gone. There is nothing the Father is telling Jesus that He did not complete for all mankind.

Since God is not on a time table, we also experience Passover and Pentecost in the oneness of HIM—I AM at the same time. Father, Son, and Holy Spirit as one in the second ADAM, Christ Jesus (1 Cor. 15).

Tabernacles is our birthing identity of who we are in the second Adam, where are you? (Genesis 3, 1 Corinthians 15).

Passover is our crossing over, feet washing experience, into the position of who we are in Christ—a royal priesthood, a peculiar people, and a Holy nation. Where we live, move, and have our being is in HIM.

Pentecost is the marriage of the bride of Christ with the Father's agreement of the Torah, and both the bride and the groom drink from the same cup. Out of our bellies flow rivers of Living waters carried to the heart, the throne room of the Father, and circumcision takes place with the bridegroom asking each of us, "Who do you say I AM," for how you see me will determine the creative power released in your words and what form the preparation of the bride will take place.

As we come into Tabernacles again, we come this time as a son or daughter of the Most High God with the mind and heart of Christ to rule and reign with Him. The earth is waiting for this moment which is here now ready to be released. The Kingdom of God that has been completed in the Heavens needs the body of Christ to rise up in oneness and unity of faith in Jesus Christ. Passover and Pentecost have been completed and the Bridegroom is ready to take oneness with His bride—the church. In Peter's famous sermon in Acts 2, Joel's prophecy has been fulfilled. Peter's message was not simply a salvation message of dying and going to heaven, but "this is that," because He died once and for all, we don't have to, but we do have to be in a oneness of intimacy with the LIFE to know Him and the power of His resurrection.

Today, we have been given the identity of Jesus Christ as one new man in Christ with many members. As HE is, so are we today, resurrection LIFE in HIM. We must first know who Jesus is to us to know what power can be released by Him through us. What name do you know Him intimately as?

What are the Cherubim?

"Thou shalt not make unto thee any graven image, or any likeness of any thing that is in heaven above, or that is in the earth beneath, or that is in the water under the earth: Thou shalt not bow down thyself to them, nor serve them...," Exodus 20:4-5.

We are told by God to make no image of anything that is in heaven above, or that is in the earth beneath, or that is in the water under the earth. Is it forbidden for us to make images, but somehow okay for God to? Is God's parenting skills "do as I say, but not as I do?" NO, NO, and NO! God is good all the time, and is not double minded. If this is not the way that we are to view this situation, then there must be a new understanding of why God's tabernacle had cherubim on the curtains, and on the Ark of the Covenant. Keep in mind that God is good all the time, so what He declares for Himself He must also declare for His children.

So what are these images called Cherubim? To understand their existence we must first ask what they looked like. The mind set of Moses and the children of Israel found in the book of Exodus was an Egyptian mind. The Egyptians were famous for using different images in their religious rituals, and one of them was a cherub. The Israelites had no previous established religion before they left Egypt because of being in bondage for over 400 years. Remember the tabernacle was built after they left Egypt. What they knew of making cherubim came from what they saw of the Egyptians, and the same would be true for Moses. When God told Moses to build an ark, Moses knew he was pertaining to a coffin. For Moses to have the mercy seat and cherubim built, he knew he was building a place of authority, power, and a throne for God.

The description given in Exodus on how to build the cherubim is very limited.

Chapter 25:18-21 says, *"And thou shalt make two cherubim of gold, of beaten work shalt thou make them, in the two ends of the mercy seat. And make one cherub on the one end, and the other cherub on the other end: even of the mercy seat shall ye make the cherubim on the two ends thereof. And the cherubim's shall stretch forth their wings on high, covering the mercy seat with their wings, and their faces shall look one to another; toward the mercy seat shall the faces of the cherubim be. And thou shalt put the mercy seat above upon the ark; and in the ark, thou shalt put the testimony that I shall give thee."* In Exodus 26:1 we read, *"Moreover thou shalt make the tabernacle with ten curtains of fine twined linen, and blue, and purple, and scarlet: with cherubim of cunning work shalt thou make them."*

There are more scriptures that use the word cherubim, however, referring to the tabernacle in the wilderness, the verses don't give any more information than what these describe of them. When you read in I Kings there is a little more description for Solomon's temple, and in Ezekiel we have a vision describing a very unusual creature with several faces called cherubim.

I've never seen pictures of the Ark of the Covenant have the cherubim that Ezekiel saw, yet his is the only real detailed description of what these creations might look like.

Somehow Bezaleel, who was appointed by God to build the ark, mercy seat, and cherubim was given the wisdom to create a material image that was pleasing to God that would be placed where God would reside. God went to great lengths to give detailed instruction on how to build the ark and the mercy seat, but not what the face or the wings of the cherubim were supposed to look like. These people had a mind set of Egypt that was customary to put parts of a bird's body on a human form, but what kind of bird? Were their wings as an eagle or a dove? Was the face as a man, a lion, a bird, etc.

I'm sure by now you ask what difference does it make, why all the inquisition? God said make no image, yet we have images sitting next to God, made out of the same piece of gold that the mercy seat is made of. These images are an extension of the mercy seat. The mercy seat is Jesus Christ with all death and judgment underneath him. The cherubim are to His right and left. This is all inside the most Holy place on the earth where God resides.

In 2 Corinthians 10:5 Paul tells us, *"Casting down imaginations, and every high thing that exalteth itself against the knowledge of God, and bringing into captivity every thought to the obedience of Christ."* The word imagination in the New Testament comes from the Greek word Logismos meaning to reckon, such as calculating or considering a predetermined conduct. God says we are to cast down our imagination. In the Old Testament the Hebrew word for imagination is Yatsar. It means to form, to fashion, to devise, to frame, to produce, to create, to be predestined. The term also means to construct thoughts and purposes. In Genesis 7:20, we are told that, "the imagination of man's heart is evil."

So what are Cherubim? They are the imagination of the children of God. They sit at His throne with power and authority. They have the faces of a lion, ox, eagle, and man representing the four gospels of Jesus

Christ. They have the power of the Holy Spirit in their wings, and they are supposed to have the fullness of the mercy seat, putting all death underneath them. When we have the mind of Christ, we have the ability to reflect the mercy seat of God. When we mix the mind of Christ, the Word, with our religious mindset we have power of our imagination.

The evil of all evils is your imagination which will keep you from all that God wants you to be. It will condemn you, it will destroy you. The destroyer is in the imagination of people. The cherubim were on the veil because the veil had to be pulled back to go from the middle court to the most Holy place. The Word is covered until the Holy Spirit pulls back the veil of your imagination, revealing His truth. Adam gave over to the devil because he gave into his imagination. Nothing they imaged would be impossible. If you can pull apart imagination then you have God. Religion works from the outside in. Each place in the tabernacle you try to go to get to the throne of God is met with an imagination of "you're not worthy", but if you "clean-up your act" or "get more faith", or more knowledge you might make it to the next level of getting close to God.

Religion is Satan's greatest warrior, because if you pull back the curtain of imagination you might see God. When you see God you don't need the ritual and formality of listening to the "body" because you know the voice of God and have the mind of God. What more is there when you have come into the presence of God?

He wants to transform you into His image while in the body on the earth. In order for this to take place, the evil of all evils will have to go which is your imagination.

Satan does not create, but takes what belongs to God and imitates, intertwining judgment and imagination that has appeal to the senses of man. When man does not know truth then what is offered of the imagination becomes truth to the temple of God, bringing destruction into the Holy of Holies.

How did Adam bring sin and destruction into this world? His imagination. In Genesis 3:3, we read the woman saying, *"ye shall not eat of it, neither shall ye touch it, least ye die."* Where did the woman get these words that have been created? She claims that God said it. She is right, but not Father God, Adam god. Adam was the only other creator to exist. Adam was created in the image and likeness of God with the ability to create with the power of words. He was the son of God (Luke 3). Father God said in Genesis 2:17, *"Thou shalt not eat of it: for in the day that thou eatest thereof thou shalt surely die".* Now the serpent had two minds, the mind of Father God, and the mind of God's son, Adam, who added the word touch to the creation of what his father said.

God wants to transform you into His image while in your body on the earth.

In Genesis 3:5, we read the serpent saying, *"For God doth know that in the day ye eat thereof, then your eyes shall be opened, and ye shall be as gods, knowing good and evil".* Did the serpent really deceive the woman considering he did speak truth? In Genesis 3:22 we read, *"The Lord God said, "Behold, the man is become as one of us to know good and evil".* Yes, the serpent did deceive the woman (to us, the church, the bride of Christ). He took the words of God the Father and intertwined judgment of knowing good and evil by appealing to the senses of man with the word touch that the woman received from Adam. **When we know good and evil we bring judgment into the house of God**. We also become ruled by our imaginations trying to determine what is right or wrong. God can only live where He builds.

Turn to Genesis 11:1, *"And the whole earth was of one language, and of one speech."* Verse 6, *"and the Lord said, Behold, the people is one, and they have all one language; and this they begin to do, and now nothing will be restrained from that which they have imagined to do."* What stops the imagination? When the Holy Spirit speaks the Word of God. Our natural minds cannot understand the language, so we can't reason with what God is doing. Verse 7, *"Go to, let us go down, and there confound their language, that they may not understand one another's speech."* God gave them His language which they didn't understand because their mind was focused on themselves versus knowing the voice of their Father.

The power of life and death is in the tongue (Proverbs 18:21). It begins in the heart and mind of creation. Once it is expressed by the tongue, the words have the potential to be manifested in the natural. If you can be full of "good" then you also have an anointing to "evil". The tree of knowledge had both fruit.

On the day of Pentecost, the tongue was changed which brought transformation. A coward like Peter was given a boldness to manifest the image of his Father by his words. His whole body was transformed. To be transformed into His image requires the ability to pray in tongues, so that your natural mind can't tell the God in you how to handle a situation, but God will tell your mind and body what He wants through tongues, and you can't argue with Him. You can't make yourself into the image of God from the outside in, it must be God in you transforming the outside.

Isaiah 25:7-8, *"And he will destroy in this mountain the face of the covering cast over all people, and the veil that is spread over all nations. He will swallow up death in victory; and the Lord God will wipe away tears from off all faces; and the rebuke of his people shall he take away from off all the earth for the Lord hath spoken it."*

These scriptures were fulfilled at Calvary and the resurrection of Jesus Christ. When he went into the Holy of Holies and became our mercy seat. We sit next to him on the throne of God. The faces of the cherubim are our faces with the eyes of the Holy Spirit. We should see as God sees with the eyes of mercy. When you use the word you use it with His character so that Love, Light, and Life are manifested out of darkness. If you see the tabernacle as the temple of God that you go through from the outer court to the inner court you will not achieve the fullness of mercy to bring to those in the outer court. You must first see that you were dead, life-less, inside the Ark of the Covenant. God took you and brought transformation life in you, covering you with gold, His character. He put Himself everywhere. There is no race or sex. God is all in all. His mercy seat becomes evident. The word and miracle are inside the ark. You don't see it, but the mercy seat is manifested. There is no mercy in the outer court. Its hard to have mercy when you hang around blood and death. It takes the Holy of Holies of all God to overcome judgment.

The five-fold ministry was to role away the stone crushing of the Ten Commandments of judgment. When the law is rolled away so is the death penalty. We didn't escape the penalty, but hung on the cross with him 2,000 years ago. Genesis 29:3 tells us that all the flocks gathered. Jesus removed the demands of the law mentality. The stone that was covering the well of water in this chapter. We now can understand the real love and mercy of the Father because the stone has been removed from the grave.

You are the ark of God. Jesus is the High Priest which he took his blood and covered you with mercy so all that was in the coffin has his life, love, and light. All around the mercy seat was a crown. The crown is sitting on the head of the mercy seat, Jesus Christ. You are the body in the ark that has been given life as the body/bride of Him. The high priest in the Old Testament wore a crown that said "Holiness unto the Lord". This spoke of carrying the mind of God among the people, the mind of mercy.

A crown equals authority, power, and placement. It took a king to place the Word of God. The crown says you have to think a different way. **You are royalty, a Son of God with power and authority.** You can't think like the accuser would which spoke of judgment and death based on good and evil. We must cast down our imagination, and be who we have been created to be walking on this earth manifesting the Sons of God.

May God bless you with this message revealing His identity in you.

CHAPTER 3

WAS MOSES JUST A MAN?

*W*as Moses just a man picked out of a hat when he was assigned to bring the children of God out of Egypt, or was there something unique going on?

Moses was chosen by God because Moses knew something that was very important for the task that needed to be done. Moses knew the mind of being a son of god (Pharaoh). He didn't first learn from God when he went on the mountain, but being raised in Pharaoh's household as his son. Moses was sent to the top of authority by God from the moment he was born. Keep in mind that the first five years of a child's life are the most impressionable to learn the most. There were things that Jesus had to see, hear, and learn from Egypt has well.

Moses was raised to be a god, a supreme being in the house of Pharaoh. He had the mindset of what it takes to be a son of god. He knew that a word spoken from anyone in the house of Pharaoh (god) was a word of power and authority to move time and history. He knew that the writings he passed down of scripture had life and power in them. He knew of what took place with the afterlife and resurrection of the dead. He understood when God wanted the Ark of the Covenant built that the word ark meant coffin. He knew that death was involved for life to come forth. The whole mindset of Egypt in handling the body of a dead king or Pharaoh is that the body is prepared and buried in such a way for the journey into the afterworld, and for them to rein forever as a god. The degree of pleasantness and success with the preparations of the body, the greater the manifestation is to the Egyptian people with the prosperity of blessings on their life and land. It is to their benefit to make sure the king or Pharaoh goes into the afterlife with food, provisions, wealth, a perfect body and organs. This is the mindset Moses had when confronted with God to build the tabernacle.

The Promised Land was for those still seeking the journey of blessings. Moses had been in the presence of God. He had the mindset of God for his face shone with the light of God that it had to be veiled. When Moses walked among the people, they saw a man who was raised to be the god of Egypt transformed with the power and authority of Almighty God into the image of God. To them it was like seeing a Pharaoh that had actually died, gone through his journey into the afterworld, and come back as god.

The Levitical priesthood showed man working toward transformation that would never be attainable by the laws and rituals. Their mindset needed a someday "promise land." Moses did not need to go because he knew that when you have God, you have it all. They already had it all in the wilderness with God in their midst. Their imaginations didn't like what they saw, so God allowed them to be guided by their own mindset. They had the position and authority of being children of God, but they blended it with an Egyptian mindset. God had to get Egypt out of them. Moses already had it out of him.

Deut 34:5-7, *"So Moses the servant of the Lord died in the land of Moab, according to the word of the Lord, and he buried him in a valley in the land of Moab, over against Bethpeor: but no man knoweth of his sepulcher unto this day. And Moses was a hundred and twenty years old when he died: his eye was not dim, nor his natural force abated."* Ask yourself, if God cannot come near death, what does he mean when he buried Moses, yet in a place that can't be found?

In all of Moses' life, what was his real search and quest to obtain? He was taken as a baby from his natural father, and raised as the son of god

(Pharaoh). Then that identity is taken from him until he meets God who proclaims he is the Father of Moses which would make him the Son of God. Moses didn't need a promised land to go to as the people searched for. **His quest was to obtain his true identity. Once that was satisfied, he knew that all else would come into place by the power and authority the position held.**

Remember his Egyptian mindset, death was a transformation into the afterworld with the ability to fully bless the people in the land. Did Moses die as we know death, or did he go behind the veil with his entire body versus just his face? Moses went into the presence of God with himself of who he was with the mindset of transformation from death to life. The mindset of the people was that of the High Priest, putting on garments of righteousness to go into the Holy of Holies. Moses knew that the identity to someday be the son of God was not something to obtain in the future for him, but to declare what was already in him by knowing God as his Father.

On the mount of transfiguration when Peter, James, and John saw Jesus with Moses where did Moses come from? Could it be possible that he was there all along, but because of the veil of "imagination" the light of the Lord in him couldn't be seen? Where did this light that glorified the Lord come from? It came from within. Moses was able to walk among the people with a veil over his face. It had to be covered because it glowed with the Light of the Lord. When Moses died, he went into the presence of the Holy of Holies on the mountain, transforming not only his face, but his body as well. He died to the natural way of man to enter into the supernatural love of the Lord. He was a type and shadow, as was Elijah, to things to come for the entire world that Jesus died on the cross for.

Moses "died" for the people so that as he is transformed into the image of God, his Father, in the afterworld the people will be blessed going into the promised land. A blessing that will be greater than the provisions of their needs taken care of that they received in the wilderness. They have an opportunity to know God in a way that Moses did, as the fullness of the Light of the world. **Where there is Light, there is Eternalness, time no more.**

God's purpose from the beginning in Genesis is to create a family, to create a people in His image. Moses wrote this message given to him by God to give to us when he wrote the first five books of the Bible.

Light, Life, and Love are not descriptions of God's character, but who He is. In Him there is no darkness, no Egypt, no time. His word is eternal. He is transforming us, removing the veil of our imagination as He fills us with who He is by the teaching of the Holy Spirit. Death is not the vessel that God desires to use to bring us into His presence. Jesus died for the sins of the world to overcome the Egyptian mindset of death being necessary for the journey into the supernatural. We pacify the need for death in order to come into the presence of God as an excuse of insecurity and doubt with our relationship with God and who we are. It is the word in us that comes out of us that causes transformation to take place—transfiguration on this earth while in the natural body.

Time is for our benefit as a school master to train us into the identification of who we are. God can only live where God is. He created Adam so He could live on this earth and reproduce Himself. When we hear, read, and do the word by faith, knowing in our hearts that if our Father has said it, it's a done deal, we will be the manifestations of the Sons of God (the body of Christ) on this earth.

God, who is the author of time, made himself subject to time by putting flesh on His Word, to do away with time, and to bring forth the end of time.

CHAPTER 4

WHAT IS THE SIGN OF HIS COMING?

"Then if any man shall say unto you, Lo, here is Christ, or there; believe it not. For there shall arise false Christs, and false prophets, and shall shew great signs and wonders; insomuch that, if it were possible, they shall deceive the very elect. Behold, I have told you before" (Matt. 24:23-25).

In this famous chapter in Matthew taught by pastors as the "signs" that the end of time is near, Jesus tells us that there will be those that are anointed with the gifts of God where signs and wonders will follow. Since God gives the gifts and does not take them back, we have a key to understanding a mystery that Jesus is sharing about the coming of the Lord.

Jesus is telling us that it will be possible for an anointed one of God, **the very elect** (apostle, prophet, pastor, teacher, or evangelist) to be teaching and prophesying opposition of what God has called for them to share. Basically, they do not have a correct stand with what God called them to unveil to the body of Christ. The elect are those teaching the Scriptures in part, but interpreting the understanding of those Scriptures as if it is the fullness of the Father's thoughts. In essence, we have the building of doctrines and theologies created through a partnership with the Holy Spirit instead of the fullness of the Holy Spirit. A mystery Jesus is sharing about the end times is there will be many that have a great calling on their life to be in ministry, yet they will not be teaching and preaching according to what God has orchestrated. Yet, since they have the gift and anointing of God, signs and wonders will be seen. Selah!

Jesus calls them "false Christ's and false prophets" with a false anointing. I repeat, Jesus is telling us that it will be possible for the elect of God, those that have a calling on their life by God to be deceived teaching deception that God did not anoint them with. Some will have power and a driving force in their ministry attracting crowds, but God says it is perverted against what He called them to share. Some will even have the demonstration of the glory of God without the truth of the glory.

However, until one has been purified by the trials and tribulations encompassed in the valley of the shadow of death (the battle of Armageddon in the mind) resurrected to know intimately the fullness of God's love and peace while in the midst of the battle, one cannot give away what they do not possess, the resurrected life of Christ Jesus; the coming of the Lord. God's love is a consuming fire. We either receive it, becoming transformed into His image, or we become consumed.

The inquiry of the disciples in Matthew 24 was about the coming of the Lord. What is the sign? The body of Christ Jesus, the bride that He is coming for must be purified with the character and nature of God symbolized as gold without spot or wrinkle. Again, there will be those that have an anointing on their life by God teaching purification of the bride according to their doctrine with signs and wonders following, but Jesus says they are false Christ's and prophets. **This is a sign of the end of the cosmos or the age we are in**. This does not mean the end of the world, but the end of the system as we know it of how the church, the bride of Christ, is to be purified.

The church of the Lord Jesus Christ, His body, is not a gender issue for male interpretation. It is an equality of male and female created in the image of God and both called Adam (Gen. 5:1-2). The purification of the body of Christ is a blood issue, but the depth of understanding and cleansing the bride of Christ without spot or wrinkle can only be grasped from the blood issue of cleansing that women endure monthly that is connected to

LIFE. Until the elect recognize the spiritual balance of creation between God's image in male and female necessary for the fullness of the coming of the Lord, the elect will be deceived.

Another issue that must be taken into consideration as we consider the end of time is that all the parts of the body of Christ are in heaven and earth. One person is not the whole body of Christ. If we concern ourselves to only look out for me—will I be raptured out before the world comes to an end? Will I be going to heaven? Then the enemy of God in our head is winning the battle of Armageddon taking place within ourselves. The body of Christ is not just one person, one local church building, one particular denomination, one theological understanding, or even one country. If people in another country are hurting and being persecuted for the gospel, then the other parts of the body in other parts of heaven and earth will be affected. If my little toe on my right foot were bruised, it would affect my whole body. I would be focused on how I would be able to walk, what shoes I could wear, whether I needed to prop my foot up or bandage it, etc. My thoughts throughout my day would constantly be redirected to my bruised toe because it hurts. This is how we need to understand the fullness of the body of the Lord Jesus Christ around the world; male and female; young and old.

As a little girl, I can remember being told to clean my plate because there were children in other parts of the world that were starving, and I should be thankful that I had food. Trying to be an obedient child, I would clean my plate not questioning how eating more food than I really needed simply because my plate was overloaded was going to affect starving children in other countries.

Today, I can affect those children in other countries by giving them bone of my bone and flesh of my flesh in Christ Jesus. *"Jesus said, I have food (nourishment) to eat of which you know nothing and have no idea"* (John 4:32 AMP). Jesus' disciples did not understand the food that gives life.

We are at a time in history that has never been seen before, where we can connect with parts of the body of Christ instantly around the world while sitting in our own home. We can pray and bless other members of the body feeding them a meal from our Heavenly Father's table while we are walking in a park via cell phones, computers, and texting. In a twinkling of an eye, we have the power and capability of our Heavenly Father to bring the resurrected life of Christ to the body of Christ filling the earth with the glory of God. The famous "rapture sermons" that have been taught by the elect from 1 Thessalonians 4 and 5 are taking place today. However, since many are interpreting these Scriptures according to doctrine and theology, they are being deceived as Christians.

To begin understanding the signs of the coming of the Lord, the mature in Christ, male and female, must be in correct position as kings and priests unto the Lord. This is why intercession—prayers of the righteous—is so important. **We cannot give to others what we do not believe in ourselves.**

"They sung a new song, saying, Thou art worthy to take the book, and to open the seals thereof: for thou was slain, and hast redeemed us to God by thy blood out of every kindred, and tongue, and people, and nation; And hast made us unto our God kings and priests: and we shall reign on the earth" (Rev. 5: 9-10).

God says, *"As He is, so are you in this world"* (1 John 4:17). The natural gives us discernment of what the body of Christ needs, but if we only take care of the natural issues, then we are not allowing the body of Christ to be healed with the fullness of the life of Jesus Christ. We must first align ourselves with the heavenly body of Christ so that we can see and understand the natural issues from God's perspective to bring transformation of the whole spotless bride of Christ into manifestation.

The end of time as we know it is now. With the power of cyberspace network, the body of Christ has the ability to bring to manifestation the coming of the Lord and filling the earth with the glory of God. In a twinkle of an eye we can win the battle of Armageddon whose captain is "self" being controlled by the spirit of fear for the sake of looking out for "number one."

The time is now to allow Jesus Christ to be our captain, putting on the Spirit of faith and allowing *"the fruit of the [Holy] Spirit [the work which His presence within accomplishes] of love, joy (gladness), peace, patience (an even temper, forbearance), kindness, goodness (benevolence), faithfulness, gentleness (meekness, humility), self-control (self-restraint, continence). Against such things there is no law [that can bring a charge]. And those who belong to Christ Jesus (the Messiah) have crucified the flesh (the godless human nature) with its passions and appetites and desires. If we live by the [Holy] Spirit, let us also walk by the Spirit. [If by the Holy Spirit we have our life in God, let us go forward walking in line, our conduct controlled by the Spirit.]"* (Galatians 5:22-25 AMP).

The time is now for the coming of the Lord to be manifested in this world. There is a company of people today around the world that are filled with the Holy Spirit knowing they are a member of the resurrected body of Christ Jesus. They are ready to lay down their carnal life and unite His body in this earth by His faith transforming the atmosphere of fear into the glory of God.

Are you one of those people? Then arise and shine where God has planted you today. Your light, Christ in you the hope of glory has come (Isaiah 60). *"You are the light of the world* (the world that you are planted)*"* (Matt. 5:14). Fill your atmosphere with His love, grace, and mercy because He loved you first while you were still in darkness and ignorance. *"Seek first the kingdom of God and His righteousness"* (Matt. 6:33). *"Trust in the Lord with all your heart and lean not on your own understanding; in all your ways acknowledge him, and he will make your paths straight"* (Proverbs 3:5-6).

The Holy Spirit will equip us to do the Father's business as a son of God because we are connected to His glorious resurrected body. Today is the day to utilize the gifts and talents that He has instilled in each of us for such a time as this to be released in the earth. Today, there is no condemnation in Christ Jesus (Romans 8:1).

"Since Christ is in you, your body (old nature, ego) *is dead because of sin, yet your spirit is alive because of righteousness. Since the Spirit of him who*

raised Jesus from the dead is living in you, he who raised Christ from the dead will also give life to your mortal bodies through his Spirit, who lives in you" (Romans 8:10-11).

God wants you to utilize the amazing gifts and talents He imparted in you before the foundations of the world.

The greatest opposition existing today to the body of the resurrected life of Christ Jesus is the religious system of the church. The children of God are living in bondage of doctrines and traditions calling it the life of being a disciple of Christ, yet, being far removed from living in their inheritance as new creations in Christ as the resurrected body of Christ Jesus. This is a repeat of history of the times when Jesus walked the earth. It was not the Gentile religions that Jesus had to stand against, but those that knew the Scriptures, but did not know the love and mercy that goes before judgment and condemnation.

Jesus came to set the captive heart free. As part of His body, is this your heart?

CHAPTER 5

WHAT IS THE GOSPEL?

"Jesus said, 'I am the Way and the Truth and the Life; no one comes to the Father except by (through) Me'" (John 14:6).

The death, burial, and resurrection life of Jesus Christ IS THE GOSPEL. He is the Alpha and Omega; the beginning and the end. Today, *"in Him, we live and move and have our being; as even some of your [own] poets have said, for we are also His offspring"* (Acts 17:28 AMP). Being "in Him" does not mean "following Jesus" or "what would Jesus do?" These doctrines sound good, but we should not be the body of Christ that is following Jesus, but be His body that is connected to His head, or the mind of Christ.

"[For it is He] Who delivered and saved us and called us with a calling in itself holy and leading to holiness [to a life of consecration, a vocation of holiness]; [He did it] not because of anything of merit that we have done, but because of and to further His own purpose and grace (unmerited favor) which was given us in Christ Jesus before the world began [eternal ages ago]. [It is that purpose and grace] which He now has made known and has fully disclosed and made real [to us] through the appearing of our Savior Christ Jesus, Who annulled death and made it of no effect and brought life and immortality (immunity from eternal death) to light through the Gospel" (2 Timothy 1:9-10).

"Anyone who confesses (acknowledges, owns) that Jesus is the Son of God, God abides (lives, makes His home) in him and he [abides, lives, makes his home] in God. And we know (understand, recognize, are conscious of, by observation and by experience) and believe (adhere to and put faith in and rely on) the love God cherishes for us. God is love, and he who dwells and continues in love dwells and continues in God, and God dwells and continues in him. In this [union and communion with Him] love is brought to completion and attains perfection with us, that we may have confidence for the day of judgment [with assurance and boldness to face Him], because as He is, so are we in this world. There is no fear in love [dread does not exist], but full-grown (complete, perfect) love turns fear out of doors and expels every trace of terror! For fear brings with it the thought of punishment, and [so] he who is afraid has not reached the full maturity of love [is not yet grown into love's complete perfection]. We love Him, because He first loved us" (1 John 4:15-18).

If people live their life never knowing the awesomeness of the Gospel of Jesus Christ, it does not change the fact that God loved us first. Today, in the sight of God, we have already been redeemed, saved, and sanctified in Christ Jesus for He died once, and for all. *"Even the Father judges no one, for He has given all judgment (the last judgment and the whole business of judging) entirely into the hands of the Son"* (John 5:22). *"If anyone hears My teachings and fails to observe them [does not keep them, but disregards them], it is not I who judges him. For I have not come to judge and to condemn and to pass sentence and to inflict penalty on the world, but to save the world"* (John 12:47). *"Whoever receives His testimony has set his seal of approval to this: God is true. [That man has definitely certified, acknowledged, declared once and for all, and is himself assured that it is divine truth that God cannot lie]"* (John 3:33).

"When we are among the full-grown (spiritually mature Christians who are ripe in understanding), we do impart a [higher] wisdom (the knowledge of the divine plan previously hidden); but it is indeed not a wisdom of this present age or of this world nor of the leaders and rulers of this age, who are being brought to nothing and are doomed to pass away. But rather what we are setting forth is a wisdom of God once hidden [from the human understanding] and now revealed to us by God—[that wisdom] which God devised and decreed before the ages for our glorification [to lift us into the glory of His presence]" (1 Cor. 2:6-7).

"For [as far as this world is concerned] you have died, and your [new, real] life is hidden with Christ in God" (Col. 3:3).

"It is from Him that you have your life in Christ Jesus, Whom God made our Wisdom from God, [revealed to us a knowledge of the divine plan of salvation previously hidden, manifesting itself as] our Righteousness [thus making us upright and putting us in right standing with God], and our Consecration [making us pure and holy], and our Redemption [providing our ransom from eternal penalty for sin]" (1 Cor. 1:30).

"By this we shall come to know (perceive, recognize, and understand) that we are of the Truth, and can reassure (quiet, conciliate, and pacify) our hearts in His presence, whenever our hearts in [tormenting] self-accusation make us feel guilty and condemn us. [For we are in God's hands.] For He is above and greater than our consciences (our hearts), and He knows (perceives and understands) everything [nothing is hidden from Him]. And, beloved, if our consciences (our hearts) do not accuse us [if they do not make us feel guilty and condemn us], we have confidence (complete assurance and boldness) before God, and we receive from Him whatever we ask, because we [watchfully] obey His orders [observe His suggestions and injunctions, follow His plan for us] and [habitually] practice what is pleasing to Him. And this is His order (His command, His injunction): that we should believe in (put our faith and trust in and adhere to and rely on) the name of His Son Jesus Christ (the Messiah), and that we should love one another, just as He has commanded us. All who keep His commandments [who obey His orders and follow His plan, live and continue to live, to stay and] abide in Him, and He in them. [They let Christ be a home to them and they are the home of Christ.] And by this we know and understand and have the proof that He [really] lives and makes His home in us: by the [Holy] Spirit Whom He has given us" (1 John 3:19-24).

"THEREFORE BE imitators of God [copy Him and follow His example], as well-beloved children [imitate their father]. And walk in love, [esteeming and delighting in one another] as Christ loved us and gave Himself up for us, a slain offering and sacrifice to God [for you, so that it became] a sweet fragrance" (Eph. 5:1-2).

CHAPTER 6

FUNCTIONING AT OUR FULL POTENTIAL

*E*verything that God creates has the ability to function by the law of God for that particular creation to manifest what it was created to be. Within its DNA God gives the creation also the possibility to reach its maximum full potential. When the creation reaches its full potential it then produces its greatest value. However, the science behind the system of God's creation is that each creation depends on another to reach its full potential.

Example: A seed planted in the soil that has lost its nutritional value will not produce a healthy plant. The plant will not produce quality fruit. The fruit will not contain the fullness of nutritional value for the person eating it. The person will not have their fullness to function at optimal level because they are lacking a particular nutrient in their diet that was inadequate in the fruit. Everything functions by God's law of creation.

Now, let us take this and apply it to our position we have today in Christ as His body. Since we are a part of the body of Christ, this same law applies where if one part of His body, a person in Christ, is not doing their part functioning at full potential, then there will be a strain on other parts of the body, other members, making it difficult for them to function at optimal level because they are either lacking or having to over compensate carrying the responsibility of another part of the body.

Another example: If a person cannot chew their food properly because of bad dental issues, then it will make it hard on the esophagus for the food to be swallowed. The stomach will have to send extra enzymes to try to break the food down causing it to work harder. The small intestines will have to use extra energy trying to pull from the inadequate processed food the correct nutrients that the body needs. Lastly, the large intestines will be working overtime trying to get rid of the excess food that really should have been absorbed into the body, but could not because it was not masticated properly to begin with. Otherwise, the body could have potential problems of either constipation or diarrhea which would cause an imbalance of necessary fluids the body needs. This shift of the body's natural function can all be related to poor dental health.

When Jesus Christ died on the cross and rose again the old Adamic nature of the first Adam was crucified. Jesus Christ ended the existence of the first Adam as the last Adam and brought into manifestation a new creation in Christ. *"The fact is that Christ (the Messiah) has been raised from the dead, and He became the firstfruits of those who have fallen asleep [in death]. For since [it was] through a man that death [came into the world, it is] also through a Man that the resurrection of the dead [has come]. For just as [because of their union of nature] in Adam all people die, so also [by virtue of their union of nature] shall all in Christ be made alive. But each in his own rank and turn: Christ (the Messiah) [is] the firstfruits, then those who are Christ's [own will be resurrected] at His coming"* (1 Cor. 15:20-23 AMP).

When we personally accept and receive the reality of what Jesus Christ accomplished at Calvary removing the old Adam, we receive the same nature that is Christ. *"Consequently, from now on we estimate and regard no one from a [purely] human point of view [in terms of natural standards of value]. [No] even though we once did estimate Christ from a human viewpoint and as a man, yet now [we have such knowledge of Him that] we know Him no longer [in terms of the flesh]. Therefore if any person is in Christ (the Messiah) he is a new creation (a new creature altogether); the old [previous moral and spiritual condition] has passed away. Behold the fresh and new has come!"* (2 Cor. 5:16-17 AMP).

Within the principle of God's law, when we are born again, there is the requirement to learn from the position of birth as a newborn baby how to be Christ, even though our natural body may be fully developed as an adult. If we try to live as new creations in Christ by our old life, we will be bringing into our Christ identity habits of yesterday causing mixture and confusion reducing the excellent potential of quality fruit of the Holy Spirit to be manifested.

Unfortunately, most Christians do not live to their full potential because they hang on to memories of the old nature not realizing that when Jesus Christ was crucified, He not only died for us, but as us. Being born again is not something that we made a choice to obtain. It was already given to us over 2,000 years ago, but we needed to be awakened out of our ignorance by the quickening of the Holy Spirit. Again, the quickening of our spirit was not a moment in time where we had a choice, but God chose to unveil the truth of who we are. *"He hath chosen us in him before the foundation of the world, that we should be holy and without blame before him in love: Having predestinated us unto the adoption of children by Jesus Christ to himself, according to the good pleasure of his will, to the praise of the glory of his grace, wherein he hath made us accepted in the beloved"* (Ephesians 1: 4-6).

The "step-child" identity of the Adamic nature of adoption into the family of God does not exist with HIM and is not who we really are. It is the imagination of an old nature that we have given power and place to instead of living out of our Christ name and nature that Jesus reestablished when we were created in His image and kind before we were conceived in our mother's womb (Jer. 1:5). When we attempt to adapt our true identity in Christ into an old Adamic nature there is no power and authority of Christ flowing through us. It may be head knowledge, but the passion and heart identity is lacking. For quality fruit of the Holy Spirit to be manifested, the head of the body, Jesus Christ, must be the life of the body, the church flowing through the many members (1 Cor. 12:12).

Christians are identified as the bride of Christ Jesus. Jesus is the beloved bridegroom who has already prepared a place for His bride

(John 14:2). His desire is to procreate the marriage of the lamb joining the head with His body. God will not share His temple with another because He will not allow another identity to make claim to be the father of His fruit. *"A married woman is bound by law to her husband as long as he lives; but if her husband dies, she is loosed and discharged from the law concerning her husband. Accordingly, she will be held an adulteress if she unites herself to another man while her husband lives. But if her husband dies, the marriage law no longer is binding on her [she is free from that law]; and if she unites herself to another man, she is not an adulteress. Likewise, my brethren, you have undergone death as to the Law through the [crucified] body of Christ, so that now you may belong to Another, to Him Who was raised from the dead in order that we may bear fruit for God"* (Romans 7:2-4 AMP).

Therefore, God waits till the bride grows up from being a child of God, and is ready to come into the bridal chamber to consummate the marriage that officially took place at Pentecost when Jesus Christ gave us His Holy Spirit. Unfortunately, most Christians do not even know that they have already been wed, and therefore we have yet to see the corporate bride take off her veil identity as the corporate bride/body willing to accept the seed of her beloved.

This awakening has begun individually around the world. However, it takes a corporate bride to remove the control of an atmosphere of fear into an atmosphere of faith manifesting the kingdom of God in the earth. This great day of the Lord will come when believers in Christ come together in the unity of faith, the wife of the WORD, as one body knowing they are a new creation in Christ, no longer focused on what is in heaven for them, but the life we now live is about HIM. This is the mind of a bride ready to become one with her beloved as a wife and mother anticipating the coming of the fruit of her womb: *"The Word (Christ) became flesh (human, incarnate) and tabernacled (fixed His tent of flesh, lived awhile) among us"* (John 1:14 AMP).

As the Bride, we must remove fear in order for the Kingdom of God to manifest in the earth.

The fruit of this union is the manifestation of: *"The fruit of the [Holy] Spirit [the work which His presence within accomplishes] is love, joy (gladness), peace, patience (an even temper, forbearance), kindness, goodness (benevolence), faithfulness, gentleness (meekness, humility), self-control (self-restraint, continence). Against such things there is no law [that can bring a charge]. And those who belong (accept Him as their husband) to Christ Jesus (the Messiah) have crucified the flesh (the godless human nature) with its passions and appetites and desires"* (Galatians 5:22-24 AMP).

This covenant marriage we have with the Lamb is SPIRIT. Now the questions we desire to ask connected with this marriage are, "Is SPIRIT male or female? Can sons of God be brides of Christ? Is this a coming marriage in the future, or is it the inheritance of our full potential today as one body of Christ Jesus?"

Let us take a look at what the Scriptures say in John chapter four:

Jesus said to her, *"Woman (church, my body), believe Me, a time is coming when you will worship the Father neither [merely] in this mountain (mixture) nor [merely] in Jerusalem (grace and the law). You [Samaritans, a mixed up body of Christ] do not know what you are worshiping [you worship what you do not comprehend]."* You mix the DNA of being a child of God with the mind of an old nature.

The woman, church answers, *"We do know what we are worshiping [we worship what we have knowledge of and understand], for [after all] salvation comes from [among] the Jews (we know that we are children of God as believers in Christ)."*

Jesus answers her, *"A time will come, however, indeed **it is already here**, when the true (genuine) worshipers (those that are intimate with the Lamb) will worship (giving of their spirit, soul, mind, and body) the Father in spirit and in truth (reality); for **the Father is seeking just such people as these** as His worshipers (the true bride of Christ that is ready to be the carrier of His seed). God is a Spirit (a spiritual Being) and those who worship (intimate with) Him must worship (experience intimacy with) Him in spirit and in truth (reality)."*

"The woman (the church, body of Christ) said to Him, I know that Messiah is coming, He Who is called the Christ (the Anointed One); and when He arrives, He will tell us (give us more head knowledge for us to comprehend) everything we need to know and make it clear to us."

"Jesus said to her, I who now speak with you am He" (John 4:21-26 AMP).

The Scriptures unveil to us a conversation Jesus Christ had with a woman who had five husbands (grace), and at this moment was now living with a sixth man. This may have been written as a historical moment, but because the woman has no name, we are given this story as a metaphor where woman is a connection to the church, body of Christ Jesus, and helpmate to the image of God. She was carrying the seed of grace (5 husbands DNA) mixed with a man she was living with (6 is the number of man). This is the position that most of the body of Christ exists and functions in today as the church and bride of Jesus Christ. They are still waiting for the bridegroom to come someday while living with the old Adam. Most Christian's doctrines accept that we are living in the time of grace, but they still mix grace under the old Adamic nature.

Jesus has already prepared a place for us to join Him. His desire is to hear the heartbeat and passion of His beloved bride to be ready to consummate the marriage that took place when we took His name receiving Him as our Lord and Savior. He has been courting His bride for over 2,000 years but most of His body is still living below their full potential as His bride and wife because their minds are stuck in the past with their dead husband Adam.

Behind the personality and essence of God, the creator of all, is a Fathering Spirit desiring to be a Father to His Kind. The Holy Spirit of God is the Fathering Spirit that presents itself as a gentle dove that does not prey on another, but comes to the rescue identifying the need, heals the wounded, and delivers the bound setting the captive free.

"Happy (blessed, fortunate, enviable) is he who has the God of [special revelation to] Jacob for his help, whose hope is in the Lord his God, Who made heaven and earth, the sea, and all that is in them, Who keeps truth and is faithful forever, Who executes justice for the oppressed, Who gives food to the hungry.

The Lord sets free the prisoners, The Lord opens the eyes of the blind, the Lord lifts up those who are bowed down, the Lord loves the [uncompromisingly] righteous (those upright in heart and in right standing with Him). The Lord protects and preserves the strangers and temporary residents, He upholds the fatherless and the widow and sets them upright, but the way of the wicked He makes crooked (turns upside down and brings to ruin). The Lord shall reign forever, even Your God, O Zion, from generation to generation. Praise the Lord!" (Psalm 146:5-10 AMP).

Many times God holds back the blessings He has for us as a Father simply because we have not prepared our hearts to receive the fullness of what that would entail. Because of the hardness of our own hearts to the Father we limit our potential blessings causing us more harm than good. Many believers in Christ would rather hold on to their doctrines and traditions of old justifying their position of what they think God desires rather than giving place to having a relationship with God as Father and coming to know the Father's business.

"When they [Joseph and Mary] saw Him, they were amazed; and His mother said to Him, Child, why have you treated us like this? Here your father and I have been anxiously looking for you [distressed and tormented]. And He said to them, how is it that you had to look for me? Did you not see and know that it is necessary [as a duty] for me to be in My Father's house and [occupied] about My Father's business? But they did not comprehend what He was saying to them" (Luke 2:48-50 AMP).

We can know God as Almighty, Creator of all as most other religions know Him. This position allows us to identify a unity with other religions of where man came from. We can know God as the Father of Jesus Christ as Christians do. This brings us to a more personal relationship with God as a follower of Jesus Christ. These are good positions in a relationship, but they are not the full potential that God created and desired for us to experience while in our natural body. His desire is for us experience and manifest "Christ in you!" These are not just sweet words of someday when I get to heaven, but the ability to intimately know Jesus Christ as a bridegroom knows His beloved bride in the bridal chamber. It is this relationship that the Fathering Spirit is drawing us to desire so that the WORD that Jesus Christ impregnates into our spirit will produce manifested LIFE as flesh.

Jesus is not just interested in us being His followers and disciples, but to live our lives with an intense passion of oneness as His wife carrying His child, the WORD, within our inner most being so that out of us will flow rivers of living water. Out of our heart, Spirit to spirit, LOVE to love wills the creative life of Christ to be released from our mouth and tongue. It is here that the fruit of the HOLY SPIRIT, the child (the WORD) of the seed of God will come forth as LIFE into the world from the consummated marriage with the LAMB.

Today, God only sees one man, Jesus Christ, the son of God. From the Father's perspective, humanity on this earth is not another man that came from Adam, but a child bride called the church in preparation to be the beloved wife of the Lord Jesus Christ to produce His LIFE filling the earth with sons of God. Selah.

In the beginning…the earth (the embryo of God kind) was without form and an empty waste, and darkness was upon the face of the very great deep (what does God kind look like?). The Spirit of God was moving (hovering, brooding) over the face of the waters. And God said," Let there be light (ME); and there was light (God Kind)….

"There is a spirit in man: and the inspiration (breath, quickening, last Adam, life giving, Christ) *of the Almighty gives them understanding"* (Job 32:8).

A Fathering Spirit behind all creation is the personality, essence, and image of God being manifested in His kind. God is Spirit. The expression of His Holy Spirit is Love. When we hunger and thirst for righteousness, intimacy with our Beloved Savior, the fullness of LOVE, LIFE, LIGHT responds, and the Holy Spirit unites with the spirit of man (the bride, the church, the wife of the Lord Jesus Christ) to bring forth LIFE.

"The Word was made flesh" (John 1:14).

"Out of his (the body of Christ) *belly* (womb, where life is carried) *shall flow rivers of living water. (But this spoke he of the Spirit, which they that believe on him should receive: for the Holy Ghost was not yet given; because that Jesus was not yet glorified.)"* (John 7:38-39).

"The abundance of the heart (full of LOVE) *his* (the church) *mouth speaks* (creation is manifested)*"* (Luke 6:45).

"Death and life are in the power of the tongue (the spoken word that originated in our belly and flowed through our heart)*: and they that love it shall eat* (give birth to) *the fruit* (fruit of our husband, the Holy Spirit, or the fruit of Adam) *thereof"* (Proverbs 18:21).

"He that is joined unto the Lord is one spirit" (1 Corinthians 6:17).

When the Spirit and soul are joined there is a consummation of the marriage of the Lamb. To experience the Fatherhood of God, He sent His Son, Jesus Christ, unveiling the Father's heart unveiling His grace, love, and salvation. The Father foreknew you before you were conceived in the womb and He accepted you and named you before you knew Him as your Father. The greatness of His love drew you to Him to develop a relationship as His son in unity with Jesus Christ as one body in Christ.

Living in the full potential of our inheritance is living beyond mercy and grace manifesting the authority of God as sons of God in the earth bringing the Kingdom of God into our NOW. We move out of "what can I get from God" to "what can I release in me of the Father's heart to give God the glory."

Functioning at our Full Potential = Eternal Life Now.

Being able to function in the image of our Heavenly Father while in our natural body on a consistent basis so that the limitations of time have no effect on us.

"WHEN JESUS had spoken these things, He lifted up His eyes to heaven and said, Father, the hour has come. Glorify and exalt and honor and magnify Your Son, so that Your Son may glorify and extol and honor and magnify

You. [Just as] You have granted Him power and authority over all flesh (all humankind), [now glorify Him] so that He may give eternal life to all whom You have given Him. And this is eternal life: [it means] to know (to perceive, recognize, become acquainted with, and understand) You, the only true and real God, and [likewise] to know Him, Jesus [as the] Christ (the Anointed One, the Messiah), Whom You have sent" (John 17:1-3 AMP).

"PAUL, A bond servant of God and an apostle (a special messenger) of Jesus Christ (the Messiah) to stimulate and promote the faith of God's chosen ones and to lead them on to accurate discernment and recognition of and acquaintance with the Truth which belongs to and harmonizes with and tends to godliness, [Resting] in the hope of eternal life, [life] which the ever truthful God Who cannot deceive promised before the world or the ages of time began. And [now] in His own appointed time He has made manifest (made known) His Word and revealed it as His message through the preaching entrusted to me by command of God our Savior" (Titus 1:1-3 AMP).

"As for you, keep in your hearts what you have heard from the beginning. If what you heard from the first dwells and remains in you, then you will dwell in the Son and in the Father [always]. And this is what He Himself has promised us—the life, the eternal [life]" (1 John 2:24-25 AMP).

There are two ways of understanding what we are going through: our own interpretation or God's. God's vision incorporates past, present, and future into now. We take our now and try to predict our future based on our past. We see trials but God sees great responsibility. We see being cast away and rejected but God sees chosen and selected. We see contradiction but God sees preparation. We see challenges but God sees victory.

"For My thoughts are not your thoughts, neither are your ways My ways, says the Lord. For as the heavens are higher than the earth, so are My ways higher than your ways and My thoughts than your thoughts. For as the rain and snow come down from the heavens, and return not there again, but water the earth and make it bring forth and sprout, that it may give seed to the sower and bread to the eater" (Isaiah 55:8-10 AMP).

The purpose of God is to position us to "live by faith." **God will not put us through anything that He is not going to use for us.** *"We know that all things work together for good to them that love God, to them who are the called according to his purpose"* (Romans 8:28). *"As for you, you thought evil against me, but God meant it for good, to bring about that many people should be kept alive, as they are this day"* (Genesis 50:20 AMP).

Since God's nature and character is ALWAYS good, He will always bring to pass what was meant for evil and bring forth the goodness as a furthering expression in our life of who He is. God does not ordain evil for our good, but will take the broken stiches in our lives and weave a master piece of Excellency that will be seeds for the next generation.

"The LORD shall give that which is good; and our land shall yield her increase. Righteousness shall go before him; and shall set us in the way of his steps" (Psalm 85:12-13). *"All [these] things are [taking place] for your sake, so that the more grace (divine favor and spiritual blessing) extends to more and more people and multiplies through the many, the more thanksgiving may increase [and redound] to the glory of God"* (2 Corinthians 4:15 AMP).

Do not let your past keep you from your inherited destiny of your Heavenly Father's blessings for your life today.

The truth that you know is what will set you free.

Your biggest enemy is not your future, but the fear of the unknown you choose to hang on to.

CHAPTER 7

THE ETERNAL WORD OF GOD

"In the beginning was the Word, and the Word was with God, and the Word was God." (John 1:1)

We know that God is the Word. It isn't God over "here" and the scriptures over "there." We also know that the Word is Jesus. The Word was with God; the Word is God.

God is eternal, all light, no darkness, all life, no death. Therefore, the Word must be the same. We take God out and fill in religion when we take the Word as literal, laced with judgment and condemnation.

The mindset that God gave us with the writings of the scriptures came through a Jewish mindset. Even though the New Testament was written in Greek, Jesus and the disciples spoke and thought with a Jewish mind. The major difference between the Greek and Jewish mind is that the Greek sees scriptures as philosophical. The natural mind must make sense of the things of God, and the more education a person has in theology and philosophy, the greater chance he will try to understand the Word through these means of understanding what God was trying to express.

The Greek mindset puts aside the fact that it is the Holy Spirit who reveals the mysteries of God. He does not need educational degrees, and can reveal God through anyone.

The Hebrew mind will ask "What is God saying to you?" It gives respect to the fact that wisdom of the Word brings life, and light to different parts of the body in different ways. There is no "I'm right and your wrong" with the interpretations of what the Holy Spirit is revealing to an individual. There is a walk of faith that there is only one Holy Spirit and One God. Even though there are many members of one body, it is only the blood of Jesus, the Word, which gives life to the many members. This kind of faith declares that it is the responsibility of the Holy Spirit to bring unity to the body.

I have shared the above for the purpose of giving some insight to the Word of God that I hope will expand and encourage a hunger to allow the Holy Spirit to reveal mysteries in the Word that you didn't see before. Here are some thoughts to consider:

I have started taking a few lessons in learning the Hebrew language. The first thing I've noticed about the language is that every letter of their alphabet is a word in itself, not just a letter. Each letter also has a numerical value. Each Hebrew word has either a masculine or feminine form which represents a spiritual or soul emphasis that is not gender related. It gives a new meaning to the words male or female used in scripture.

Let's take one of the letters of the Hebrew alphabet to show other alternatives in viewing the word of God.

The last letter of the alphabet is the "tav." It is transliterated as the "t" sound. In the New Testament it was interpreted as the Greek letter "omega." Unfortunately, translating from Hebrew to Greek took away the expansion of potential meaning for this letter.

The letter "tav" has the numerical value of 400. It is the end of all the other letters. The number 4 can represent the four corners of the earth, or four directions, or fullness. The number "0" is an eternal number with no ending or beginning just as God is. The double "0"s can represent a double witness, or even the old and new testaments. The original writings would use the "tav" with a silent "h" to separate the "tet" letter of the alphabet which also had the "t" sound. The "h" was later dropped in translating, but if the "tav" was used it was known to expect the "h" to be there which was given as the breath of God.

The "vav" or "v" sound in the word "tav" has a numerical value of 6, which is the number of man. It is used as a connecting letter for the word "and" to bring two or more thoughts together as one.

The Torah uses the "tav" not the "tet". It has been misinterpreted as the Jewish Law; but correctly translated, according to the Jewish Publication Society of America's "Holy Scriptures" it means: teachings, instructions, directions, rituals, and obligations. Very rarely is it ever used as law.

In Matthew 5:18 Jesus says, "till heaven and earth pass, one jot or one tittle shall in no wise pass from the law, till all be fulfilled." He is referring to God's instructions given to Moses to pass on to man for living a life of blessing and joy, not a matter of law and commandment. God gave the Torah as guidelines for a whole way of life.

Putting all this information together gives insight to the letter "tav." It has more significance than just making a "t" sound. We have the numbers 4+0+0 and 6. The number 10 represents God's creativity. The usage of it can also mean the fullness of the earth and heavens coming together with the instructions of life between God and man, so that God can be manifested all in all.

The insight of the letter "tav" is not limited to this teaching, but an example of going beyond the limited English version of using the letters in the alphabet to understanding God's word. God is eternal, and each letter of His Word has eternal ability to be manifested. It is up to us to open our hearts with a teachable spirit allowing the Holy Spirit to pull the veil away to reveal the eternal goodness of our heavenly Father through His letters to His children. May God bless you with this teaching and draw you to His eternal love.

CHAPTER 8

MOVING FORWARD IN CHRIST: OUR DIRECTION AND HEIGHT

"Our citizenship is in heaven. And we eagerly await a Savior from there, the Lord Jesus Christ, who, by the power that enables him to bring everything under his control, will transform our lowly bodies so that they will be like his glorious body" (Philippians 3:20-21).

We are told by Papa God through our brother Paul that we are citizens of heaven NOW while living in our flesh on the earth. "As we eagerly wait for our Savior" is not about someday when we cross over to the other side and leave our natural body, but the unveiling of who we truly are in Christ NOW. Our Savior, Christ Jesus, is with us today ready to rule and reign in our natural body, eager to take authority over all strongholds that do not align with our position that has been already established in heaven.

"And God raised us up with Christ and seated us with him in the heavenly realms in Christ Jesus" (Ephesians 2:6).

"Since, then, you have been raised with Christ, set your hearts on things above, where Christ is, seated at the right hand of God" (Colossians 3:1).

When God put us into Christ as being born again from the quickening Spirit of the last Adam (1 Corinthians 15), we were given an elevated status on this earth. This means that we live from the place of above, heaven, while in our natural body as we are going through issues of the world. Connecting with LIFE in the Spirit is not only about our direction of moving forward, but what height are we functioning from? What height does Papa God want you to travel at as you enter into your next season?

Jesus gave us permission that whatever is bound in heaven we can bind on earth, and whatever is loosed in heaven we can loosen on earth today. We must be prepared for the enemy of God to come at us like a flood, but also to be prepared in this season for God to lift us up!

"When the enemy shall come in like a flood, the Spirit of the Lord shall lift up a standard against him" (Isaiah 59:19).

When we receive visions from the Lord that give us forward direction, but not height, we miss a hidden part of the vision that will unlock the inner mysterious of our identity in Christ. The best we end up with are prophecies of promises of God to come to us versus the truth that the fullness of those promises are already within us because God goes with us wherever we are.

The Apostolic ministry of the body of Christ has a purpose to release the paradox of height and direction for the body. Be aware of your territory the Lord has placed you in. What is the atmospheric condition? Much of the body of Christ is busy dealing with storms and crisis from the position of fear and exhaustion wondering when it will end. The Lord tells us to fight the battle from His position of rest, praise, joy, love, righteousness, and peace. What we find out is from that position, the battle has already been won. So we come down from the height we were at in intimacy with the Father to be sabotaged with the pressures of this world. Next thing we know we are exhausted trying to give others encouragement and love. Even Jesus had to spend quality time daily with the Father to re-energize Himself with the washing of LIFE (John 17).

Father God desires for us to rule and reign on this earth as kings and priests unto His glory. We each have an allotted territory to take authority over the strongholds of this world. *"As He is, so are we NOW in this world"* (1 John 4:17).

As we move between being sons of God/bride of Christ we have times in our life that we go forth in the position of decreeing heavenly authority as rightful heirs of the Father's' kingdom. This is our kingship/Sonship position. However, there must also be times when we have oneness with Christ Jesus who is our King and also our Beloved. This is intimacy on the highest level allowing the seed of our Beloved to impregnate us that we know we are carrying His name, nature, and character to birth a son as His wife and authority in this world. This is our position as priests/brides/wife. The son in us is able to establish the Kingdom of Heaven, not fighting battles for the King of kings, but as His authority established already in us.

Most of the body of Christ are fired up to go forth and conquer, but not willing to take the quality time of intimacy to know that the battle is not ours, but His and it is already finished. Our real responsibility is to go forth and multiply filling the earth with HIS KIND, God KIND, taking dominion and authority of all that is not Christ from our heavenly position where we are seated and resting in Christ Jesus (Genesis 1:26-28).

My husband and I are building a new house, but for the past month we have been challenged with every excuse of why we still have not gotten our temporary electric power pole and hook up established. After going around and around for an hour with the company on the phone, not getting any more information than I already knew, I decided to go down to the local office and talk with someone face to face. As I was driving to the building I took a deep breath and shifted my thought position of coming up higher unto the Father's presence. (I know, I really should have done this first). I heard Papa say, "So are you ready to do it my way?" I laughed and said yes.

He then helped me get clarity of what was really going on. It was the power company's internal communication system, not my problem but theirs, and I didn't need to own it. If anyone working within the company were to be in my position of needing a temporary power pole they would have face to face communication to get the problem resolved, but outsiders are treated differently. The Lord reminded me that ALL outsiders were treated that way and not to make it personal, but, if I were someone like the Mayor or President they would instantly give me the VIP treatment. Papa said to me, you are royalty, act like it so they know. I shifted my thoughts of who I AM, not in arrogance, but the fact of BEING a daughter of the KING. As soon as I walked in the front door, I received the VIP treatment being taken straight to the CEO who kept apologizing for the incompetence of their communication issues, assuring that I would have the power connected within the next few days. Then he gave me his personal cell number for my husband to contact him directly if we had any further problems.

That is an example of how we should be shifting our territory for bringing in the Kingdom of God Now.

How many of our leaders in the body of Christ are willing to go to a new height? Moses had to give way to Joshua; David had to give way to Solomon.

How much of another fight do we have in us willing to allow the joy of the Lord to lead? Most of us worship the Lord from tradition and customs from the formality of familiarity we hang out with of a particular part of the body of Christ. If they raise their hands we raise our hands, if they dance and sing in tongues then so do we. We get into worship by what the worship leader and band has orchestrated and determined. However, would that song and dance be the instrument and tool you would take to the front line to defeat your enemy?

Yesterday, my husband and I visited a very large church. The service was great, but after we left, we had to exit onto a major road where there was a law officer controlling the light signals for traffic. The reason was not just because of the heavy traffic exiting the church we just attended, but because there was also a church about the same size on the other side of this major road, and they were exiting from their service at the same time. My thoughts were taken to Jesus going to Samaria and visiting the woman at the well who had five husbands and was now living with a man. The truth of her circumstance was identified, but the real truth that Jesus wanted her/body of Christ to identify with was not which mountain to worship on, but that He was the living water:

"The water/the seed that I will give shall become a spring of water welling up (flowing, bubbling) [continually] within him/MAN (male and female) unto (into, for) eternal life" (John 4:14).

"He who believes in Me [who cleaves to and trusts in and relies on Me] as the Scripture has said, from his innermost being shall flow [continuously] springs and rivers of living water." (John 7:38).

This is bedroom, Holy of Holies, intimacy with Christ Jesus. In the natural world it is the male who carries the seed of life, but in the Kingdom of God there is only one male heir carrying the seed of God and that is Christ Jesus. The body must understand their position as a woman's issue of blood in order to worship in Spirit and Truth. Natural man does not have blood issues dictated monthly by their body which determines readiness to accept the seed, and most male leaders in the church don't want to talk about this because they don't know what to do with it since they don't have the experience.

We are kings and priests unto the Lord. Levi priests worshipped 24/7, not just when they were gathered together, but also in the quiet time with the Lord. They worshipped while they worked, rested, ate, slept, and fellowshipped. Worship was not something they did, but who they were. **True worshippers are atmosphere changers simply by their presence in the room**. They don't need to be announced or wear the most elaborate clothes with bells and whistles, they simply radiate with the Life and Love of God because of who they are in Christ, carrying His name.

If we are pursuing the presence of God, we will recognize true worshippers among us. We will be drawn to them as a light in this world that takes us to a higher level in our spirit, drawing us to the Father. They may be on the street corner or the grocery store. The obvious place one would think inside a church building may be where only a few are found hidden in the back of the sanctuary.

The attention will not be about them, but the awareness that they are missing something in their relationship with the Father that they desire knowing; it takes entering into the secret place of their heart.

God has not seen a sinner since Calvary.

If you have been single and go to a friend's wedding to celebrate their marriage, often times there is a moment in your heart that you recognize an internal love in the atmosphere that this couple have found, and you are happy for them, but there is a part of you that is still searching for the perfect mate. Oh, we allow justification to come in saying to ourselves, "been there and done that" and now you're dealing with the pains of a divorce, or you're so focused on your career you don't have time for real love, just non-committed relationships. These are just veils we place over our hearts not allowing ourselves to truly search within and be vulnerable before God because we don't want to deal with unmet expectations.

Our beginning when we entered this world as a baby was to pursue unconditional LOVE that we were born and created for, but our finish line is to BE in the presence of LOVE in oneness with HIM while in our natural body in the earth.

Paul says it to the church in Philippi, "*[For my determined purpose is] that I may know Him [that I may progressively become more deeply and intimately acquainted with Him, perceiving and recognizing and understanding the wonders of His Person more strongly and more clearly], and that I may in that same way come to know the power outflowing from His resurrection [which it exerts over believers], and that I may so share His sufferings as to be continually transformed [in spirit into His likeness even] to His death, [in the hope] that if possible I may attain to the [spiritual and moral] resurrection [that lifts me] out from among the dead [even while in the body].*"

Our relationship and reflection of being Christ Ones on earth should be a demonstration of our citizenship we already have in Heaven, but if our relationship with Heaven is always from a position of trying to get there someday instead of who we already are, then when we enter an atmosphere of unfamiliarity, we don't have the weapon of worship that brings joy in the midst of our challenges to overcome our enemy. A Levi priest was not supposed to see judgment or condemnation in the People of God, but to be in a position of intercession and authority that could overcome that sin and death. When they were called into action to stand in the gap, they had to be fully armored with their identity and the position they held. If they saw the sins of the world upon the children of God, they were supposed to judge themselves asking, "What is in me that I see the sin in you?"

The number one phrase Christians identity themselves and other believers with is, "I'm a sinner saved my grace." **Papa God has not seen a sinner since Calvary**, just children that are living in ignorance and darkness of who they truly are in Christ.

As citizens of Heaven, we are in this world, but not of it. There are no sinners in heaven. This world is built upon negativity from the enemy of God, but greater is He that is in you, than he that is in the world. We often are looking for Jesus to return and make everything beautiful, however, He gave us the scepter of His authority to do greater works. He breathed upon us His Holy Spirit to calm the storms, heal the sick, find hidden coins in unusual places, and raise the dead back to life while in the natural. Papa God has not dealt with sin since the cross in which Jesus took it ALL, and gave us His righteousness. It is His righteousness in us that Papa God is pulling through our natural body to be unveiled.

As sons of God, we have the direction of Father God's authority, but we first must know the height and intimacy of HIM as our beloved Bridegroom in the position that we are His Bride. It is the Bride that receives the seed identity to create the son. This is the true challenge the church/body of Christ is faced with today. We have come through the season and many years of being trained and equipped by the male side of God's kind, but there is not one male in history able to share the EXPERIENCE of the brideship intimacy that Jesus desires with His church/His body. There is not one male in church history that has experienced the internal changes the female side of God goes through in pregnancy and birthing a child.

When God created MAN in HIS image, He created THEM male and female in unity and equal necessity to go forth and produce His KIND, taking dominion and authority over all creatures. When the Spirit of MAN (male/female) and Christ rested together on the seventh day as one (Genesis 2), together they produced a man/son. They encouraged the man to grow up and take authority naming the creatures, which also gave wisdom and understanding of what was NOT like man/son. Yet the pattern man saw was Christ Jesus and MAN/Bride of Christ together as one. Man could find no helpmate outside himself, hence, Wisdom comes in and unlocks the mystery "Christ in YOU, bone of HIS bone and flesh of HIS flesh."

The world is under an identity crisis. All of creation is waiting eagerly for the manifestation of the sons of God as one body in Christ. However, Christ is waiting for His Bride to make herself ready without spot or wrinkle. Let us come up to where He is seated in Heavenly places (height) to get proper direction for the manifestation of the sons of God. Ego and world issues that both men and women are camping around cannot be a part of what is brought into the bridal chamber of intimacy with the KING. It is only the image of Christ that our Beloved Bridegroom seeks to consummate the marriage to produce sons of God.

Right now this is happening all over the world where men are putting aside their Scripture understanding and relationship with Jesus from their previous theology, recognizing the necessity to be part of a Bride company. Yes, it is a challenge, a warfare is in the hearts and minds because of the identity crisis the world is challenged with on sexuality. Sonship and Brideship of GOD do not identify sexual preference issues the world struggles with. I can be a son of God, but in the natural I am a mother, wife, and daughter. I learn how to be a son of God by appreciating the unique differences of who I am compared to my brothers, husband, father, and my sons. What makes them tick? How do they handle situations differently than me? Could I properly do a job the way they would if the challenge was there? However, no matter how well I can do a job that might be something a guy usually does, I have body parts and functions that cannot be changed to reclassify me of being anything but a female. The same thing goes for men. Men may enjoy doing things that most women do so they think that makes them attracted to men, but men together or women together cannot fulfill the basic foundation of reproducing after one's own kind while in the act of intimacy.

If the body of Christ is only receiving wisdom and understanding from a masculine perspective, we will wait for another generation until the feminine side of the body of Christ rises up to unlock the mystery of how to bring into the world the manifestation of the finished work where the Spirit and the Bride say come. Intimacy involves a blood issue that carries the Life of the flesh. Men can know about the involvement of reproduction and the blood, but they cannot internalize or experience what is truly taking place. It is necessary for women to teach men in love the experience of carrying and birthing the seed of Christ to produce sons of God. Women were created to receive unconditional love. Men were created to be the manifestation of giving unconditional love as Christ loves the church. Together a LOVE CHILD/God Child is produced (Ephesians).

So you can't find your car keys, and you're sure that your wife did something with them. Think like a woman, oh yes, she went out the back door that was locked yesterday evening to see the SON resting over the water!

"For it is written, I will destroy the wisdom of the wise, and will bring to nothing the understanding of the prudent. Where is the wise? Where is the scribe? Where is the disputer of this world? Has not God made foolish the wisdom of this world? For after that in the wisdom of God the world by wisdom knew not God, it pleased God by the foolishness of preaching to save them that believe" (1 Corinthians 1:19-21).

"The testimony of Christ is now confirmed in you: So that you come behind in no gift; waiting for the coming of our Lord Jesus Christ: Who shall also confirm you unto the end, that you may be blameless in the day of our Lord Jesus Christ. God is faithful, by whom you were called unto the fellowship/intimacy of his Son Jesus Christ our Lord. NowI beseech you, by the NAME of our Lord Jesus Christ (I AM), that you all speak the same thing, and that

there be no divisions among you; but that you be perfectly joined together in the same mind and in the same judgment" (1 Corinthians 1:6-10).

Where was the male unconditional love that should have told Eve that she was already as God? Thinking more with his soul than the Spirit of Christ.

Eve had a void in her relationship that another voice was filling, and so adultery and false identity came in.

CHAPTER 9

BUILDING THE CITY OF GOD: THE NEW JERUSALEM

Psalm **40:7** *"Then said I, Behold, I come* (Jesus Christ)*; in the volume* (body of Christ) *of the book it is written of me."*

Hebrews 10:7, *"Then I said, Behold, here I am, coming to do Your will, O God—[to fulfill] what is written of Me in the volume (Genesis to Revelation) of the Book* (Christ's autobiography; Husband and Wife; Jesus Christ & the church)*."*

2 Corinthians 3:3, *"you are an epistle (pages in the book) of Christ, ministered by us, written not with ink but by the Spirit of the living God, not on tablets of stone but on tablets of flesh, that is, of the heart."*

Epistles, chapters in the book... testimonies, are personal experiences of what Jesus Christ did for you while you were in a situation that only God could receive the glory.

Revelation 15:5, *"After this I looked and the sanctuary of the tent of the testimony in heaven was thrown open."*

A personal experience, a testimony, becomes a city by the actions of joining together as one with other testimonies. This is the church of the city of the

New Jerusalem we read in Revelation that John wrote about. The city of God or the bride/wife of Jesus Christ on the earth filling the earth with His glory.

God is not interested in words from the churches that bring division and separation to the body of Christ, but THE CHURCH that has a covenant spirit of unity with the foundation that Jesus Christ is Lord.

Matthew16:16-18 AMP, *"Simon Peter replied, you are the Christ, the Son of the living God. Then Jesus answered him, blessed are you, Simon Bar-Jonah. For flesh and blood [men] have not revealed this to you, but My Father Who is in heaven. And I tell you, you are Peter, a large piece of rock, and on this rock I will build My church, and the gates of Hades (the powers of the infernal region) shall not overpower it [or be strong to its detriment or hold out against it]."*

Each person is a chapter, a testimony, in the book of Jesus Christ. Each time we read a name in the Bible, we are reading a testimony of the personal experience that person had with their relationship to Christ. Matthew, Mark, Luke, John, Paul, Peter, James, and the many other witnesses of Jesus Christ each shared their experiences and relationship of personal understanding with Christ Jesus. No one person had the full understanding, but together, their testimonies have laid the foundation for the church, the body of Jesus Christ to be manifested; the New Jerusalem, the city of God on the earth to rule and reign with Christ.

If we took 20 women sharing their experiences of preparing for their wedding, the actual wedding, and the day after the wedding we would hear similar events but a personal story that only that bride could share. No one would be able to contradict her experience. The same thing holds true if you asked 20 women of their experience of having their first child. Being a bride/wife as the church of the Lord Jesus Christ is an experience that must come through the natural understanding of being a woman. The masculine side of the body of Christ has done a wonderful job of bringing the church into repentance, salvation, and justification as children and sons of God, but to be a bride and wife it takes teaching the body of Christ from the feminine side of the image of God HE created in Adam.

"So God created mankind in his own image, in the image of God he created them; male and female he created them" (Genesis 1:27). *"This is the book of the generations of Adam. In the day that God created man, in the likeness of God made he him; male and female created he them; and blessed them, and called their name Adam, in the day when they were created"* (Genesis 5:1-2).

The Old Testament gave us a pattern pointing the way for Jesus Christ to be manifested. The New Testament gives us the testimony of personal, covenant experiences becoming joint heirs with Christ. Our lives are not created to be about ourselves and what we can do, but about being joined as a wife to her husband, Jesus Christ, to create a family. When we use the inheritance of the testimony we have in the Bible to justify the means of building a denomination, decree, or doctrine that divides the body of Christ, we come under our own judgment with the WORD of God.

"For it is time for judgment to begin with God's household; and if it begins with us, what will the outcome be for those who do not obey the gospel of God?" (1 Peter 4:17).

The world is experiencing a shaking that has never been seen before as God is cleansing and purifying His bride, the church of the Lord Jesus Christ. For a season, God has allowed separation and division with races, religions, genders, ages, cultures, economics, traditions, and customs. He is now removing the boundaries that have once separated His boy to come together as one body in the unity of His faith that will manifest the WORD made flesh and dwells among men.

God is removing the boundaries to open our eyes to the unity of All in All.

As we discern the times and the seasons, we realize that no one area has a greater voice or monopoly than another and the ability to express our voice can instantly be heard around the world. The church of the Lord Jesus Christ is no longer a literal building place to come together to fellowship, but claims unity and dominion over the air, the sea, and under the earth by the WORD of the testimony of Christ within.

The WORD is Spirit which comes and goes as the wind with no building, place, or man's name to identify with for God does not share His glory with anyone or anything. The Spirit reveals itself through man by love, joy, peace, forbearance, kindness, goodness, faithfulness, gentleness and self-control.

The WORD is LIFE which has no death, no issues of right, wrong, good or bad connected with knowledge.

The WORD is LIGHT which has no darkness or limitation involving time. It is NOW, which comes in faster than a twinkling eye where once darkness or time may have thought it controlled, does not even exist.

The WORD is LOVE which unveils itself with unconditional patience and kindness. It does not envy, or boast, nor is it proud. It does not dishonor others and is not self-seeking. Love is not easily angered, or keeps record of wrongs. Love does not delight in evil but rejoices with the truth. It always protects, always trusts, always hopes, and always perseveres. Love never fails.

"When I shut up the heavens (harden the hearts of men) *so that there is no rain* (revelation of the WORD), *or command locusts* (government, leaders, and religious officials) *to devour the land* (the people's inheritance) *or send a plague* (taxes) among my people, if my people, the *bride/wife of Jesus Christ, who are* ***called by my name****, will humble themselves, judge their own hearts, and pray and seek my face and turn from their wicked ways,* (stop bringing the ego into the covenant relationship) *then I will hear from heaven* (the heart of my beloved), *and I will forgive their sin and will heal their land. Now my eyes will be open and my ears attentive to the prayers offered in this place* (the marriage bed, the place of consummation between the Spirit and the bride, the HOLY of HOLIES). *I have chosen and consecrated this temple* (the hearts of my beloved) *so that my Name* (CHRIST) *may be there forever. My eyes and my heart will always be there."* (2 Chronicles 7:13-15).

In Daniel chapter six we read a familiar story about King Darius who is a good king, but still had an ego issue in the way he rules which allowed a spirit of control and manipulation to enter in. He surrounds himself with many advisors including Daniel, but unfortunately the other advisors who had ego issues of their own do not care for Daniel and want him out of the committee because he does not go along with the crowd. They try to find some personal issues against Daniel to take to the king that would disqualify him to be a part of the advisory committee, but nothing could be found. The only possible way they were able to come up with was to address what was most important in Daniel's life and that was his relationship and allegiance to God. Now Darius didn't have a problem with Daniel worshipping God, but the others did. However, through a manipulative decree working towards King Darius's ego created by those that wanted Daniel out, they were able to get the King to establish a law that they knew would come against Daniel. Due to King Darius's ego, he was blinded to the impact this decree would have on Daniel, who was his most faithful and loyal advisor, until it was too late.

"So the king gave the order, and they brought Daniel and threw him into the lions' den. The king said to Daniel, "May your God, whom you serve continually, rescue you!" King Darius was forced to put Daniel in the lion's den by his own word. *"A stone was brought and placed over the mouth of the den, and the king sealed it with his own signet ring and with the rings of his nobles, so that Daniel's situation might not be changed."* He grieved at the position he was placed in, but recognized that it was his own fault. *"Then the king returned to his palace and spent the night without eating and without any entertainment being brought to him. And he could not sleep."* The next day at first light he went to the lion's den and called out to Daniel. *"When he came near the den, he called to Daniel in an anguished voice, "Daniel, servant of the living God, has your God, whom you serve continually, been able to rescue you from the lions?"*

I believe that the king repented and cried out to God all night while Daniel was in the pit of hell with the lions, but when the LIGHT of God is with you, and you know who you are in Christ the King, you have the covenant right of being one with the KING in HIS decree to call out the name that is in bondage, hell, and identifying with bone of His bone and flesh of His flesh.

Daniel responds, "May the king live forever! My God sent his angel and he shut the mouths of the lions. They have not hurt me, because I was found innocent in his sight. Nor have I ever done any wrong before you, Your Majesty."

Daniel tells the king the words that were used against him, "may the king live forever," but now it comes from the heart of glorifying God in unity with King Darius and not King Darius's ego.

This is the position that God is calling His church; His beloved wife. If My people called by My name. Are you called by the name of Christ? Are you a Christ one bone of His bone and flesh of His flesh? There is only one husband whose name is Jesus Christ. He gives the SEED of LIFE. The church; the wife of Christ; male and female are to prepare the soil with prepare to receive the consummation of the marriage to the Lamb of God so that out of our bellies will flow rivers of living water and the WORD of God becomes flesh as the LIGHT of the world among men that choose to live among the tree of Knowledge and what seems right in their own eyes, but will become their own destruction.

Come Lord Jesus in the volume of your book. Let Your banner over us be Love, and may your mercy and grace go before your judgment and truth. Let the Spirit and the Bride say come! (Rev. 22:17).

CHAPTER 10

THE FATHER OF SPIRITS: GOD

"Moreover, we have had earthly fathers who disciplined us and we yielded [to them] and respected [them for training us]. Shall we not much more cheerfully submit to the Father of spirits and so [truly] live?" Hebrews 12:9 AMP

Father of Spirits: the highest revelation we can experience is to know God as Father. It comes from a generational impartation that began with Jesus coming in the flesh and unveiling to us the Father (Luke 3: 25-38). Until we know God as our Heavenly Father, we are as children tossed around sharing God with other religions for there is, *"ONE GOD and Father of all* (religions, race, genders, cultures, nationalities, denominations, beliefs), *who is above all, and through all, and in you all. But to each one of us* (believers in Christ Jesus) *grace was given according to the measure of Christ's gift"* (Eph. 4:6-7).

Jesus came to show us the Father, His Father and our Father (John 20:17). The DNA that was in Jesus Christ is in us (Luke 3:38). This is eternal LIFE; when we know God as Father, then truth is unveiled that our true identity is not a sinner saved by grace, but spirit life in Christ. Our flesh is where the Holy Spirit of our Father abides in us.

All the other realms and avenues we connect to Jesus are added blessings (savior, healer, redeemer, etc.) we receive when the Holy Spirit quickens our spirit and we accept Jesus Christ personally. However, the main objective for Jesus coming into the earth, dying on the cross, opening up the grave of death, and bringing resurrected Life back into our lives was to unveil to us our true identity as gods, children of the Most High God (John 10:34, Psalm 82:6).

Everyone wants God to do something, but the fact is, God has already done everything.

Man does not live by bread alone, but by every word that proceeds out of the mouth of God. This does not mean every word that we read. The word is the letter which is able to leap off the pages of the Scriptures and ascend into the realm of spirit and open the mouth of God. The Word creates; it has the ability and the power to change things: create. However, it must first be launched from the platform of the written word. For this reason, studying the word and showing we are approved by God, allows the breath of God in us to unveil His creativity through us as the written Word becomes life in our flesh. We must first find ourselves in the written word of God by hearing (Romans 10:17).

People are waiting for God to do something or miracles to happen, playing a game of hit and miss as children of God. When miracles happen, it is because the Word in us is witnessing to the hearing and seeing of TRUTH by the Spirit of God. This can happen by the words in the pages of the written word of God becoming Life in us, leaping off the pages as the Holy Spirit speaks to us, bringing forth the transformation of Christ in us into the world.

This also happens when we hear His Holy Spirit speaking to our spirit through others as they speak the written Word in the character and nature of our Father drawing us to Him. In the midst of the double witness taking place within our body (hearing and seeing), there He is. "*Again, I tell you that if two of you on earth agree about anything you ask for, it will be done for you by my Father in heaven. For where two or three come together in my name, there am I with them*" (Matt. 18:19-20 NIV).

Not everyone can read the Scriptures with the understanding of the Father's character and nature: LOVE, LIGHT, and LIFE. There are many who have memorized verses in the Bible, but they do not allow the word to become flesh in them. They know they are saved and going to heaven, but when it comes to handling situations on earth, they fall apart. Yes, they can start quoting Scripture, and they can start praying, but they do not believe in their heart the Truth that God is their Heavenly Father. They only know that Jesus made a way for them to spend eternity in heaven instead of hell. This is one of many reasons we have "prayer chains" and "prayer lists" leaning upon quantity instead of quality of faith. They are hoping that someone will have the faith of the Father to call forth the power of transformation, manifesting miracles in the earth.

Not everyone has the exposure to read the Scriptures because they simply do not have the written word, or they do not know how to read it in the language it is presented. There are many believers in Christ with the desire and heart to share the Gospel of Jesus Christ out in the mission fields around the world. The first obstacle they have to confront is the ability to communicate. If the missionaries are trying to share the Gospel in English and the people only understand another language, they will not only reject the written word, but also the verbal sounds.

Can communication happen? Can the mission be successful? YES! When the missionaries BECOME the written word, and share the character and nature of the FATHER by giving the people His LOVE, LIFE, and LIGHT, communication takes place spirit to spirit with Jesus Christ in the midst. To be equipped to do this kind of missionary work, we must first know who we are in Christ Jesus and the power of His resurrection. We cannot give away the love and life of our Father if we do not know God as Father.

Philippians 3:7-11 AMP:

> *"Whatever former things I had that might have been gains to me, I have come to consider as [one combined] loss for Christ's sake. Yes, furthermore, I count everything as loss compared to the possession of the priceless privilege (the overwhelming preciousness, the surpassing worth, and supreme advantage) of*

> *knowing Christ Jesus my Lord and of progressively becoming more deeply and intimately acquainted with Him [of perceiving and recognizing and understanding Him more fully and clearly]. For His sake I have lost everything and consider it all to be mere rubbish (refuse, dregs), in order that I may win (gain) Christ (the Anointed One), And that I may [actually] be found and known as in Him, not having any [self-achieved] righteousness that can be called my own, based on my obedience to the Law's demands (ritualistic uprightness and supposed right standing with God thus acquired), but possessing that [genuine righteousness] which comes through faith in Christ (the Anointed One), the [truly] right standing with God, which comes from God by [saving] faith. [For my determined purpose is] that I may know Him [that I may progressively become more deeply and intimately acquainted with Him, perceiving and recognizing and understanding the wonders of His Person more strongly and more clearly], and that I may in that same way come to know the power out flowing from His resurrection [which it exerts over believers], and that I may so share His sufferings as to be continually transformed [in spirit into His likeness even] to His death, [in the hope]That if possible I may attain to the [spiritual and moral] resurrection [that lifts me] out from among the dead [even while in the body]."*

John 5:38-40 AMP:

> *"And you have not His word (His thought) living in your hearts, because you do not believe and adhere to and trust in and rely on Him Whom He has sent. [That is why you do not keep His message living in you, because you do not believe in the Messenger Whom He has sent.] You search and investigate and pore over the Scriptures diligently, because you suppose and trust that you have eternal life through them. And these [very Scriptures] testify about Me! And still you are not willing [but refuse] to come to Me, so that you might have life."*

1 John 1:1-3 AMP:

> *"[WE ARE writing] about the Word of Life [in] Him Who existed from the beginning, whom we have heard, whom we have seen with our [own] eyes, Whom we have gazed upon [for ourselves] and have touched with our [own] hands. And the Life [an aspect of His being] was revealed (made manifest, demonstrated), and we saw [as eyewitnesses] and are testifying to and declare to you the Life, the eternal Life [in Him] Who already existed with the Father and Who [actually] was made visible (was revealed) to us [His followers]. What we have seen and [ourselves] heard, we are also telling you, so that you too may realize and enjoy fellowship as partners and partakers with us. And [this] fellowship that we have [which is a distinguishing mark of Christians] is with the Father and with His Son Jesus Christ (the Messiah)."*

Paul tells us in 1 Corinthians 4:14-16 AMP:

> *"I do not write this to shame you, but to warn and counsel you as my beloved children. After all, though you should have ten thousand teachers (guides to direct you) in Christ, yet you do not have many fathers. For I became your father in Christ Jesus through the glad tidings* (the Gospel)*."*

In the letters of John, he addresses three levels of growth to the churches in Asia Minor. He mentions that some people are children of the Father, some are young men, and some are fathers. John is not talking about literal children, young men, and fathers, but maturity levels of both men and women in the body of Christ.

At a basic child level relationship of being a Christian, a person should know that their sins are forgiven and that they have an advocate to come boldly to the throne of God through Jesus Christ which allows them to have a relationship with God as Father. As simple as this should be in sharing the Gospel, many, long time believers in Christ Jesus are willing to accept Jesus as Lord and Savior of their life, but they refuse to accept that God is their Heavenly Father. They may receive this revelation with head knowledge, but struggle from their, heart causing them to work out their salvation of being a god, child of the Most High God. This sounds like blasphemy, yet it was Jesus who presented these same words to the Jews (John 10:33-34).

> *"Jesus said to them, "I tell you the truth, unless you eat the flesh* (acknowledge that you have the same DNA, the same spirit) *of the Son of Man and drink his blood* (life giving word), *you have no life in you* (no power and authority to be a Christ one). *Whoever eats my flesh and drinks my blood has eternal life, and I will raise him up at the last day* (today is the day of salvation, eternity in your Now). *For my flesh is real food and my blood is real drink. Whoever eats my flesh and drinks my blood remains in me, and I in him. Just as the living Father sent me and I live because of the Father, so the one who feeds on me will live because of me. This is the bread that came down from heaven. Your forefathers ate manna and died, but he who feeds on this bread will live forever."*
>
> *"Many of his disciples said, "This is a hard teaching. Who can accept it?"*
>
> *"Aware that his disciples were grumbling about this, Jesus said to them, "Does this offend you* (to accept that ye are gods, children of the Most High God)*? What if you see the Son of Man ascend to where he was before* (does it takes you seeing truth with your natural eyes before you will believe by faith)*! The Spirit gives life; the flesh counts for nothing. The words I have spoken to you are spirit and they are life. Yet there are some of you who do not believe." For Jesus had known from the beginning which of them did not believe and who would betray him. He went on to say, "This is why I told you that no one can come to me unless the Father has enabled him* (in other words, saying a sinner's prayer does not qualify you to get into heaven)" (John 6:53-65).

How often do believers in Christ Jesus try to share the Gospel, yet fall short because what they are really sharing is another religion in the name of Christianity? They have no resurrection power in them because the Holy Spirit has not impregnated them to do the Father's business. Many places we call the church only know God as God, and Jesus as the Savior for a future eternal life in heaven. They do not know God as Father. To try to justify keeping their doors open, they function as a non-profit organization. This has the same outcome the children of God encountered over 2,000 years ago when the religious leaders were doing their temple rituals. If we were to do as Jesus responded by overturning the money changers' tables and taking away the offerings, how many in "full time ministry" would really be called by God to be Fathers (or mothers)?

John addresses young men (or women) who understand that they are saved and that God is their Heavenly Father. These believers in Christ Jesus have a zeal of strength and ambition which is wonderful to be around. They know who they are in Christ Jesus. However, in their maturity understanding, the relationship they have with their Heavenly Father is focused on them. They are strong and have overcome the evil one acknowledging that God is their Heavenly Father, but their point of reference is themselves (1 John 2:14). This is not a bad place to be, but it is also not a place of growth to be a parent doing the Father's business.

John addresses fathers as a stage of maturing in Christ that requires living by faith and resting in the knowing relationship of BEING in Christ. This is not a stage of gender issue only for men, but to function in the fullness of parenting as the vessel God created in you, whether male or female. It is a stage of fellowship in His suffering where His death operates in our souls so that we may also know the power of His resurrection through our spirit, soul, and body. The life that we NOW live, we live by the faith in Jesus Christ (Gal. 2:20). To be a father/mother means that you have a responsibility as a parent to the children and young men/women. A parent gives their unconditional love to their child whether or not that child receives their love or acknowledges them as parents. They are willing to give their life for another, just as Jesus Christ gave His life for them.

Jesus Christ came to show us our Heavenly Father. God loves us, you and me, with an unconditional love, that while we were in ignorance and darkness to the greatness of His love, He still gave His own life through Jesus Christ to bring us back home into His presence as DAD because we have always been His child (Luke 3:38) created in His image (Genesis 1:26).

For us to change the world, we must first change ourselves, to step into the fullness of who we are in Him.

Are you truly sharing the Gospel of Jesus Christ to those that are lost, or are you sharing another religion? When others see you, do they see their Heavenly Father? Do you forgive others as the Father has forgiven you, or do you place judgment and condemnation until they do the "religious prayer" of your doctrine?

If we truly want to change the world, we must first change ourselves allowing the life that we now live to be so that only our Heavenly Father is glorified as the WORD becomes flesh in us. Children don't care about the issues of LIFE giving. They want their needs met and they want to play. Young men and women desire to mature in Christ to promote a better quality relationship with their Father, but they are still not ready to be parents. They see the gifts of the Holy Spirit as a focus on their own growth and development in the Kingdom of God, not necessarily a means of glorifying the Father.

Those that are ready to be parents in the Kingdom of God must KNOW they are spirit beings able to hear the voice of their Heavenly Father. They must understand what it means to BE a bride of Christ, not as a gender issue, but as the body of Christ Jesus with the willingness and desire to be intimate with the WORD, allowing His identity to impregnate the soul. Then, after exiting the mercy seat located in the bridal chamber of the Lamb of God, and entering into the world, you know that you are no longer a bride of Christ because a bride is only for a day, but an expectant parent (wife) carrying the WORD to be released as the *"The Word became flesh and made his dwelling among us. So that the world shall see his glory, the glory of the One and Only, who came from the Father, full of grace and truth"* (John 1:14).

"For to you a Child is born, to you a Son is given" (Isaiah 9:6).

> *"I, Jesus, have sent My messenger (angel) to you to witness and to give you assurance of these things for the churches (assemblies). I am the Root (the Source) and the Offspring of David, the radiant and brilliant Morning Star.* ***The [Holy] Spirit and the bride (the church, the true Christians) say, Come!*** *And let him who is listening say, Come! And let everyone come who is thirsty [who is painfully conscious of his need of those things by which the soul is refreshed, supported, and strengthened]; and whoever [earnestly] desires to do it, let him come, take, appropriate, and drink the water of Life without cost"* (Rev. 22:16-17 AMP).

> *"When Jesus therefore saw his mother* (the place where HIS life was conceived in the flesh), *and the disciple* (the first Adam linage) *standing by, whom he loved* (unconditionally), *he said unto his mother, Woman* (bone of my bone and flesh of my flesh), *behold thy son* (give LIFE to Adam because we are one as the Father and I are one (John 17:21)! *Then Jesus said to the disciple* (first Adam), *behold thy mother* (the bride of Christ)! And from that hour that disciple (first Adam) *took her* (woman) *into his own home* (accepted his identity as a son of God created in His image). *After this, Jesus knowing that ALL THINGS were NOW accomplished* (completed), *that the Scripture was fulfilled, said, I thirst. Now there was set a vessel full of vinegar: and they filled a sponge with vinegar, and put it upon hyssop, and put it to his mouth. When Jesus therefore had received the vinegar, he said, IT IS FINISHED: and he bowed his head, and gave up the ghost"* (John 19:26-30).

"And the LORD God said it is not good that the man should be alone; I will make him a help meet for him" (Gen. 2:18).

"And God said, Let us make man in our image, after our likeness: and let them have dominion over the fish of the sea, and over the fowl of the air, and over the cattle, and over all the earth, and over every creeping thing that creepeth upon the earth. So God created man in his own image, in the image of God created he him; male and female created he them. And God blessed them, and God said unto them, be fruitful, and multiply, and replenish the earth, and subdue it (with my image, children of the Most High God)" (Genesis 1:26-28).

"In the day that God created man, in the likeness of God made he him; Male and female created he them; and blessed them, and called their name Adam, in the day when they were created" (Genesis 5:1-2).

While we were in ignorance and darkness, the last Adam, Jesus Christ, gave birth (rejuvenation of spirit, soul, and body) to the first Adam at Calvary when He said "It is Finished."

CHAPTER 11

IN SEARCH OF THE FATHERS OF THE FAITH

"Behold, I will send you Elijah the prophet before the coming of the great and dreadful day of the Lord: And he shall turn the heart of the fathers to the children, and the heart of the children to their fathers, lest I come and smite the earth with a curse" (Malachi 4:5-6).

These verses are the last two verses found in the Old Testament. Between the Old and New Testament there was approximately a 400-year span that the voice of the Lord was not heard through any prophets. This prophetic word from Malachi comes during a time period after the temple in Jerusalem had been completed. Abuse had come into the sacrificial system of the priesthood, and the overall spiritual state of the people was in decline. Divorce was widespread (Malachi 2:14), mixed marriages were being contracted (Malachi 2:10-12), there were offerings of blemished sacrifices (Malachi 1:6-14), and people failing to pay tithes (Malachi 3:8-10), were all part of the lifestyle during these times. Many theologians believe that God was silent during these 400 years, allowing mankind to take charge of his own self-destruction.

After this prophecy was given to the people of God, it became a custom while celebrating the Feast of Pentecost, for the Jewish people to place an empty chair at their table with a glass of wine in anticipation that

Elijah would return. When the spirit of Elijah returned, the people would anticipate the fulfillment of this prophetic word. They would eagerly look for the return of fathers to their children and children to their fathers so that the earth would not be cursed. Centuries of restoration have been taking place, yet even today, the Jewish people are still looking for Elijah. They believe that this will be the sign of knowing that the Messiah's coming is near, and then, there will be peace on earth.

As I was doing research on this topic I found it interesting that the name "Malachi" means "messenger of the Lord." Following the end of the Old Testament we begin with the book of Matthew. His name means "gift of Jehovah." Matthew begins where Malachi left off four hundred years later, with fathers having sons from Abraham to Jesus Christ.

Many people skip over the first chapter of Matthew because it seems boring with just a generational history lesson. What appeals to me is that the four hundred years that theologians consider God to be silent, He is actually putting the fine tuning into manifestation of the coming of the Lord. Each of the fathers in Matthew, Chapter One is recognized because they produced (begat) a son. Whether or not they were recognized for anything else in history, the one thing they did which was of great significance is to keep the lineage from Abraham going of a father to a son, and then a son becoming a father to produce a son until the birth of Jesus Christ. This tells me that God was very busy when others thought He was silent. He was putting the fine touches of completion to the salvation of mankind. Each father had to have an understanding of the vision and significance of the Abraham covenant to keep the desire to father a son; and each son had to have a relationship with their father to want to inherit that vision to give to their own son as expressed in Malachi 4:5-6. This is a heart's desire that comes from knowing God and believing God by faith as Abraham did.

Today, God speaks to us by His Son, Jesus Christ, through the power of the Holy Spirit versus the prophets. The difference between a Son and a child of God is a Son must mature into the position of doing the Father's business. His passion and heart cry must be to glorify His Father, and not himself, so that all that he says and does will be to draw others to the Father. As Sons, we are to be the expressed image of God's glory, His person. We are the tangible Father's image to the world. Do people hear the voice of their Heavenly Father calling them by name in love into a closer relationship with Him through our hearts and mouths? Do others see unconditional love, forgiveness, and peace when we speak; or do they hear Scripture quoted bringing justification and condemnation?

In I Corinthians 4:14-16, Paul considers it his responsibility of being a father to the Corinthians by referring to them as his sons. He does not desire to shame them, but to warn them of the direction they were taking in their Christian walk. What is interesting is that he points out that there are ten-thousand instructors in Christ, but not many fathers among them. If we apply this today we could say we have lots of men and women on the platform in our churches, but how many of them would be considered as fathers? Please keep in mind that in scripture, the term father is a spiritual identity of maturity in the natural, just as the word son is. We are given natural fathers as a type and shadow for understanding spiritual implication, but God is both male and female according to Genesis 1:27.

So what kind of person is this "spiritual father" that Paul refers to? In the natural, a father is one that has raised his children, passing on his genes, and the goodness of his identity. The children recognize their identity as the father's sons because of his name which carries honor and authority. The father does not look for glory and recognition, but knows that when his children come to a point in their lives where they talk and do their business as he did, then his own glory will come. Fathers get taken advantage of when their children are still children. There is no honor to a father to see his grown children still living as a dependent child not able to handle his own affairs. However, when a father sees his children working through their lives in the way they were taught by their parents, there is great joy to the parents.

Anyone can come and mesmerize a congregation with revelation knowledge from the Lord that will impregnate their spirit. However, Paul tells us in I Corinthians 4:15 that very few teachers are there to nurture the birth of this revelation allowing the spirit to grow and develop. This leaves a child with spiritual power, but no one to help them grow in wisdom, and know how to give glory to the Father. Galatians 4:1-2 tells us that it takes the heart of a father's love and wisdom to help the child grow up with understanding of Son-ship of our Heavenly Father. Many times we are asked, "What would Jesus do?" but few of us really allow the Son-ship of Jesus Christ to flow through our minds and bodies because we are not taught how to be sons. Jesus did not consider it robbery to be equal with God, yet very few churches will acknowledge that this should be our mind as believers of His body. Instead, we are as children searching for our identity of where we fit. We know who Jesus is, but we are not able to consider our true identity as His brother/sister in Christ, and the power and responsibility of that position.

Individuals with a calling to be an evangelist, teacher, prophet, apostle, or pastor are supposed to walk in their gifting with the heart of a father. However, many of them share wonderful Biblical wisdom on a platform, and then disappear in a crowd. The church was given the five-fold ministry as the hand of God to be "fathers" to the children. How many of these "fathers" are staying home raising their children versus coming to preach on Sunday mornings, stirring the children up with a good time party, and then taking off when a bigger and better opportunity arises? A father has a responsibility to seek out the children: watching, praying, staying awake late at night with concern about EACH one, letting none of his children lack or suffer in any way that he has been given responsibility for. He knows with an intimacy of knowing, and loves with a passion that cuts to his heart for each of the members of his congregation. He worries when the children are rebellious wanting to go in a different direction that is not like Jesus.

Jesus illustrated this for us when he prayed to the Father in John Chapter 17. This prayer tells us that Jesus knew his responsibility was to show the disciples the Father through himself. He made sure that his work was completed and none of the disciples were lost that the Father gave him to minister to.

The church is a family affair. Fathers should be "hovering" over the children of God to protect and discipline them in love rather than "ruling" them with judgment and condemnation. Paul told the Corinthians in I Corinthians 4:15 that he fathered them through the gospel; that his ways are in Christ, which is what he taught everywhere, in every church. The Corinthians were manifesting the gifts of the Spirit of God, but they were not reflecting the heart of the Father which is why Paul was correcting them. Paul was not withdrawing the significance of the gifts, but without love, they were just showing off and glorifying themselves. This is what we see even today in much of the church and the gifting God has given to the body.

Churches today lack the supernatural power of God because they have not kept the pattern of father and son relationship in Jesus Christ. When others see a Christian they should be seeing Jesus, and in turn be drawn unto their Heavenly Father. Jesus showed us that the life of God is manifested at the midnight hours of our lives where there is no yesterday nor tomorrow. It is a moment of eternity in the midst of time that comes forth. If you go to your past to search for answers then you are out of covenant, and if you move forward with your own thoughts and ideas you are out of covenant. It can only be Jesus, not Jesus "plus" our own way. It is at this moment, that the supernatural power of God is manifested in the Sons of God.

In Matthew 16:15-18, Jesus asked the disciples who they thought he was after they had just discussed that the people considered Him to be either John the Baptist, Elijah, Jeremiah, or one of the other prophets. Peter spoke up and said, "Thou art the Christ, the Son of the living God." Jesus responds to this revelation that Peter received saying that it came from the Father of Jesus, and it is with this wisdom that JESUS will build His church, not man. Jesus shares in John 20:17 that his Father is our Father, and his God is our God. Jesus keeps the father and son covenant continuing with the lineage of Abraham by telling us that as the Father sent him, he sends us (John 20:21). This type of relationship crosses over from Old Testament to New Testament showing us that God is eternal and not limited to time. It was by faith that Abraham rested believing God that his seed would bless all the nations of the earth (Genesis 22:18).

God came to Abraham to initiate His ways beginning in Genesis Chapters 12-22. If the fathers/leaders (the five-fold ministry covering of your church) are not in Christ, following after Jesus to build the church, then you won't see Christ. When people say, "I am a servant of the most High God," or "I am a sinner saved by grace," yet they have been a believer for a season in the body of Christ, they may sound religious, but in reality they are still children and not mature as Sons. They are not edifying the Father and building up the body of Christ with His power and authority, but are using their own ability in works to keep the body of Christ together. They are staying focused on themselves in a religious way versus moving forward to maturing and bringing the reflection of Jesus Christ for the world to see. Instead, they reflect immature behaviors of self-centeredness, rebellion, hurt feelings, pride, discomfort, and are easily offended. They are as children without power, authority, or influence lacking the ability to manifest the supernatural power of the Father (Galatians 4:1-2).

The kingdom of God is as the smallest seed becoming the largest tree. Abraham's faithfulness is what has kept the promise. Scripture shows us that each generation has a double portion of inheritance as illustrated by Elijah giving his mantel to Elisha because he stood with his father (2 Kings). The spirit of Elijah spoken of in Malachi represents kingdom order of a Father and son relationship. This prophecy was fulfilled with John the Baptist according to Luke 1:17. What will save the earth from a curse is getting the earth in proper alignment. God is after the father's heart to turn it toward the children, and then the children's hearts will be turned to the Father. When we go through life trying to possess the land our way, we have a mindset of telling God how to be God. God will not bless our mess. The most destructive answer we can get from God in answer to our prayers is for Him to say nothing, but allow us to continue in our own self destruction until we realize it is ALL God, and only God in ALL.

As Christians, we pray asking God to bless our confusion, but we are not willing to align ourselves up to the order of God for the blessings to flow. We play a game of hit and miss with God by dying to ourselves for a moment, and then after He has taken over the situation, we raise up the old man to live with the new, and wonder why God isn't answering prayers.

We then try to justify our natural understanding by saying, "maybe it is not God's will for me to be healed, or maybe He wants me to go through this because I must suffer first before being blessed." We justify the circumstance by what we see versus walking in faith of what we should believe Scripture tells us. We also look at things from the level of a child or at the foot of the cross, rather than the position of Sonship which is resurrection power from death, hell, and the grave.

John the Baptist was the son doing the Father's business declaring for all to "prepare ye the way." His life was an illustration of how "the way" is prepared with his own head being cut off. This is a type and shadow to teach us that we are to have the mind of Christ by beheading ourselves as believers, and being crucified with Christ (Galatians 2:20). The life we now live in the flesh is Christ by the faith of the Son of God. We are to take on the mind of Christ, and not our natural understanding. This mind is the key to our inheritance of aligning our spirit, soul, and body with His. We must protect this inheritance by the words of our mouth and the mindset of our heart anxiously desiring to develop this inheritance, to pass it on with a double portion of blessing to our children. **The inheritance of the Sons of God is not the cross, but the resurrection** (Galatians 2:21-3:3, 13).

Jesus is the firstborn to bring the pattern of the old into redeeming the world. He is not just a savior or redeemer. He is the FIRST BEGOTTEN SON of GOD. He gave us the covenant of a Son. Being a child of God does not give a believer automatic access into the inheritance of God. Everyone is given the power to become Sons of God, but not everyone succeeds (John 1:12). A Son of God is revealed by the power of God being manifested in love, not personal edification. Signs and wonders follow behind Sons of God (Acts 5:15). Children are looking for them (John 4:48), and then running to and fro trying to possess them (Daniel 12:4).

In Genesis, Chapter 9, we read about the story of Noah and his sons after the flood. Life is starting over for his family. They plant a vineyard, make some wine, but then Noah indulges a little too much, and is found drunk and naked by his son Canaan. Did you ever wonder why, when Noah finds out that Canaan went and told his brothers about what he saw, that Noah cursed him, but blessed the other two sons? It wasn't that Noah loved the other two sons more than Canaan, but that Canaan was just as much a son as his brothers, yet he refused to grow-up, and therefore would be a servant versus a son. When Canaan saw his father drunk and naked the first thing he did was to play the childish game of telling a secret. He disgraced his father versus standing in the gap as a covering. Once the other brothers became aware of the situation, they took covering on their shoulders and walked backwards so they didn't see their father's nakedness, and then they covered him. The shoulders represent authority. Shem and Japheth were not making judgment on Noah by walking backwards, but acting as a shield of sonship to protect their father from anything while he was in a vulnerable state.

The church of Jesus Christ is to be built where the gates of hell cannot prevail against it. Satan should not be allowed in the house of God for there is no place for the devil (Ephesians 4:27). Yet, he is welcomed in through the doors of: gossip, complacency, denominational doctrines, theology, religious rituals, and self-centered Christianity. Churches today do not align themselves with the Son-ship of Jesus Christ which is why there is no power. There is an abundance of sickness, disease, poverty, depression, divorce, etc. inside most churches. Many times when people have exposed their personal struggles, conflicts, and sins for prayer request, this information becomes passed on as gossip in the name of needing prayer. A true Son of God would take what has been shared, lift it up to the Father, and declare by the power and authority of the name of Jesus that it is a finished work (healed, completed, satisfied, restored) according to John 19:30. Most people are still in a vulnerable state, and therefore it is up to the Son that received the prayer request to also be the intercessor, as a hedge of protection to believe by faith, that the issues are a finished work until the full manifestation is seen. The church should be setting an example for the world as a place of healing, wholeness, life, love, and peace. When a person comes into a place where the Sons of God are present, there should be a distinguishing presence of heaven on earth.

It took thirty years for Jesus to grow and develop into the understanding of his true identity as the Son of God, and his purpose on this earth. In Luke 3:21-22, we are told that heaven was opened when Jesus was baptized in the Jordan River. When a person is baptized, it means that the person you were a few seconds before going into the water, and who you are coming out of the water after being immersed, are two different people. The Jordan River represents death of the old man. When Jesus came up from being baptized, a voice came from heaven saying, "Thou art my beloved Son; in thee I am well pleased" (verse 21). From that moment on, Jesus had a responsibility to be about the Father's business so that when others saw Him, they saw the Father. Before the Jordan, he was living a life as the child of Mary and Joseph, but after his baptism, His whole focus was to reflect his identity as the Son of God.

Today, we have many children of God refusing to grow up. They believe that if they have received Jesus as their personal savior, they go to church, read their Bible, and try to be a good person for their family and community, that they consider themselves to be mature Christians. This is not the Biblical definition of being mature in Christ.

A mature Christian is one that has the confidence and wisdom of our Heavenly Father to know His power and authority, and apply it to everyday life situations. They walk by faith, not by sight, knowing that their Father judges no man (John 5:22), and that His mercy endures forever (Psalm 136). They look unto Jesus (to see the Father) to learn how to respond to the world issues, to pray, and to seek wisdom of unconditional love, mercy, and forgiveness without bringing attention to self. They believe that it is their Father's will that none shall perish (2 Peter 3:9), and that they have a responsibility to stand in the gap of intercession for the lost sheep until ALL one-hundred percent have come back to the Father. The body of Christ cannot be blemish-free without ALL of the "lost Adam linage" being returned to the Father.

Where do you fit in with the growth and development of being a Christ One? Are you about doing the Father's business, or are you looking out for yourself, being a good Christian and waiting to get to heaven someday?

"Finally, be ye all of one mind, having compassion one of another, love as brethren, be pitiful, be courteous: not rendering evil for evil" (I Peter 3:8-9a). Peter tells us that we are all to have one mind, the mind of Jesus Christ. As the bride of Christ, we are a corporate body. If one person is lost, whether in the flesh, or out of the flesh, the body of Christ cannot be complete until we intercede to bring them out of hell or darkness. Jesus didn't send them there; we did with our thoughts and words by believing in tradition and denominational religion instead of allowing Jesus to build His church.

If we truly have a heart's desire to see the return of Jesus, we must be willing to change allowing the Sons of God to come forth bringing unity and wholeness to His body.

CHAPTER 12

CHANGING YOUR ATMOSPHERE WILL CHANGE THE WORLD

"The heavens are recounting the glory of El, and the atmosphere is telling the work of His hands. Day after day is uttering a saying, and night after night is disclosing knowledge. There is no audible saying, and there are no words; their voice is unheard. Yet into the entire earth their voice goes forth, and into the ends of the habitance their declarations. For the sun He has placed a tent in them" (Psalm 19:1-4 CV).

What is the glory of God the heavens are recounting?

Jesus speaks of this when He prays to the Father before going to Calvary in John 17. Let us read these together for they hold a necessary key to understanding our purpose and position in Christ:

1 WHEN JESUS had spoken these things, He lifted up His eyes to heaven and said, Father, the hour has come. Glorify and exalt and honor and magnify Your Son, so that Your Son may glorify and extol and honor and magnify You.

2 [Just as] You have granted Him ***power and authority over all flesh*** *(all humankind), [now glorify Him]* ***so that He may give eternal life*** *to all whom You have given Him.*

[3]***And this is eternal life***: *[it means] to know (to perceive, recognize, become acquainted with, and understand) You, the only true and real God, and [likewise]* ***to know Him***, *Jesus [as the] Christ (the Anointed One, the Messiah), Whom You have sent.*

[4]*I have glorified You down here on the earth* ***by completing the work*** *that You gave Me to do.*

[5]*And now, Father, glorify Me along with Yourself and* ***restore Me to such majesty and honor in Your presence as I had with You before the world existed.***

[6]***I have manifested Your Name*** *[I have revealed Your very Self, Your real Self] to the people whom You have given Me out of the world. They were Yours, and You gave them to Me, and they have obeyed and kept Your word.*

[7]*Now [at last] they know and understand that all You have given Me belongs to You [is really and truly Yours].*

[8]*For the [uttered] words that You gave Me I have given them; and they have received and accepted [them] and have come to know positively and in reality [to believe with absolute assurance] that I came forth from Your presence, and they have believed and are convinced that You did send Me.*

[9]***I am praying for them***. *I am not praying (requesting) for the world, but for those You have given Me, for they belong to You.*

[10]***All [things that are] Mine are Yours, and all [things that are] Yours belong to Me; and I am glorified in (through) them***. *[They have done Me honor; in them My glory is achieved.]*

[11]*And [now] I am no more in the world, but these are [still] in the world, and I am coming to You. Holy Father, keep in Your Name [in the knowledge of Yourself]* ***those whom You have given Me, that they may be one as We [are one].***

[12]***While I was with them, I kept and preserved them in Your Name*** *[in the knowledge and worship of You]. Those You have given Me I guarded and protected, and not one of them has perished or is lost except the son of perdition*

[Judas Iscariot—the one who is now doomed to destruction, destined to be lost], that the Scripture might be fulfilled.

13And now I am coming to You; I say these things while I am still in the world, so that My joy may be made full and complete and perfect in them *[that they may experience My delight fulfilled in them, that My enjoyment may be perfected in their own souls, that they may have My gladness within them, filling their hearts].*

14I have given and delivered to them Your word (message) and the world has hated them, because they are not of the world [do not belong to the world], just as I am not of the world.

15I do not ask that You will take them out of the world, but that You will keep and protect them from the evil one.

16They are not of the world (worldly, belonging to the world), [just] as I am not of the world.

17Sanctify them [purify, consecrate, separate them for Yourself, make them holy] by the Truth; Your Word is Truth.

18Just as You sent Me into the world, I also have sent them into the world.

19And so for their sake and on their behalf ***I sanctify (dedicate, consecrate) Myself, that they also may be sanctified (dedicated, consecrated, made holy) in the Truth.***

20Neither for these alone do I pray [it is not for their sake only that I make this request], but also for all those who will ever come to believe in (trust in, cling to, rely on) Me through their word and teaching,

21That they all may be one, [just] as You, Father, are in Me and I in You, that they also may be one in Us, so that the world may believe and be convinced that You have sent Me.

[22]I have given to them the glory and honor which You have given Me, that they may be one [even] as We are one:

[23]I in them and You in Me, in order that they may become one and perfectly united, that the world may know and [definitely] recognize that You sent Me and that You have loved them [even] as You have loved Me.

[24]Father, I desire that they also whom You have entrusted to Me [as Your gift to Me] may be with Me where I am, so that they may see My glory, which You have given Me [Your love gift to Me]; for You loved Me before the foundation of the world.

[25]O just and righteous Father, although the world has not known You and has failed to recognize You and has never acknowledged You, I have known You [continually]; and these men understand and know that You have sent Me.

[26]I have made Your Name known to them and revealed Your character and Your very Self, and I will continue to make [You] known, that the love which You have bestowed upon Me may be in them [felt in their hearts] and that I [Myself] may be in them.

The prayer Jesus is praying to the Father is from Jesus, Son of God Son of Man.

We have been called into a global infusion as a many-membered body called Christ to fuse together as one body so that the world will experience the manifested presence of the tangible reality of Jesus Christ on the earth. *"For we [no matter how] numerous we are, are one body, because we all partake of the one Bread [the One Whom the communion bread represents]"* (1 Corinthians 10:17AMP).

Let us re-read John 17:21-23, *"That they all may be one; as thou, Father, art in me, and I in thee, that they also may be one in us: that the world may believe that thou hast sent me. And the glory which thou gave me I have given them; that they may be one, even as we are one: I in them, and thou in me, that they* ***may be made perfect in one****; and that the world may know that thou hast sent me, and hast loved them, as thou hast loved me."*

Jesus Christ gave us the glory and honor that was given to Him by the Father so that we would be one with them. The pattern that was given is that Christ is in us and the Father is in Christ so that together we are perfectly united. In this position the world will know and recognize that the Father sent Jesus Christ because the Father loves each of us in the same respect as He loves Jesus Christ.

There is a union by fusion such as when Jesus prayed in verse 23, "they may become one, be made one, and perfect (complete/finished) as one."

What is this glory of God that was given to Jesus Christ which He has given to us that we would be made perfect and one with Him and the Father**? It is the weight or power and the Light of God that causes and brings change.**

This prayer in John 17 is the WORD made flesh talking: Christ Jesus, Son of God/Son of Man.

In Genesis 1:2 when the WORD spoke and said, "Let there be Light and there was light." Here, the WORD is speaking again as one with the Father.

The Apostle Paul writes, *"But to those who are called, whether Jew or Greek (Gentile), Christ [is] the Power of God and the Wisdom of God." (1 Corinthians 1:24). "That together you may [unanimously] with united hearts and one voice, praise and glorify the God and Father of our Lord Jesus Christ"* (Romans 15:6 AMP).

The power of God and the wisdom of God, Christ, becomes a man. Christ is the manifestation of the invisible God. In John 17 we have the WORD of GOD talking in the manifestation of the person Jesus in the flesh speaking the WORD into creation LIFE. Jesus is not just saying a spiritual prayer that sounds sweet and kind for others to hear, but He is decreeing a global fusion of LIFE as in Genesis 1:2, "Let there be LIGHT." This is the LIGHT that was lit before the sun, moon, and stars were created. This is glory, a fusion, a creation taking place.

Jesus Christ is talking about the glory of God that was before the world began (John 17: 5, 24). This glory is the Father's image, God Himself. Jesus is describing the science of creation—in the beginning before the world was formed. He is unveiling the LIGHT, the POWER, and the ENERGY that brought LIFE into a manifested, tangible form; the glory of God Himself in Christ Jesus is now given to us.

Let's read this again: *"Unto them which are called, both Jews and Greeks,* ***Christ the power of God, and the wisdom of God****"* (1 Corinthians 1:24). This power and wisdom became a person. They are the elements of God that create something new. This is the same power that came into our lives when we received Jesus Christ as our personal Savior and Redeemer, bringing us back to our rightful inheritance to be one with the Father. This power and wisdom of God in us has the same ability to be manifested as resurrected LIFE in Christ today in our natural bodies.

"If we are in Christ we are a new creature: old things are passed away, dead, removed; behold, ALL things are NOW new" (2 Cor. 5:17). These are not just poetic words in a book. As part of the body of Jesus Christ, we are the brightness of His glory, the express image of His Person, the upholding of His WORD.

The Apostle Paul's writing to Philippi shares these thoughts in Philippians 3:8-11AMP:

"I count everything as loss compared to the possession of the priceless privilege (the overwhelming preciousness, the surpassing worth, and supreme advantage) of knowing Christ Jesus my Lord and of progressively becoming more deeply and intimately acquainted with Him [of perceiving and recognizing and understanding Him more fully and clearly]. For His sake I have lost everything and consider it all to be mere rubbish (refuse, dregs), in order that I may win (gain) Christ (the Anointed One),

And that I may [actually] be found and known as in Him, not having any [self-achieved] righteousness that can be called my own, based on my obedience to the Law's demands (ritualistic uprightness and supposed right standing with God thus acquired), but possessing that [genuine righteousness] which comes through faith in Christ (the Anointed One), the [truly] right standing with God, which comes from God by [saving] faith.

[For my determined purpose is] that I may know Him [that I may progressively become more deeply and intimately acquainted with Him, perceiving and recognizing and understanding the wonders of His Person more strongly and more clearly], and that I may in that same way come to know the power outflowing from His resurrection [which it exerts over believers], and that I may so share His sufferings as to be continually transformed [in spirit into His likeness even] to His death, [in the hope]

That if possible I may attain to the [spiritual and moral] resurrection [that lifts me] out from among the dead [even while in the body]."

The writer of Hebrews shares, *"God in these last days spoken unto us by his Son, whom he hath appointed heir of all things, by whom also he made the worlds; Jesus Christ being the brightness of his glory, and the express image of his person, and upholding all things by the word of his power;"* (Hebrews 1:2-3a).

It is this same power that is Christ in you, the hope of glory to be manifested out of you while you are in your natural body for the world to see (Col. 1:27). If Christ is in you, you are a new creation (2 Cor. 5:17) with the same power and wisdom that Jesus had demonstrated on the earth to uphold all things by the power and wisdom of God in you. It is this same power that raised Jesus from the dead that is in you today. This power is the goodness of Christ and the LIFE of Christ seeded in you. *"God has made everything beautiful for its own time. He has planted eternity, HIMSELF, in the human heart"* (Eccl. 3:11a NLT).

Who do you say "I AM?" These two words are your identity with the Father through Jesus Christ. They carry the weight and the power in you to change the atmosphere of time and space. What we do with these two words will determine whether we create Life or Death for it is the words that follow "I AM" that will determine if we are sowing seeds of LIFE or seeds of death into our atmosphere and domain.

"Death and life are in the power of the tongue: and they that love it shall eat the fruit thereof" (Proverbs 18:21).

"The fear of the LORD and the law of the wise is a fountain of life, to depart from the snares of death" (Proverbs 13:14, 14:27).

When we accepted Jesus Christ as our personal savior we did not sit down and have a cup of coffee with Him. We did not visibly see Him walk into the room from an invisible place. We did not have a tangible experience that determined the evidence of accepting Jesus as our redeemer. Yet, we each personally experienced a transformation of our spirit, quickened into a new life that was so real and personal to each of us that we know that we know. This power and wisdom of God that came into our lives was so real, though not visible or tangible, that it caused a change in our lives, turning us into a new creation. These are spiritual elements that God uses to create and has given to us to change our atmosphere for His glory.

Peter writes about this in 2 Peter 3: 10-11, 17-18, *"But the day of the Lord will come like a thief, and then the heavens* (our hardened heart) *will vanish (pass away) with a thunderous crash* (the sound released when lightning strikes), *and the [material] elements [of the universe] will be dissolved with fire* (the presence of God), *and the earth* (carnal knowledge and understanding) *and the works that are upon it will be burned up. Since all these things are thus in the process of being dissolved, what kind of person ought [each of] you to be [in the meanwhile] in consecrated and holy behavior and devout and godly qualities... Let me warn you therefore, beloved, that knowing these things beforehand, you should be on your guard, lest you be carried away by the error of lawless* (judgment and condemnation) *and wicked [persons and] fall from your own [present] firm condition [your own steadfastness of mind].* ***But grow in grace (undeserved favor, spiritual strength) and recognition and knowledge and understanding of our Lord and Savior Jesus Christ (the Messiah).*** *To Him [be] glory (honor, majesty, and splendor) both now and to the day of eternity. Amen (so be it)!"*

If Christ BE in you, then you are a new creation in Christ (2 Cor. 5:17). This didn't happen because you read the Bible, but because you experienced this fusion while you were in ignorance and darkness (Acts 26:18, 23). When we read the Scriptures, our spirit takes in a fresh breath of life which makes the Bible more than just a history book or a book of do's and do not's. The Scriptures themselves become alive to our spirit because it is a Spirit to spirit experience in conversation, an intimacy that brings transformation for us to be LIFE while in our earthen vessels. This is not for our own ego, but so that others that are spiraling in a pit of hopelessness are given HOPE by the presence of Christ radiating in our mortal bodies (2 Cor. 4:11).

The Apostle Paul refers to this as, *"The LIGHT of the glorious gospel of Christ, who is the image of God"* (2 Cor. 4:4). It is not the man Jesus from Galilee that we had a personal experience with, but the LIGHT of the glorious gospel of Christ who is the image of God that spoke into our darkness, confusion, ignorance, and face of our deep secrets and said, "LET THERE BE LIGHT." Then suddenly... our inner being is changed. Our heart was at peace and calmness that could not be explained. There is a joy coming out of our inner most being that moments earlier could only think of negative thoughts.

"For God, who commanded the light to shine out of darkness, hath shined in our hearts, to give the light of the knowledge of the glory of God in the face of Jesus Christ" (2 Cor. 4:6). Paul is borrowing the words from Genesis 1 when he says "light to shine out of darkness." *"In the beginning God created the heaven and the earth. And the earth was without form, and void; and darkness was upon the face of the deep. And the Spirit of God moved upon the face of the waters"* (Genesis 1:1-2).

The face gives identity. Paul continues in 2 Corinthians 4:7 saying, ***"But we have this treasure in earthen vessels, that the Excellency of the power may be of God, and not of us."*** Paul continues in this chapter sharing the process of how we are being transformed daily into the resurrected LIFE of Jesus Christ while in our mortal bodies. This is not a someday experience when our natural body dies, but the scientific, life transforming power of the thought becoming the fact by the renewing of our minds.

"Be not conformed to this world: but be ye transformed by the renewing of your mind, that ye may prove what is that good, and acceptable, and perfect, will of God" (Romans 12:2).

This treasure that Paul says is within us is the Divine energy, LIGHT, power of Christ that is our DNA given to us by our Heavenly Father. It is not of our carnal flesh and blood. *"To the intent that now unto the principalities and powers in heavenly places might be known by the church the manifold wisdom of God"* (Ephesians 3:10).

In 2 Corinthians 4:8-13, after Paul informs us that we have this power and wisdom of God in us, he continues by sharing the process of how spiritual fusion happens:

8 *We are troubled on every side, yet not distressed; we are perplexed, but not in despair;*

9 *Persecuted, but not forsaken; cast down, but not destroyed;*

10 *Always bearing about in the body the dying of the Lord Jesus, that the life also of Jesus might be made manifest in our body.*

11 *For we which live are always delivered unto death for Jesus' sake, that the life also of Jesus might be made manifest* ***in our mortal flesh****.*

12 *So then death worketh in us, but life in you.*

13 ***We having the same spirit of faith****, according as it is written, I believed, and therefore have I spoken; we also believe, and therefore speak;*

This is a day to day occurrence that is taking place NOW in our mortal bodies so that:

[14]*Knowing that he which raised up the Lord Jesus shall raise up us also by Jesus, and shall present us with you.*

[15]*For all things are for your sakes,* ***that the abundant grace might through the thanksgiving of many redound to the glory of God****.*

[16]*For which cause we faint not; but though our outward man perish, yet the inward man is renewed day by day.*

[17]*For our light affliction* (jobless, sickness, negatives in life), *which is but for a moment, worketh for us a far more exceeding and eternal weight of glory;*

[18]*While we look not at the things which are seen, but at the things which are not seen: for the things which are seen are temporal; but the things which are not seen are eternal.*

This is spiritual fusion in operation. Verse 14 states that this is the power that raised Christ Jesus from the dead, and this same power is now working in your mortal body today to raise you from the death of the natural world! When Jesus died on the cross and rose again, everything in the natural responded; the earth quaked. So it is within each of us. Our earthen vessels are quaking as Christ in us is being raised from the death of our mortal bodies.

The global environment is experiencing the impact of this heavenly fusion taking place around the world with the shifting and quaking of the earth as the heavens shift in the hearts of the sons of God. Creation is being changed! The person of Christ is the body of Christ of those chosen with Him, the cells of His body, before the foundation in which Jesus Christ is the head. The head needs the body, the ELOHIM, the completion of God to bring into the manifestation of the new creation of Christ Jesus.

The events happening around the world are a two-fold shift: The bringing down the towers of Baal (politics, race, gender, religion, ego control), which include Sodom and Gomorrah and the spirit of anti-Christ. *"For thus saith the LORD of hosts; yet once, it is a little while, and I will shake the heavens, and the earth, and the sea, and the dry land"* (Haggai 2:6).

Simultaneously, as Baal is coming down and the people are being brought to their knees, we will see revivals to turn to Almighty GOD as they seek Truth, the WAY, and the LIFE that will bring PEACE. *"If my people, which are called by my name* (I AM), *shall humble themselves, and pray, and seek my face* (Jesus Christ), *and turn from their wicked ways; then will I hear from heaven, and will forgive their sin, and will heal their* (earthen vessels, flesh) *land"* (2 Chronicles 7:14).

This healing will result in the manifestation of His glory filling the world as the waters cover the sea. *"They shall not hurt nor destroy in all My holy mountain: for the earth shall be full of the knowledge of the LORD, as the waters cover the sea. And in that day there shall be a root of Jesse, which shall stand for an ensign of the people; to it shall the Gentiles seek: and his rest shall be glorious"* (Isaiah 11:9-10).

The intensity of people's daily life and death issues around the world is causing the stirring on the face of the deep (Genesis 1:2), and the love and passion of Christ in the heart of man (Eccl. 3:11) is creating a fusion of heaven and earth coming together. The manifestation of this is being seen by the global earth shifting as the atmosphere of cyberspace is being filled with the WORD of God. Our social networking capability is having a supernatural power touching the heart of the Father to move mountains.

This takes us back to John 17:23 when Jesus prayed, *"I in them, and thou in me, that they may **be made perfect in one**; and that the world may know that thou hast sent me, and hast loved them, as thou hast loved me."*

"Thou shalt be perfect with the LORD thy God." (Deut. 18:13).

CHAPTER 13

TOXIC ENERGY BEGINS WITH TOXIC THOUGHTS

"So many enemies against one man. All of them trying to kill me. To them I'm just a broken-down wall or a tottering fence. They plan to topple me from my high position. They delight in telling lies about me. They praise me to my face but curse me in their hearts. (Selah). Let all that I am wait quietly before God, for my hope is in him" (Psalm 62:3-5 NLV).

People need people, but connecting to the right people will determine how we grow and develop our God given destiny of why we were born at a certain time in His story.

The natural pattern of socialization with those that we connect with to help us to grow and mature begins usually with our parents and siblings. Then we reach out to our extended families of grandparents, aunts, uncles, and cousins. From there we have friends, teachers, bosses, co-workers, acquaintances, and strangers that are part of our everyday lives. Most churches teach their members to prioritize their lives by putting God first, spouse second, then children, and extended family. Afterwards are friends, co-workers, acquaintances, and strangers.

This may be the pattern of a nuclear society, but when it comes to overcoming acute death at the door issues of life, Jesus did not use this pattern.

After Jesus was filled with the Holy Spirit, prepared to do the Father's business on the earth, he surrounded himself with a company of people. This company included both men and women. It included members of his biological family. There were times when Jesus would address twelve men. There were times when he would speak to seventy. There were times when he would talk with both men and women, and sometimes to just women. There were times when he would surround himself with over five thousand, and then there were times when he would require only three. It is the times when Jesus would appoint three men that I would like to share my thoughts about.

In Mark, Chapter Five, a story is told about a twelve-year-old girl that is the daughter of a synagogue leader who is sick, and the father goes to Jesus to heal his daughter. Take note that this man was high up the rank in the official religious, law governing system, yet when it came to life and death within his personal family, he is seeking outside help. He did not go to the High Priest of the day or any intercessory prayer warriors. He also did not go to the medical connections of the day. He went to Jesus.

As Jesus followed Jairus to his home, he was confronted with a crowd of people who also wanted to somehow connect with him, including a woman that had an issue of blood that had been chronic for twelve years. This issue of blood caused the woman to be an outcast in society not allowing her to be around people, nor having a man in her life to take care of her because she was considered defiled and unclean. She was treated with total abandonment as if she had leprosy. For her to be there in the midst of a crowd seeking a touch from the hem of Jesus' garment was a life and death matter. She had placed herself in a position with the law to be put to death for being in that crowd, yet in her heart, she has been dead for twelve years since she had not had the ability to bring forth a son because of her issue of blood.

It is not a coincidence that around the time the twelve-year-old little girl was born into the world, this other woman who wasn't too far away had begun having a blood issue that had lasted as long as the life of this twelve-year-old girl of the leader of the religious system in the area. Here we have two women; the young girl was at the stage of her life beginning puberty and the opportunity for her body to carry a child, but due to life circumstances she was dying. The other woman had experienced life in her body for herself, but was considered dead because her body did not allow her to have a relationship with a man to produce a child due to a continuous blood issue that the law says qualified her to be unclean and defiled.

Touching the hem of Jesus' garment was touching LIFE. The fringes of a person's garment identified the person of their status and position they held in society. The fringes on Jesus' garment would have represented that He was LIFE; the Son of God. When LIFE has made contact with you, anything that is anti-LIFE must leave.

After the woman touched the fringes of His garment, she was healed. She was not looking for attention but in the desperation of needing Life for her body, she had been willing to risk everything. Jesus did not allow her to leave without making a public statement that she had been redeemed and in every way whole. Jesus publicly acknowledged the woman's healing by saying virtue had left Him. The seed of His LIFE had just been with her to bring LIFE transformation within her. This is an intimacy position declared publically.

Jesus continued on to the home of the Jairus, the leader of the synagogue. From the perspective of society of Jairus seeking Jesus for his daughter, this would be like the president of the USA seeking help from a fortune teller instead of his cabinet counsel; or a medical doctor seeking help from a witchdoctor for his own healing. Keep in mind that Jesus was not a colleague or friend to the synagogue counsel. They were looking for ways to keep Jesus silent even to the point of trying to kill Him. For Jesus to enter into the leader's home and declare that his daughter was not dead was a total mockery and insult to the natural intellect and high authority of that day.

However, notice what Jesus did. He did not challenge or justify His position and statement to the people. He simply took authority and showed them the door telling them to get out. No argument or discussion whether the girl was asleep or dead. He did not try to make an authority position as an expert over life and death issues. He simply told them all to get out with the exception of the girl's father, mother, Peter, James, and John.

Jesus had five people in His inner circle. The inner circle of our life is what is the heart issue of the situation? Who would you share your bed with? (For further study, Paul addresses this in Romans chapter seven).

This young girl had not known a man, but was at the border of her life to be bodily transformed into being capable of producing Life, and then she dies.

The number five means grace. *"For the law was given through Moses; grace and truth came through Jesus Christ"* (John 1:17). The leader of the synagogue represented the law; the inner circle is the witness of grace, and Jesus Christ is "*the way, the truth, and the Life. No one comes to the Father, comes into the Holy of Holies, except through Him*" (John 14:6).

We now have the necessary portions to bring forth resurrection Life from the dead. Only God can come into the presence of God and live. There is no death, time, or conditional love in the presence of God.

So why did Jesus choose these five people as His inner circle?

Would it be our choice if we were faced with life and death matters?

Who do you want by your side when you are sick or at the hospital or facing a life and death crisis?

Jesus had with him members of his biological family: His mother and his brothers James and Jude. They had seen and could testify to the many miracles that Jesus had already done. They were family. Shouldn't that have had priority of who's in the inner circle? Why didn't He choose them?

Let's think about each of these five people. Please keep in mind that this is not a comprehensive evaluation of each of these people, but some thoughts to consider for our own life issues when we are faced with life and death circumstances.

There is no death, time, or conditional love in the presence of God.

We have the girl's father who knew and practiced the law. He is in a high position of authority. He would be like the doctor you would go to if you were sick, or the minister you would seek out to get closer to God, yet he goes to the person his congregation wants to kill, and then he brings him into his home... interesting!

Jesus kept telling the father "have faith." A life-giving Faith needs to be in the inner circle.

Then we have the mother of the girl. She does not have a voice that was recorded, but she has the experience of oneness with "faith" that produced the life of the girl from her own body. She has the "works" that must accompany "faith" to bring forth transformation into a new creation of LIFE. *"Faith without works is dead. For as the body without the spirit is dead, so faith without works is dead also"* (James 2:20, 26).

Next, we have Peter. This is the vessel in the earth that established the decree that Jesus Christ was the Christ, Son of the Living God. It was on this rock foundation that Jesus established His church, His bride, His wife. Remember we have two women—an issue of blood, and life and death. This is the whole Bible foundation for the Old Testament and the New Testament. It does not matter the personal issues that Peter travailed through. Those are the many journeys of life that we all struggle with. For God to come through the heavens as LIGHT giving LIFE there must be an earth grounded conduit resource.

Now we have James on one side and John on the other. Remember these two brothers were called "sons of thunder." What is the purpose of thunder? It is the atmospheric voice when Lightning strikes. These are the two disciples that the request was given to Jesus if they could sit on His left and right side when He entered into His kingdom. This only shows the limitations of their natural minds while God was already using them in His Kingdom, but they did not know the full extent. They only believed and responded to what they knew about being with Jesus.

The name James has several attributes that we can pull from of why Jesus may have chosen him as one of the inner circle. Keep in mind that Jesus also had a half-brother with this same name. The name James is connected with the name Jacob meaning supplanter. It carries the challenges between the ego and the Christ identity in the body; what is best for self, versus giving one's self for others.

The name James also carries the attribute of Wisdom. King Solomon wrote much about "wisdom" emphasizing that it is a "woman issue." When we get wisdom, we receive understanding; resurrection life for that wisdom of revelation. *"The LORD by wisdom* (impregnated the woman/church) *hath founded the earth* (the image of God in the flesh); *by understanding hath he established the heavens*" (Proverbs 3:19).

After the ascension of Jesus Christ, this disciple was the first to be beheaded of the twelve. He was also the first to travel the furthest from Jerusalem, carrying the Gospel of Jesus Christ before he was martyred. Shortly after, a foundational leadership was established for the church or bride of Jesus Christ by Jesus' brother James in Jerusalem. This is the author of the Epistle of James in the Bible. It is considered the first book of the New Testament.

We have two James; two Jacobs, struggling with wisdom to get understanding in the womb of man. *"Jacob was left alone; and there wrestled a man with him until the breaking of the day"* (Genesis 32:24). When he received understanding, he also had his old identity removed and replaced with a new one. This is all incumbent with the position James held in the inner circle of a Life and Death issue.

Last, we have John. We know much about John as the closest to the heart of Jesus. Where others would evaluate and share their experience and knowledge about Jesus, John shares Jesus from the heart of the Father. His name is connected with LOVE as the beloved. It is an intimacy connection of oneness in Spirit. The attribute of the name John is the GRACE and MERCY of God. Though John is a male, he brings the heart and soul helpmate of the church/bride of Christ.

Is James on the left side and John on the right? We tend to think of goats and sheep with this picture, but the reality is that just as James and John are of the same family, so are goats and sheep. There are times when it is good to be a sheep following the shepherd, but there are also times to be a goat; a giver of milk, an apostolic heart, and a sacrificial life as on the Day of Atonement. This is the scales of balance and justice. *"Justice and judgment are the habitation of thy throne: mercy and truth shall go before thy face"* (Psalm 89:14).

So now in this room where death lies in a young woman we have Jesus Christ: LIFE, LOVE, and LIGHT surrounded by FAITH, WORKS, the rock foundation of I AM the WAY, the TRUTH, and the LIFE, WISDOM & UNDERSTANDING, and GRACE & MERCY.

DEATH cannot stay in the place where there is the totality of LIFE giving Spirit.

"Mercy and truth are met together; righteousness and peace have kissed each other" (Psalm 85:10). *"They shall see His face, and His name shall be on their foreheads"* (Revelation 22:4).

When death and sickness are at the door of your life, who do you have in your house, your heart to overcome the enemy of the body of Christ Jesus in you?

"The power of life and death are in the tongue and they that love it shall eat the fruit" (Proverbs 18:21). *"Out of the abundance of the heart the mouth speaks"* (Matthew 12:34).

"Let a man [thoroughly] examine himself, and [only when he has done] so should he eat of the bread and drink of the cup. For anyone who eats and drinks without discriminating and recognizing with due appreciation that [it is Christ's] body, eats and drinks a sentence (a verdict of judgment) upon himself. That [careless and unworthy participation] is the reason many of you are weak and sickly, and quite enough of you have fallen into the sleep of death" (I Corinthians 11:28-30 AMP).

Do you have an inner circle that will discern the Lord's Body and intercede with LIFE giving affirmation to overcome sickness and death?

Today is the day of our salvation and the finished work that Jesus Christ completed on the cross, bringing into perfection His body, His beloved bride, the resurrection LIFE of Christ while in our natural body.

"That I may [actually] be found and known as in Him, not having any [self-achieved] righteousness that can be called my own, based on my obedience to the Law's demands (ritualistic uprightness and supposed right standing with God thus acquired), but possessing that [genuine righteousness] which comes through faith in Christ (the Anointed One), the [truly] right standing with God, which comes from God by [saving] faith. [For my determined purpose is] that I may know Him [that I may progressively become more deeply and intimately acquainted with Him, perceiving and recognizing and understanding the wonders of His Person more strongly and more clearly], and that I may in that same way come to know the power outflowing from His resurrection [which it exerts over believers], and that I may so share His sufferings as to be continually transformed [in spirit into His likeness even] to His death, [in the hope] That if possible I may attain to the [spiritual and moral] resurrection [that lifts me] out from among the dead [even while in the body]" (Philippians 3:9-11 AMP).

Each member, each cell of the bride, the church, must be LIFE in Spirit and Soul to bring forth the coming of the Lord in the flesh. Our lives today are not about us, but about HIM and the power of His resurrection flowing through us that has overcome death, hell, and the grave.

As believers in Christ Jesus and our beloved husband, we must unite together in His Spirit around the world to birth the coming of the Lord as we rule and reign on the earth with Him. His Life must become our Life. His WORD must come forth from our inner most being, the womb of man (male and female) as rivers of living water, circumcised by the heart, so that out of our mouths the likeness and image of Christ will take form.

"Beloved, now are we the sons of God, and it doth not yet appear what we shall be: but we know that, when he shall appear, we shall be like him; for we shall see him as he is. And every man that has this hope in him purifies himself, even as he is pure" (1 John 3:2-3).

"Then He showed me the river whose waters give life, sparkling like crystal, flowing out from the throne of God and of the Lamb" (Revelation 22:1)

"The [Holy] Spirit and the bride (the church, the true Christians) say, Come! And let him who is listening say, Come! And let everyone come who is thirsty [who is painfully conscious of his need of those things by which the soul is refreshed, supported, and strengthened]; and whoever [earnestly] desires to do it, let him come, take, appropriate, and drink the water of Life without cost" (Revelation 22:17).

At the end of the Bible we have the Spirit of God and the Bride as one, creating Life by the WORD released. Jesus Christ is the Alpha and Omega, the beginning and the end. What is ended is also the beginning.

Jesus said "it is finished" when He was crucified on the cross (John 19:30). When He rose from the dead overcoming death, hell, and the grave, He was the first, the head of many to follow. The book of Revelation is the revelation of Jesus Christ, the body, the bride of Christ being prepared without spot or wrinkle.

What comes after the Spirit and the bride say "come?" The church is no longer a bride of self-focus, but impregnated as a wife with the seed of her husband and with the desire to produce a son that is the image of the Father.

"So God created man in His own image, in the image and likeness of God He created him; male and female He created them. And God blessed them and said to them, be fruitful, multiply, and fill the earth, and subdue it" (Genesis 1:27-28).

"We are of God: he that knows (experienced intimacy with) *God hears us; he that is not of God* (has not consummated with the WORD) *hears not us. Hereby know we the spirit of truth, and the spirit of error. God is love; and he that dwells* (in intimacy with) *in love dwells in God, and God* (has impregnated the WORD) *in him. Herein is our love made perfect, that we may have boldness in the day of judgment* (accusing voices within our ego causing judgment, condemnation, and fear)*: because as he is, so are we in this world. There is no fear in love; but perfect love casts out fear: because fear hath torment. He that fears is not made perfect in love. We love him, because he first loved us"* (1 John 4:6, 16-19).

The earth has been dominated by the father of lies, the spirit of fear and condemnation by the air we breathe and the thoughts we create and speak. Today is a new day. Let us begin taking authority and dominion over the spirit of fear bringing forth the spirit of faith.

Let every breath you breathe praise the LORD! If you are breathing, then begin praising Him in your going and comings of LIFE.

CHAPTER 14

SALVATION OR JUDGMENT

"Blessed be the God and Father of our Lord Jesus Christ, who hath blessed us with all spiritual blessings in heavenly places in Christ: According as he hath chosen us in him before the foundation of the world, that we should be holy and without blame before him in love: Having predestinated us unto the adoption of children by Jesus Christ to himself, according to the good pleasure of his will, to the praise of the glory of his grace, wherein he hath made us accepted in the beloved." (Eph. 1:3-6)

According to these scriptures and Jeremiah 1:5, we began in Him in the very beginning, before the foundations of the world found in Genesis, Chapter One. Now, come with me to John, Chapter Three. We have a discussion taking place between Nicodemus and Jesus about being born again. Jesus states in verses 5-7, "*except a man be born of water and of the spirit he cannot enter into the kingdom of God. That which is born of the flesh is flesh; and that which is born of the spirit is spirit. Marvel not that I said unto thee, you must be born again.*"

Jesus specifically is telling Nicodemus not to be concerned of how this will take place; don't marvel, or be surprised. Jesus and the Father had the situation handled. Being a religious leader for the Jews, Nicodemus is questioning the details, but can only see the physical realm of possibilities. He immediately brings up the physical birth of an individual, but Jesus is saying there is something beyond that. Being born again does not mean a physical birth, but a spiritual. The real individual, the real "I am" is spiritual.

In the beginning Adam came into the creation of God as an immortal flesh, as the image of God. Adam brought sin into creation by the flesh. The Spirit of God that was in him literally had to be veiled from Adam because of Adam's denial of who he really was, preferring to eat off of logic and reason instead of life. Afterwards, Adam heard the voice of God walking in the garden, outside of Adam instead of within him. Since the Spirit of God had to be veiled from Adam, his body no longer had the force within him to manifest eternal life. (All things in the beginning came from God, and it was the Spirit of God in him which made his flesh immortal). Adam brought mortality into existence to where man could die physically. Jesus came to the earth to restore all things (there's that word ALL again, Selah.). Man was first restored back to be a spiritual being by the resurrection of Jesus from the death on the cross. The real me today is a spirit, not a body. The body is the house the Spirit of God lives in. The more revelation I receive by the Holy Spirit, of who I am, the more transformation of Christ in the body will take place. **We must demand that our flesh be obedient to the mind of Jesus Christ**, and that our mind is His mind hearing the Spirit of God in us.

To be born again is to declare that the real you is the Spirit of God resident in you. Where God lives He doesn't share His house with anyone (Satan, sinner, flesh, human, etc.). When we identify ourselves with these words, we are lifting up an antichrist spirit and denying our true identity. Sounds like something the Woman did with the serpent in Genesis 3.

The day you found out that the real you is the Spirit of God in you was the beginning of the revelation of your true identity that took place in Galatians 2:20. When Jesus was on the cross, you were there with Him; and when He was in the tomb you were buried with Him; and when He rose from death and lives forevermore you rose with Him. Being a believer declares the knowledge that you were a part of what Jesus did

2,000 years ago on the cross. The flesh is only a house, but not the real you that already died on the cross with Him.

Let's read Hebrews 9:24-28:

"For Christ is not entered into the holy places made with hands which are the figures of the true; but into heaven itself, now to appear in the presence of God for us: Nor yet that he should offer himself often, as the high priest entered into the holy place every year with blood of others; For then must he often have suffered since the foundation of the world: but now once in the end of the world hath he appeared to put away sin by the sacrifice of himself. And as it is appointed unto men once to die, but after this judgment: so Christ was once offered to bear the sins of many; and unto them that look for him shall he appear the second time without sin unto salvation."

Wow! As I write these scriptures there is so much our Father is saying, but let me highlight just a few points to get you thinking. To understand the work that Jesus did as a sacrifice of Himself, and then entering the Holy of Holies once and for all, takes some understanding of what the High Priest did on the Day of Atonement for the children of God. The High Priest wore a garment called the ephod made of stones that represented all of God's people separated into different tribes. This was worn everyday as an intercessor to bring mercy and forgiveness to the people from God. On the Day of Atonement it was removed, and only white garments were worn. The entire formality of the ceremony performed by the High Priest going into the Holy of Holies was the total cleansing and remission of sins for all the nation of Israel. Since the sacrifices used were of a different kind, the cleansing of sin and restoring of a relationship with God had to be done yearly. In Hebrews 9:25, we read the word "others." This word is referring to the same kind. Jesus had the same blood as us which allowed the putting away of sin to be done once for all. It was not the blood of animals of a different kind that had been previously used by the High Priest.

"It is appointed unto men once to die," men died 2,000 years ago, but after this the judgment. The judgment is mercy that is supposed to come forth. Verse 28 follows: "and unto them that look for him shall he appear the second time without sin unto salvation." This is for today. You look in the Bible to see how God sees you in Christ, through the finished work. Jesus Christ' identity is in you.

Now, let's back up a moment to this word "judgment." It is appointed unto men once to die which was done on the cross according to Galatians 2:20, then the judgment. What does scripture say in reference to this word? Turn to John 5:22, "For the Father judges no man, but hath committed all judgment unto the Son." There's that word *all* again. If this scripture is true—that God doesn't judge anyone because He gave it all to the Son—then the great white throne of judgment needs to be re-thought out. God is not sitting on this huge throne somewhere, out there in space, ready to place sentence on mankind, Selah. Go to John 5:27, "and hath given him authority to execute judgment also, because he is the Son of Man."

Let's continue on with more scripture: John 7:24, "Judge not according to the appearance but judge righteous judgment." This is the judgment of God that He gave to Jesus to execute on men. John 8:15, "Ye judge after the flesh; I judge no man." Can this be true? Jesus says he judges no man. It doesn't distinguish between believers and non-believers. It says NO MAN. He confirms this with the next verse: "And yet if I judge, my judgment is true: I am not alone, but I and the Father that sent me. It is written in your law that the testimony of two men is true" (John 8:16-17). John 5:22 tells us the Father doesn't judge, and John 8:15 tells us the Son doesn't judge, Selah.

Let's continue on in scripture to John 9:39, and Jesus said, "For judgment I am come into this world that they which see not might see; and that they which see might be made blind." Very simply, those that do not judge will see Jesus, and those that judge will be blinded by the truth of who Jesus is and the work he did on the cross.

John 12:31-33, "*Now is the judgment of this world. Now shall the prince of this world be cast out. And I, if I be lifted up from the earth, will draw all men unto me. This he said, signifying what death he should die.*" (Funny how we like to skip over the 3 letter words like now and ALL). He states the "now" occurred at his death, burial, and resurrection. The work that he finished was judgment of sin that separated us from a relationship with the Father. The deceiver, utilizing the Tree of Knowledge was cast out of the world. He has no more power except what we give him through the power of words we create that are not His creation. Jesus' death and resurrection fulfilled the will of God that none would perish (2 Peter 3:9), and by the finished work all men will draw unto him.

Revelation 14:7, *"Fear God and give glory to him; for the hour of his judgment is come: and worship him that made heaven, and earth, and the sea, and the fountains of water."*

Revelation 18:10, *"Standing a far off for the fear of her torment, saying, alas, alas, that great city Babylon, that mighty city! For in one hour is thy judgment come."* Babylon is the adulteress church that takes God's word to bring judgment and condemnation instead of unconditional love and forgiveness. The one hour of judgment is when Jesus hung on the cross. He hung on the Tree of Knowledge of Good and Evil to do away with that tree. He declared "IT IS FINISHED" (John 19:30).

John 19:7-8, The Jews answered him, *"we have a law, and by our law he should die, because he made himself the Son of God. When Pilate therefore heard that saying, he was the more afraid; and went again into the judgment hall and saith unto Jesus, whence art thou? But Jesus gave him no answer."* The Jews represent religion speaking. **True faith has no laws**. The judgment hall was a place that all nations were judged.

In one point of time we have the government of God, the government of religion, and the government of the world congregating in the same area. The government of religion is justified by legalism; the government of the world is justified by power motivated by fear (read verse 10). The government of God is silent. God is not intimidated by religion, law, power, or fear. When you know who you are in Christ Jesus there is no need for proof. The fruits of His Spirit spring forth and override all other natural manifestations. The Spirit of God in Christ Jesus has NOW no condemnation (Romans 8:1).

To close this teaching we repeat John 19:30 where Jesus says "It is finished." He completed all of the will of God, and restoring all which began in the beginning. John 19:31-36 shows us that religion does not accept the finished work of Jesus. There is always something more that Jesus has to do. They don't see themselves as Paul describes in Galatians 2:20, "I am crucified with Christ: nevertheless, I live, yet not I, but Christ in me: and the life which I now live in the flesh I live by the faith of the Son of God, who loved me, and gave himself for me." Religion is still looking up at the cross, seeing Jesus hanging there. "They shall look on him whom they pierced" (John 19:37).

*Reference to the priesthood ceremony of Day of Atonement was taken from: Richman, Chaim. A House of prayer for All Nations, The Holy Temple of Jerusalem (The temple Institute & Carta: Jerusalem)1997.

CHAPTER 15

LIFE LESSONS FROM THE BOOK OF NEHEMIAH

The Old Testament was not written for the purpose of providing history lessons, but to give instructions, illustrations, definitions, and types/shadows for us to see God's plan in bringing forth the sons of God on the earth. It shows us the way to walk and also how not to walk. God uses the Old Testament to express truths that are present today, for with God there is no past tense. What the children of Israel walked through in the Old Testament is still being walked out by the church today.

Jerusalem signifies the house of God, the city of God. It is a city surrounded by a wall with gates. Today we hear of the "golden gates" which will surround Jerusalem when the Lord returns. This is a city that has gone through destruction and rebuilding more than any other city around the world. However, the wall that God is building today is not a part of the literal city of Jerusalem, but the people, or church. We are the temple of God today (I Corinthians 3:17).

God is bringing forth a remnant of people around the world today to declare His city; His Holy Nation (Isaiah 62:12). In these scriptures this is represented by the people that have escaped the bondage of Babylon. They were free but had lost the foundation and understanding required to have a relationship with God. Religious confusion had replaced relationship.

The first concern that Nehemiah had was to rebuild the walls of Jerusalem. Those that had returned to Jerusalem had no way to defend themselves. Rebuilding these walls was accomplished over a 25-year period, which took place several hundred years before Christ. It didn't just happen within a few years, but was a vision that was diligently pursued for a long time with many people having to put aside their own issues of fatigue. They didn't have the miracles of Jesus or the letters of Paul to encourage them. It was the faith and vision God gave Nehemiah that allowed them to persevere.

Today, there is a loud trumpet call being given to rebuild the walls of Zion, the people of God, His Holy Nation under the headship of Jesus Christ. The vision that Nehemiah was given to rebuild the wall of the city of God had been a trumpet call as well. This is the same trumpet that is heard in the book of Revelation to return and establish the foundational walls of Christianity.

Nehemiah faced a tremendous amount of hardship in taking on this project. His workmen had to defend themselves from their enemies while they were trying to work to rebuild the wall. They were continually ridiculed with words that demeaned their craftsmanship being told by outsiders that what they were doing would not stand the test of time, and that their work was irrelevant to the city of God. This was a very long, tedious project that was draining on the people emotionally, physically, and spiritually. Theologically, building this wall compares to us today building the temple of God, Christ in us, so that deception of religion, economics, and government bondages cannot penetrate the revelation of LIFE that the Holy Spirit has revealed to us.

There were military attacks which tried to deter the children of God from building this wall. This book of Nehemiah illustrates the persistent will that took place when God placed a vision in the heart of those that He had called. The wall was intended to secure the city so that it would be possible to inhabit the Holy City again. For us today, our "Holy City" is being in the presence of God and knowing the UNCONDITIONAL love that He has for us as Father despite the opposition where scriptures are used to bring condemnation and justification.

Nehemiah's vision was not only the preparation of the walls to inhabit the city safely, but to bring restoration to the temple on Mount Zion. The other concern he had was the recovery of the Law of Moses, and the faithful interpretation and observation of the sacred word. The vision the Lord gave him was not only to protect the city, but to have the truth of the word of God be restored in the city. The people would need spiritual food to grow and develop to be able to keep the city.

Nehemiah was a builder and an administrator. The Scribe Ezra, who lived during this time, was given the responsibility by Nehemiah to re-establish the Law of the Covenant. Ezra had spent his whole life copying and studying the law. He knew it better than any other person that lived. They were concerned about the proper interpretation of the law that had gone astray during exile.

Hundreds of years before this time when God's people were in the wilderness with Moses, there was only a remnant that crossed over into the Promised Land even though the word of the Lord had been given to them. What God gave them was more than the laws of Moses. It included the Law of the Covenant that all the children of Israel had received. Yet, while in the wilderness, sin and contamination entered into their lives. Just like Moses and Joshua, Nehemiah and Ezra came to renew the Covenant of God with the people. They desired to bind the people to God on the basis of the Word, and reestablish Truth.

The people had been without the wisdom and knowledge of what God originally established among His people for such a long time that it was necessary for them to go back to the foundation to re-establish the Law of the Covenant. Ezra took on the responsibility to establish the law in the hearts of the people keeping out sin and disobedience. He called the assembly together as Moses did to establish the Covenant by reading the words likened to a trumpet sound. He then sprinkled the blood of sacrifice upon the altar first, and then upon the people, binding them together in covenant unto God.

We begin with the Book of Nehemiah, Chapter One, using the Amplified Bible:

With verse 3 – 11, we read that Nehemiah was given a message about what is taking place in Jerusalem with the people of God. When he heard that the people were in great affliction and reproach, it stirred his heart to the point that he wept taking upon himself to pray, fast, and plead before God for the people's situation. He then began to intercede for the people reminding God of His words to Moses:

Verse 8-9: "Remember (earnestly) what You commanded Your servant Moses: If you transgress and are unfaithful, I will scatter you abroad among the nations; but if you return to Me and keep My commandments and do them, though your outcasts were in the farthest part of the heavens (the expanse of outer space), yet will I gather them from there and will bring them to the place in which I have chosen to set My Name."

Nehemiah came to Jerusalem to restore the city with rebuilding the wall. The word "wall" means to join and protect. The wall that God is rebuilding today is not a physical place called Jerusalem, but people. However, these people must show the rebuilding of His temple as a type/shadow of the real. God is not going to permit the rebuilding while we just sit and wait for the Lord's return. He is making sure that there will be those that He has called to personally qualify for what only God will do. This book is full of specifics about the people that God chose to build what portion of what gate and what location of the wall. A whole teaching could be done about each person's name that is listed in this book declaring something unique and specific in the way God built the wall and re-established the city.

A wall represents the standard and boundaries of a city. It is the protection, limitation, and expression of a city. Today, Christ is living within a people. We are the temple of God. His coming forth will not be from the sky, but from within His temple. If we miss the coming of Christ it is because we were not looking in the temple of God, but somewhere else. Christ IN YOU is the hope of glory (Col. 1:27).

The golden gate that theologians say will be opened in Jerusalem when the Lord returns is a type and shadow for us to look within ourselves for a gate to be opened and the manifestation of Christ in us to be released. The Book of Nehemiah gives us a pattern to follow in the opening of this gate within the heart of each of us.

The wall that Nehemiah is called by God to build is a standard being set within a company of people that have been pulled aside by God to establish for His kingdom. However, whether we speak of the wall in China or in Jerusalem, they both make a specific statement to the world which is: This is the city and here is the expression of it. Here are the gates and entrance to enter into it and here is the place of exit. The walls state that within them there is protection and unity of like mind.

Nehemiah groans for the city and seeks the Lord for the repairing of it, including the walls that protect it. The overwhelming task set before him is a project that he knows must be accomplished, but he also must depend on God for the resources and manpower to make it happen. He had served under a heathen king, but God touched the heart of Artaxerxes so that he was willing to supply Nehemiah with the means to rebuild Jerusalem.

Chapter 2: Nehemiah begins to encourage the people, showing the king's letter, which gained access to supplies to rebuild the wall. In verse 11, we see that he was in Jerusalem for three days, which spiritually speaks of resurrection or a new beginning.

He then got up in the night after everyone else was asleep taking just a few men with him and an animal to ride on. What Nehemiah did not do is go about telling a lot of people what God had put in his heart, trying to get a committee or church group's approval.

He went out by the Valley Gate toward the Dragon's Well and to the dung Gate inspecting the gates that had been destroyed by fire. He then went to the Fountain Gate and to the King's Pool, but couldn't pass because the destruction was so great. So he rode by the brook (Kidron) in the night, inspecting the wall, and then returned to the Valley Gate (13-15).

Verse 16 tells us that no one knew what Nehemiah was doing including the rulers, Jews, priests, nobles, officials, or even the people that did the work. God gave him a secret work to survey the situation and destruction that exists. No one had a clue that he was making an observation of the situation for God.

When Nehemiah had a good understanding of what the circumstance was with the city of Jerusalem and the wall that had been torn apart, he presented the situation to the people. In verse 18 we read, "Then I told them of the hand of my God which was upon me for good, and also the words that the king had spoken to me. And they said, Let us rise up and build! So they strengthened their hands for the good work."

Whenever God is doing a good work through us we can expect opposition of some kind. The same thing occurred for Nehemiah and the people that were supporting him to rebuild the wall. In verse 19, Nehemiah and the people were mocked with the words of Sanballat the Horonite, Tobiah an Ammonite servant, and Geshem who were Arab. They laughed, scorned, and despised Nehemiah and the people by saying "What is this thing you are doing? Will you rebel against the king?"

They didn't just express their opposition once and then walk away. We read in Chapter 4, verses 1 and 2, "But when Sanballat heard that we were building the wall, he was angry and in a great rage, and he ridiculed the Jews. And he said before his brethren and the army of Samaria, what are these feeble Jews doing? Will they restore things (at will and by themselves)? Will they (try to bribe their God) with sacrifices? Will they finish up in a day? Will they revive the stones out of the heaps of rubbish, seeing they are burned?"

Since his mockery didn't do anything against Nehemiah, Sanballat gathered the strength of the Samaritan army. Samaritans represent Jews that did not want to submit to the ways of God. They set up their own standard instead of God's.

Nehemiah was receiving the opposition of all those that were against what God had shown him. There is a parallel with the Jews and Samaritans that is relevant for us today. For example, we can see all the many Christian denominations that refuse to work together as one body, yet insist that their doctrine is the path to life according to the word of God. Nehemiah was going against all ridicule and enemy forces to do what God had shown him.

These people that worked on the rebuilding did not turn their backs to the enemy. While they worked, they carried swords and shields to fight off any attacks (vs. 17). They had to continually keep themselves protected as they were rebuilding. Keep in mind; this was not a 6-month or one-year project, but took place over a 25-year period. Many people died of old age before seeing the finished work, yet by faith they persevered.

With all the opposition around Nehemiah and the men that were rebuilding, they prayed to God and set a watch against their enemy's day and night. Those carrying the most burdens began to weaken, so Nehemiah set armed men behind the wall in places that were less protected. He used the people as families with their swords, spears, and bows.

In Chapter 4, verse 4, we read, "(And Nehemiah prayed) Hear, O our God, for we are despised. Turn their taunts upon their own heads, and give them for a prey in a land of their captivity."

The parallel that we see happening is what we go through today: God will be calling us out to do something that may not agree with church doctrine. We must pray about it waiting for His counsel while searching His word. Once we know in our heart without any question what God is commissioning, we must put on the armor of God, expecting to be attacked with words of ridicule that will try and convince us that we are not really hearing from God.

The voice of the enemy will say things such as, "If God is in this: why hasn't He told everyone else; why is there so much financial struggle; why is it difficult to get the supplies that are needed; why are you and a few people the only ones hearing; why is there so much confusion; why are things going backwards after taking a few steps forward; why is there delay?"

These questions are not meant to be answered, but to weaken the vision and call of God. Therefore, it is vitally important to be equipped with the armor of God (Ephesians 6:13-18), expecting confrontation while moving towards what God has called us to do for His glory and His kingdom to be manifested NOW.

Nehemiah 4:13-14, "So I set (armed men) behind the wall in places where it was least protected; I even thus used the people as families with their swords, spears, and bows. I looked (them over) and rose up and said to the nobles and officials and the other people, do not be afraid of the enemy; (earnestly) remember the Lord and imprint Him (on your minds), great and terrible, and (take from Him courage to) fight for your brethren, your sons, your daughters, your wives, and your homes."

Further down in this chapter we read that the destruction of the wall was great and spread out. The workers were individually armed, but because of the distance between workers, they were to press on in diligence to the cause and vision God had given them independently. This issue is addressed by Nehemiah in verses 19-21:

"And I said to the nobles and officials and the rest of the people, the work is great and scattered, and we are separated on the wall, one far from another; in whatever place you hear the sound of the trumpet, rally to us there. Our God will fight for us. So we labored at the work while half of them held the spears from dawn until the stars came out."

When God calls us to do something, He equips us individually in accordance to the vessel that we are created for that purpose. Though it will be the same equipment, it may fit a little differently on each person because we are all a unique portion of the body of Christ. However, once the trumpet sound is heard within our spirit (vs. 18), we will come together as His body for the same call that God has placed in each of our hearts.

In Chapter 5, the people began to complain about their debt and what it is costing them to build this wall. The kingdom of God requires a certain standard of excellence. God is not looking for a people that are interested in doing a "patch job" for His Kingdom to be manifested. He does not need a "buddy" to give Him an opinion of what works and doesn't work. Christ is all and in all (Col. 3:11). It takes those that know they are a new creature in Christ (Gal. 6:15) ready to do the Father's business. They believe in their heart that as He is so am I in this world (I John 4:17). The old man (Adam) is gone and all things are new in Him (2 Corinth. 5:17). God requires perfection from those that He has called.

The people's complaints to Nehemiah were about a burden they were carrying as a debt that was way beyond THEIR ability to pay. They were armed from attacks from their enemy on the outside, but they were feeling the pressures that come from within their soul of the cost to rebuild the wall.

When we come to Chapter 6, verse 5, we see that the people are influenced from the words of outsiders, causing them to start forming their own opinions and views of what God called Nehemiah to do. They were ideas and thoughts like "this rebuilding project was not from God, but to build a kingdom for Nehemiah." The workers grouped together to come against him because of their own burden, but they were blaming the situation on Nehemiah. They tried to justify their position by emphasizing that they already had a king and didn't need Nehemiah to be one. They threatened to take matters to the Persian king.

Verse 8-9: "I replied to him, no such things as you say have been done; you are inventing them out of your own heart and mind. For they all wanted to frighten us, thinking, their hands will be so weak that the work would not get done. But now strengthen my hands!"

The people that had been called by God began to make an impact on those outside. Not understanding the ways of God, those in leadership felt threatened by what building this wall might mean to their personal situation and rulership. God's people tend to doubt God when natural opposition, which may sound logical, causes insecurity, anxiety, fear, and confusion to the vision that God has given. Again, the "why" questions enter into the mind of the people. Many people leave what God has called them to do as a result of the conflict and troubles they encounter, thinking that in doing so their troubles will leave.

Nehemiah responds by telling the people that the reports are not true. The people must strengthen the weakened areas where doubt and insecurity have tried to penetrate by tightening the armor of God around them.

In verses 15-16, the wall is finished. "When all our enemies heard of it, all the nations around us feared and fell far in their own esteem, for they saw that this work was done by our God."

The wall has now been built. Around the wall there were gates established that were part of the rebuilding of the wall. Each gate had a designated team of people that were assigned for a specific purpose at the gate of which they were to be in charge. Each gate had a unique position for the city's purposes, yet had to work in unity with the other gates to establish strength and power as one wall around the city.

In Chapter 7:1, we read, "Now when the wall was built and I had set up the doors, and the gatekeepers, singers, and Levites had been appointed..."

Notice who is watching over the gates: gatekeepers are those who serve; singers are those who lead in praise to God; and Levites are the priests or sons of God. The post watch of the gates was a 24/7 responsibility. In other words, these gates were manned with the armor of God continually by those that had been crucified with Christ. Their life was not their own, but in a position of strategy for the Kingdom of God.

When we go to verse 3, Nehemiah says, "Let not the gates of Jerusalem be opened until the sun is hot; and while the watchmen are still on guard, let them shut and bar the doors. Appoint guards from the people of Jerusalem, each to his watch (on the wall) and each opposite his own house." The word "sun" can be replaced with "SON" in applying these scriptures for us today. This means that there will not be a releasing of the gates until the SON is red hot, or until it is "high noon" when the LIGHT is shining at HIS brightest. It also means that the pressures we incur in the natural realm will be at their hottest point; when we think we can't take it any longer and we are ready to give up or quit whatever God has called us to do.

Those that will be in the city cannot go out, and those on the outside will not be able to come in until God says it is "high noon." We read in this same verse that the guards take their position on the wall opposite their own house, yet in verse 4 their houses were not yet built! In verse 5 we read that the people that are counted in the city have a genealogy connection to the city which qualified them to be inside the wall.

Let's get this picture: The people that are within the city are there because of being a son or daughter of someone that was connected to the city of God, not because they had years of experience in being a guard; however, they don't yet have a house. Until the gates are opened so their house can be built, they are to establish themselves as a guard on the wall opposite where their house will be. How many times do you think these people went through their days visualizing their dream home within the city walls while they stood guard? How often did they long for the gates to be opened so that they could start building their homes?

These people had already gone through many trials trying to build the wall while dealing with the attacks from their enemies. They were tired. When the wall was finished, they were ready to rest, yet God was calling them to come to a place higher, the top of the wall, and guard the place where their house would be in the city, not telling them how long they would have to continue watch. They would know by a sign when things were at their hottest and the sun was at its brightest. When the SON is red hot, everyone will be steaming and sweating uncontrollably. Water will be pouring out of the flesh. It is the trials and tribulations of our life that this experience occurs. Selah.

The gates to the city each had a particular purpose for entering into the city:

Sheep Gate: Those that are migrating in the world needing to be gathered together by the shepherd. This gate is a place of collecting or coming together. They began to collect the sheep.

Fish Gate: The souls of people that have been seeking for the deeper things of God not satisfied with what tradition or denomination has taught. There are numerous squirming souls ready for harvest gathering. God is repairing and recollecting.

Old Gate: Symbolic of something that has always been in existence. Represents truth that has always existed; but alienated from the lives of the people.

We can go back today through history and find a company of people that God has used to preserve His word and truth as a seed to be carried into the next generation. God's present truth has always been and will always be. There is nothing new with God.

God is collecting the sheep that have gone astray, and the souls that are squirming with the word of God that has always been in them, but because of traditions and doctrines, has been hidden except for a few that have carried the genealogy seed which qualifies them to stay within the walls.

Valley Gate: The main entrance in the west wall (West Gate or Jaffa Gate). This gate symbolizes arrogance. In the Old Testament, if there was an ego issue that God needed to deal with, that person was brought into the city through this gate. They had to go down into the valley to find humility before coming up into the city of God. He is bringing about restoration where there was arrogance.

Dung Gate: Represents a heap of rubbish or filth; a sense of scraping. God is drawing the rejects and outsiders of society into the city. Through all the rejection they have experienced, they are finding their true identity with their Heavenly Father as being a child of God. They are finding out that God loves them unconditionally, and that they are wonderfully and fearfully made!

Fountain Gate: The place of the eye; a place that is obvious. The center or display that catches your eye that everything else evolves around. It is supposed to be the Church; however, what should be a display of Christ has been a reproach. The outside world sees the church as a mockery and insult to God. God is restoring the eye or center display so that when others see the church, His body, they will see HIM and be drawn to HIM.

Water Gate: Spring or new beginning which comes from the word sperm. The restoration of the "seed" of the word of God. The restoring of intimacy, childbirth, and multiplication of the word of God as sons of God ready to do the Father's business. The restoration of creating after our own kind that Adam was originally commanded to do by God in Genesis 1: 27-28a:

"So God created man in His own image, in the image and likeness of God He created him; male and female He created them. And God blessed them and said to them, be fruitful, multiply, and fill the earth, and subdue it (using all its vast resources in the service of God and man)."

Horse Gate: Skipping and leaping for joy; the restoration of joy.

Miphkad Gate: Also known as the Muster Gate. The assignment, the mandate, or command. The repairing of the net for recapturing the commandment of God:

Matthew 22: 37-40: *"You shall love the Lord your God with all your heart and with all your soul and with all your mind (intellect). This is the great (most important, principal) and first commandment. And a second is like it; you shall love your neighbor as (you do) yourself. These two commandments sum up and upon them depend all the Law and the Prophets."*

When we come to Chapter 9, Nehemiah tells us how the Israelites came together and separated themselves from all foreigners. They stood and confessed the sins and iniquities of their fathers; read from the Book of the Law of the Lord; and worshipped God by singing praises and lifting up His name.

In verse 8 of this chapter there is a list of "ites" from which the people had been set free. They were released from the following:

- Canaanite: Freedom from being humiliated or belittled.
- Hittite: Freedom from being terrorized.

- Amorite: Freedom from a place of publicity and pride.
- Perizzite: Freedom from rusty; from being separated or in the wilderness.
- Jebusite: Freedom from being trodden.
- Girgashite: Freedom from being trampled and possessed or ruled over.

A very prevalent disease during Bible history was Leprosy which is symbolic of the "disease of the mind." It was a disease that the people were very fearful of being around. Those that had it blamed someone other than themselves for the responsibility of their condition or negative circumstances. Their praises to God included the recollecting of how His people were a "stiff-necked" group complaining constantly, yet God was ready to pardon, gracious and merciful, slow to anger, and of great steadfast love. He did not forsake them and allotted to them the Promised Land (vs. 17, 22).

Something we must consider is; there were those that were called to rebuild the wall; those that were called to guard the gate; those that were called to guard their home; and then those that were princes, Levites, and priests to set the standard for the city. Each of these people were called by God. Chapter 10 gives a list of these people. Their names teach a lesson.

These people had a passion to reestablish the covenant of God and walk in His Law which was given to Moses (vs. 29). They desired to see lost souls come into the city and have a safe place they could reside with their brothers and sisters. This is what all the gates represent.

There is a restoration today calling the people that have labored through this process to bring ALL into the kingdom of God. Each of us has a "gate" that we have come through. Each gate is important and not any greater than another gate. God calls us to come with a spirit of unity and understanding of the importance of the assignment each person has.

God calls us to come with a spirit of unity and understanding of the importance of the assignment each person has.

We each have a list of "ites" or the Leprosy of our mind that will try to justify why we can't do our portion to what God has called to bring the unity of the family. However, there is a trumpet call that will be heard, and is being heard even now, for each of us to wake up and realize that the purpose of our being is not about us, but about Him. When this happens in each of us; when we experience our "high noon," we will rise up beyond our "ites" to do the Father's business in filling the earth with His glory, setting the captive free and bringing unity to the family of God.

In Revelation Chapter 21:2-3 we read, "And I saw the holy city, the new Jerusalem, descending out of heaven from God, all arrayed like a bride beautified and adorned for her husband; Then I heard a mighty voice from the throne and I perceived its distinct words, saying, See! The abode of God is with men, and He will live (encamp, tent) among them; and they shall be His people, and God shall personally be with them and be their God." The gates were opened resurrection morning when Jesus Christ rose from the grave for all to come through with whatever situation is going on in our lives. Each gate is separate, yet built of one pearl. (Rev. 21:21). Pearls represent a transformation through trials and tribulations coming through as a stone of righteousness.

"I saw no temple (natural building) in the city (body of Christ), for the Lord God Omnipotent (Himself) and the Lamb (Himself) is its temple. And the city has no need of the sun nor of the moon to give light to it (natural or carnal understanding), for the splendor and radiance (glory) of God illuminate it, and the Lamb is its lamp. The nations (all mankind) shall walk by its light and the rulers and leaders of the earth shall bring into it their glory. And its gates shall never be closed by day, and there shall be no night (sorrow, ignorance) there. They shall bring the glory (the splendor and majesty) and the honor of the nations (our Christ identity) into it" (Revelation 21:23-26).

These are they that have moved into place of overcoming by His grace and faith any hindering circumstances and have come to a place of higher understanding in God. They know it is not about lifting themselves up, but about establishing their true identity and the unconditional love of God.

"I have been crucified with Christ (in Him I have shared His crucifixion); it is no longer I who live, but Christ (the Messiah) lives in me; and the life I now live in the body I live by faith in (by adherence to and reliance on and complete trust in) the Son of God, who loved me and gave Himself up for me" (Galatians 2:20).

"In this (union and communion with Him) love is brought to completion and attains perfection with us, that we may have confidence for the day of judgment (with assurance and boldness to face Him), because as He is, so are we in this world. There is no fear in love (dread does not exist), but full grown (complete, perfect) love turns fear out of doors and expels every trace of terror! For fear brings with it the thought of punishment and (so) he who is afraid has not reached the full maturity of love (is not yet grown into love's complete perfection). We love Him, because He first loved us" (I John 4:17-19).

CHAPTER 16

THE KIND PRINCIPLE

God established a law in Genesis the first chapter called the "Kind Principle". It states that the seed of that kind is within, and able to produce more of the like kind.

Adam is the only creation that can produce creativity by words that are spoken. Once words are spoken they have the power to produce life or death. Genesis 2:19 tells us God formed every beast, every fowl, and brought them to Adam to give them a name. The name he gave was forever instilled as the identity of that creature. A dog is not a cat, a bee is not a mosquito, an elephant is not a giraffe. Anywhere in the world the name of each creature is the same, and can only produce its own kind.

Genesis 1:26 tells us that God made man in "our" image after "our" likeness (which means kind). Adam declares this image has been reproduced when he sees the creation taken out of him and says it is his bone and his flesh, calling it Woman. God's image, God's kind has reproduced and is known in the New Testament (yet before Calvary) as the offspring of God, The son of God. (Check out the genealogy of Jesus in Luke chapter 3).

Knowing this kind principle still exist today since we still see orange trees producing orange trees, cats producing cats, and people producing people, etc. Let's ask ourselves another question, does a child (offspring) have the right to choose who it's parents are going to be? Can a child change the DNA structure of its bloodline and genetic coding? Of course not. The basic laws of conception state that a male and female of the same kind come together as one. Even this act is not a guarantee of producing offspring. It begins with God. Jeremiah 1:5 tells us before God formed us in the womb, He knew us in an intimate way, a oneness of His kind, and then before we came out of the womb He sanctified us which means to make clean, dedicate, consecrate to God. To declare us as holy. (I didn't say this, the Bible does). God declares this after the fall of Adam to Jeremiah and then confirms it to Luke when the Holy Spirit gives the genealogy of Jesus.

Knowing that it was God who created the kind principle, how does being a sinner fit into the picture? How can a sinner become a son of God? This is like saying a dog doesn't want to be a dog anymore, it wants to be a cat. Where does a man get the idea that he can become a woman, or a woman can become a man changing the kind principle that God created? It begins with a mindset. Whose mind are you listening to? When an individual has major sex change surgery to where outwardly they totally appear to be the opposite of who they were, they still can't change the cellular structure of the DNA, or the life in the blood that declares if you were born as a woman then you are a woman, and if you were born as a man then you are a man. This is why they can't reproduce the change into children.

When we receive Jesus Christ as our personal savior, what are we really declaring? Is acknowledging being a sinner a statement as a noun or a verb? Is it possible that we have been taught a lie that goes against the laws of nature, the kind principle that God created? Medical science will acknowledge that if you take a genius child, born of royal bloodline, put him in an environment that he only hears how dumb and stupid he is along with being surrounded with every negative name calling with no love or encouragement, that child will not know his true identity and inheritance. When he becomes an adult at midlife finding out who he really is, it will be very difficult to accept and change because of the life style and words that have been his identity in his mind. Another example, if you take a newborn eagle and place it in a chicken coop to be raised with the chickens it will act like a chicken as an adult. It will not know that it has the ability to fly high, to see with a depth and distance further than a chicken. It will not know that it has the natural ability to be a very powerful creature fit for survival and independence.

What is the real difference between those that declare they are Christians and those that don't? Could it be that those that don't simply don't know who their real heavenly Father is? Are we as Christians showing non-Christians their Father God? That is what Jesus did. He said when you see me, you see the Father, my Father and your Father. For all power has been given to me in heaven and earth, as my Father sent me, even so send I you (John 20). The Bible doesn't say that He is speaking to just believers, or to those that received Him first to get the ability to call God Father. He made a statement that He was your Father whether you received Him or not.

Sin has placed a bondage on God's children, removing them from the ability to have a personal relationship with Him in the Old Testament. Jesus paid the price of that bondage, removing and destroying it when He went to the cross. He said that all power in heaven and earth has been given to Him. If all means all, then Satan can't have any power. If Jesus has sent us as He is then we have that power as cells of His body. The power that Satan receives comes from us, not by who he is, but by us not knowing who we are. Many Christians still say, "I'm just a poor sinner saved by grace." There is no power of God in that mind set. Do your children stop being your children because they chose to live a life you didn't raise them as which may be headed for destruction and hurt? No, they will always be your children. What they are missing is the relationship and the ability to receive the inheritance of your wisdom. When a child realizes that things were better around mom and dad, that their parent's lives are an example of love, life, peace, etc., a veil is removed from the child's understanding that his way may not have been the best. There becomes a need to go back and get reconnected with the wisdom and relationship with his parents of who he really is. That's called repentance, simply turning around and beginning again with your true identity. Being a sinner is not a noun of identity, but an action or direction that was taken apart from the truth of who God is and who you are.

Adam and the Woman began the question of who they were in chapter 3 of Genesis. The fact that there is a conversation and question with Satan as to their identity shows their own insecurity. They were messing around in the fields instead of staying in the garden where they belonged. They were already God beings created in His image and producing sons of God as found in Genesis 6.

The Woman exchanges words with Satan, a creature that wasn't supposed to talk. She adds the word "touch"—a created word by Adam, not God, to the words God gave her opening a realm of the creation of good and evil. "If it feels good, looks good, taste good, sounds good, it must be good" or "I need to see it before I believe it" mentality. This mindset hinders the mindset of our God identity that faith is the substance of things hoped for, the evidence of things not seen (Heb. 11:1).

The Woman today is the church, the body of Christ. Jesus Christ is the second Adam. Still today we have the woman trying to dig up the tree of knowledge of good and evil. That tree no longer exist except in the mind of man. The second Adam, Jesus who is the Tree of Life, hung on the tree of knowledge, removing the penalty and bondage that the first Adam and the first Woman placed on the genealogy of God. God's children were in a spiritual prison, which was removed 2,000 years ago.

God spared not His own Son, but delivered him up for us all. All means all, not just those that believe, but those that don't know who they are yet. In Romans 8:38-39, we read, "neither death, nor life, nor angels, nor principalities, nor powers, nor things present, nor things to come, nor height, nor depth, nor any other creature, shall be able to separate us from the love of God, which is in Christ Jesus our Lord.

This covers the all, those that believe, and those that don't. We as Christians need to look within ourselves and ask, are we presenting the Father to the non-believer, which reflects unconditional love and forgiveness, or are we showing how bad they are and that they are going to hell if they don't do something by accepting Jesus as their personal savior? Many of them will tell you they are already in hell, where else can they go? Accepting Jesus and conforming to the life style of the church today becomes a works issue they can't relate to. Sometimes people change because of a fear that they are going to be left behind. Think about this, what father or mother who really loves they're children wants a relationship with them based on fear? When a child recognizes their true identity and knows in their heart that their parents will receive them back after a life of destruction with open, loving arms there is a drawing effect a child will respond to because of the inner heart's desire to be loved and accepted. There may be issues of blockage that cause hindrance to come back home, usually because of doubt and insecurity of understanding the fullness of the Father's love. It is our job as believers to show them the forgiveness and unconditional love of their heavenly Father.

"Blessed are the pure in heart for they shall see God. Blessed are the peacemakers for they shall be called the children of God" (Matt. 5:8-9).

CHAPTER 17

FEAST OF YOM KIPPUR: A DAY OF ATONEMENT

*T*oday is a very special day for all humanity: Jews, Christians, and Gentiles or a believer of another faith, for today is the day appointed by God to seal the Book of Life. The rabbinical tradition begins by the blowing of the two silver trumpets at Rosh Ha Shana. At this time, the people were to prepare themselves for the next ten days called the Days of Awe to have good deeds outweighing their sins in order to have their name written in the Book of Life. During this time, the High Priest would also be going through intense preparations to carry the responsibility of coming into the Holy of Holies three times before God with his sacrifice first and then the sacrifice of the people. If at any time one of the sacrifices were not accepted, the high priest would instantly die in the Holy of Holies before God.

Jesus Christ was our sacrificial Lamb, which took place in the spring at Passover, but fulfilled as the sacrificial Lamb required at Yom Kippur. Two calendar Holy Days fulfilled as one event. Not using the blood of bullocks and goats that was sufficient one year, but His own blood as the final scapegoat, once and for ALL.

It is a custom for the Jewish faith to fast during the 24 hours of Yom Kippur as a way of repentance, reflection, and reconciliation unto God as a bride preparing herself for her beloved for intimacy. However, as new believers in Christ Jesus, do we still need to fast? After spending time with the Lord about this question, the Lord reminded me that there were two silver trumpets blown at Rosh Ha Shana, just as there were two goats sacrificed: One goat was "unto the Lord" where this sacrifice was received in intimacy with God. The other goat took upon his horns the blood sacrifice of the first as sins of "another kind of beast" that was not God's identity that we would call sin of man. The horns of the goats represent the trumpets. The silver represents redemption. This second goat, the scapegoat, would be taken by a priest to the wilderness carrying a crimson-dyed piece of wool. Just before the priest would send the goat over the cliff to his death, he would take the wool and tear it into two pieces. He would then tie one piece to the goat's horns before pushing him over the cliff with both of his hands while the other piece of the wool was tied around the priest's wrist. As soon as the goat would be dead, a miraculous thing would happen to the wool around the priest's wrist: It would turn white as snow signifying that the sacrifices were finished and that God would bless the New Year with life and favor for the next year.

The writings in the book of Hebrews brings this through that Jesus finished this for all mankind with his own blood and body, giving us today a New Year of eternal life in Him now, not just when we get to heaven, not just based on our good works, and not just for a year at a time. When Jesus hung on the cross he cried out, "It Is Finished"(John 19:30).

So again I ask, is fasting necessary? There is a place to fast as a preparation of intimacy and oneness unto our beloved. For some it may be food or drink. For others it may be places, people, or things. Whatever is more important to you than intimacy with Jesus should be your fast "unto the Lord".

However, there is another trumpet/goat besides the one designated "unto the Lord". With intimacy comes the ability to reproduce fruit. When the high priest entered into the Holy of Holies, it was the only TIME the name of God could be pronounced, YHWH, also known as I AM. The high priest did not wear his "golden garments" at this time, but was clothed in white linen, signifying purity and holiness before God. When he came out of the temple's inner sanctuary, the people saw the representation of God in the glory of intimacy, not in royal attire. It is in this position of holiness that the high priest has the authority to take the sins of the people and place them on the scapegoat.

Once the sacrifice was completed, the high priest would descend to the Women's Court and read aloud from the Book of Leviticus before the congregation:

"For on that day shall the priest make atonement for you, to cleanse you, that ye may be clean from all your sins before the Lord. It shall be a Sabbath of rest unto you, and ye shall afflict your souls, by a statute forever. And the priest, whom he shall anoint, and whom he shall consecrate to minister in the priest's office in his father's stead, shall make the atonement, and shall put on the linen clothes, even the holy garments: And he shall make an atonement for the holy sanctuary, and he shall make an atonement for the tabernacle of the congregation, and for the altar, and he shall make an atonement for the priests, and for all the people of the congregation. And this shall be an everlasting statute unto you."

Then the high priest would close the scrolls and it was considered "sealed" with the names written in the Book of Life.

In Luke 4 we read,*"Jesus came to Nazareth, where he had been brought up: and, as his custom was, he went into the synagogue on the Sabbath day, and stood up for to read. And there was delivered unto him the book of the prophet Isaiah. And when he had opened the book, he found the place where it was written, 'The Spirit of the Lord is upon me, because he hath anointed me to preach the gospel to the poor; he hath sent me to heal the brokenhearted, to preach deliverance to the captives, and recovering of sight to the blind, to set at liberty them that are bruised, To preach the acceptable year of the Lord. And he closed the book, and he gave it again to the minister, and sat down. And the eyes of all them that were in the synagogue were fastened on him. And he began to say unto them, this day is this scripture fulfilled in your ears.'"*

From the Court of Women, the High Priest's work was finished; it was completed. It is the intimacy of the bride of Christ that leaves the inner court to release to the people the identity of Christ in her whom the Bible calls the church. She is the one given the authority to forgive sin, heal the sick, and raise the dead. Whosoever sins you forgive, they are forgiven, and whosoever sins you retain, they are retained.

What is the greatest "fast" we can give today to the world? Our time as new creations in Christ. Our world today is so busy with self-focus, easily hiding behind texting and emails that we are raising a generation that has little value of spending quality time in the presence of another. Much of our socialization is about how to be a surface friend of doing things together, but not really coming into another person's world of what they may be dealing with in their heart. Our time given to another is priceless when it produces fruit of love, patience, peace, longsuffering, kindness, gentleness, goodness, faith, hope, and humbleness into the lives of another.

For God so loves you, He gave you the life of Jesus while you were still in ignorance and self-absorbed, thinking the world revolved around you owing you something. I challenge you to fast a day, any day, giving 100% of your time devoted to whoever comes across your path that you will give them your time. Let a stranger know they are special to you and you value their life. Do you know their name? Do you see something beautiful about them that could edify and lift them up? You can't let offense enter in if they reject your time, and you can't put limitations of your time being given to them.

There is a story in the Bible where Peter and John went to pray unto the Lord. When they got to the gate called Beautiful there is a lame man that couldn't walk begging for alms. It was the best he knew to do to survive. Peter and John were preparing to worship "unto the Lord," but the Christ in them pointed out the lame man whom many others had walked by. Peter and John went to the lame man saying, "Silver, gold, money, or food I don't have (the natural level of Peter and John), but what I do have I will give to you (Spirit of Christ identity, I AM). I have

Christ in me that says your sitting by the gate called Beautiful and you don't know that the real value of Christ in you can lift you up from the begging/complacent position you are stuck in. So, what does Peter and John do? In the NAME, nature, identity of Christ Jesus, they give this to the lame man and decree that he can rise up and walk away from where he had been sitting.

Jesus closed the book in Luke 4 and sat down. The Scripture He was reading from in Isaiah 61 is longer than the two verses Jesus read. The rest of the chapter is the responsibility of His bride, bringing Heaven and Earth together as the Word being made flesh and dwelling among men on the earth.

So do you fast? Yes, but not only for purifying yourself "unto the Lord", but giving of the most precious gift every one of us has, our time into their world. Since we have the eternal life of Christ in us, we can bring heaven into someone else's time, releasing the Father's love that decrees I see you special, beautiful, and loved. Rise up and walk out of whatever is holding you back from the fullness of who God created you to be in the image and likeness of Him in the earth.

CHAPTER 18

THE TABERNACLE IN THE WILDERNESS

Contained within the tabernacle in the wilderness is the key for transformation to transfiguration. It was the first building after the Garden of Eden that God built. The minute that Adam turned on Eve, he brought expulsion into the Holy of Holies. He brought into the presence of God the law of death. We know this by the pattern of the High Priest, their life requirements to come into the presence of God for the redemption of the people of God. These requirements were commandments given to Moses to give to the Levitical Priesthood. If the High Priest were to take anything into the Holy of Holies that did not reflect the character and nature of God, then he would die. His garments had to be made of pure white linen which spoke of being sinless, his headpiece spoke of the mind of God which said "Holiness unto the Lord". It was made of gold which represented the character of God. He had to go through several purification processes to get his body, soul, and mind filled with only God. Anything of himself would bring instant death. All of his presence had to speak of God. He wore a bell around his waist so that if he entered with anything of himself that would cause him to die the other priest in the Holy area could pull him out without entering into the Holy of Holies, least they would die themselves.

Adam and Eve were one. That is my bone and my flesh. You cherish and nurture your own flesh. You protect and watch over it. They were God on this earth. When they had a relationship of intimacy together it was God to God. The real center of who God is: unfailing, unalterable, unconditional love. Only with the mind of God can we know this love.

Have you ever thought of why the Ark of the Covenant is the mercy seat, which is where God resides? God is love, there is no condition to His mercy. When a love relationship from the heart is taking place with God then the blessings of mercy come forth. A pure heart is a heart of all God which is a heart of non-judgment, full of love and forgiveness. When a pure heart is manifested, God is there being revealed face to face. Peace comes forth when God is seen, and the temple that He is seen in is reflecting itself as His child (Matt. 5).

When you accuse someone or don't cover another's sins, then you are manifesting Adam versus God. If Adam had accepted the responsibility of Eve eating from the wrong tree, then the image of who he was as God would have cleansed the unrighteousness at that time. Jesus came to do what the first Adam did not do. He said to God that every sin committed, past, present, and future was me. I did those, it was my fault. He paid the penalty on the cross 2,000 years ago of what Adam did when he brought death into the Holy of Holies.

In Romans 5:12, we read, "by one man sin entered into the world, and death by sin; and so death passed upon all men, for that all have sinned." Verse 8 of the same chapter says, "But God commended his love toward us, in that while we were yet sinners, Christ died for us." Verse 10, "For if, when we were enemies we were reconciled to God by the death of his Son, much more, being reconciled, we shall be saved by his life." Paul is saying that whether you know it or not, or whether you receive it or not, the enemy of God is gone. Jesus's death brought reconciliation to all men. This is confirmed with the role of the High Priest on the day of atonement when he went into the Holy of Holies for the sins of the people. He would go through a ritual that required taking in the blood of one goat, spotless, and then when the High Priest came out he would go to another goat that was the scapegoat. He would release it into the wilderness never to be seen again. This was to signify that God received the sacrifice offering for the sins of the people, forgiving them, never to be remembered again. They could now have a relationship with God through the intercession of the Levitical Priesthood, and the atonement of their sins. However, it was the children's choice to acknowledge the cleansing that was theirs to receive. In the eyes of God, they were clean, but in their own eyes they may still feel an unworthiness. This is how we sometimes view our relationship with God now. We don't look at ourselves and others through the finished work of Jesus Christ, but at our own unworthiness to receive what he completed on the cross. Instead, we want to keep digging up the grave of skeletons, trying to bring life into something Jesus destroyed to justify the unworthiness of God's love and mercy.

Think about when we are in a battle of war. Men have been sent out to fight the battle and find themselves in some remote area with very little outside communication. They continue to diligently fight for their country. They come against the enemy ready to do battle only to be told the war is over. It had been over for many months. You could have gone home to freedom a long time ago. The victory has already been won. We are no longer your enemy. We have accepted the gift of freedom and democracy that your country has offered. Now, you are out in this remote area with just this one person that you have been told to fight with. Do you accept and lay down your weapon, or shoot the love and freedom that stands in front of you? Does the decision you make change the fact that the war is over? No, Jesus finished the battle on the cross 2,000 years ago.

Romans 5:18-19 says, "therefore as by the offense of one judgment come upon all men to condemnation; even so by the righteousness of one the free gift came upon all men unto justification of life. For as by one man's disobedience many were made sinners, so by the obedience of one shall many be made righteous." We tend to take the word "many" as those that choose, but the true context of the word is "all" as described in verse 18.

This is not a message of a license to sin as religion will try to obtain. Paul says in Romans 6:15, "What then? Shall we sin, because we are not under the law, but under grace? God forbid." When we yield ourselves with the acceptance of the finished work that Jesus accomplished on the cross, there is a drawing effect of repentance and cleansing. The Holy Spirit in us, in all men, has the responsibility to reveal truth to us, not with a pointing of our faults, (men can do that very nicely) but with "The goodness of God leaded thee to repentance" (Romans 2:4).

Romans Chapter 7 tells us that we are no longer married to a dead man, Adam. We didn't kill him by receiving Jesus as the Son of God and the finished work. He was already killed on the cross 2,000 years ago by religion and legalism. The work was completed and the fulfilling of the law that Jesus accomplished to bring forth the kingdom of God on earth so that God could dwell with His children once and for all. Adam hasn't existed for over 2,000 years. Galatians 5:14 says, "For all the law is fulfilled in one Word (Jesus), even in this; thou shalt love thy neighbor as thyself." Galatians 6:1-2 says, "Brethren, if a man (one that committed the action sin) be overtaken in a fault, ye which are spiritual (hearing from the Father) restore such a one in spirit of meekness; considering thyself, lest thou also be tempted. Bear ye one another's burdens, and so fulfill the law of Christ." Ask yourself, what would you be tempted with? The answer is judgment! What is the law of Christ? Mercy!

As you read the love letters (the Bible) of our Father to His children consider this: God is Light, God is Love, and God is Life. In Him there is no darkness. When you come into His presence of the Holy of Holies there cannot be any judgment, condemnation, or self-issues. It must be all God with those three manifestations; light, life, and love. Now, this is the moment of truth. When do you go into the Holy of Holies? Is it a "someday" thing that happens after you physically die because the Bible says, "absent from the body is present with the Lord" (II Corinthians 5:8)? We can literally wait until we have experienced physical death to come into His presence, but we have the blessing and approval through Christ Jesus to do so now. When we come through Christ Jesus there cannot be any judgment or condemnation according to Romans 8:1. God is His Word. Jesus is the Word made flesh. When we yield our members (body, soul, and spirit) to Him allowing the Holy Spirit to bring forth the mind of Christ, we become the Word made flesh and dwelt among men. Every scripture, every word in the Bible, must be seen as Jesus carrying with it

Light, Life, and Love. If any one of these elements are missing in the way we are understanding the wisdom of our Heavenly Father, we are hearing from the wrong father. Satan cannot create, but will try to imitate to such a closeness to truth, appealing to our senses, that if you don't have an intimate relationship with Father God you may be hearing the wrong voice. Just because you read something in scripture that sounds good and appeals to the natural man does not mean it is your Heavenly Father speaking to you. Remember that Satan used scripture to tempt Jesus in the wilderness. He will do the same to us. When you have all three elements in the understanding of what God is saying to you, the natural man must mentally die because only the mind of Christ can receive by faith Life, Love, and Light. It won't make sense to the natural man's understanding which requires logic and reason. It will seem like foolishness. The creation of the body to the mind is that the mind is what directs and programs the body. If a person is brain dead, his body dies. The battle of Armageddon is taking place daily in the mind of God's children. Transformations are happening at a rapid speed as the children of God are putting aside the religious teachings of a "someday inheritance when I get to heaven," and making claim to who they are in Christ today with the power and authority the Holy spirit has given them. As the Word becomes flesh among man, we will soon see the transfiguration that all creation is crying out for; The Sons of God shall come forth manifesting the Kingdom of God, the Kingdom of Peace.

This is the wisdom of the New Age established 2,000 years ago by the disciples. The creativity to be peacemakers in building the kingdom of God. The creativity of the power of peace.

God instilled in us through the Holy Spirit, the power to create peace.

Prophets today that declare judgment and destruction are not prophets of God working under the power of the Holy Spirit. All religious prophecy is opposed to the creative power of peace. Instead, they try to blow the earth up with God's word. Satan tries to encourage this mindset to get rid of the inheritance of the children of God (Matt. 5:5) before they figure out their true identity and power.

God created the earth by His word. If He were to destroy the earth as His word has been prophesied, He would be destroying His son Jesus who is the Word (John 1).

Jesus said, "Peace be unto you" (John 20). He gave us the power and ability that man had lost to create peace because of the Holy Spirit. The Holy Spirit was given to make peace. Our mouth is trained to glorify the works of the natural man versus declaring the works of God. When sweet and sour come out of our mouths we are incorporating the kingdom of God with the kingdom of Satan. This is a violation of being a Christian, a Christ one, a child of God. We must choose whose kingdom will be manifested, for the temple of God is to be a declaration of peace.

How do you make peace? Not by acknowledging the works of the devil, but by holding no man's sins against them. To believe that God gave you the ability to forgive sins by the power of His Holy Spirit in you according to John 20:21-23. Keep in mind that this is what Jesus was being persecuted for by forgiving sins in Luke 5:20-21. Religion will persecute those that are peacemakers because to establish peace we must know our identity and power as Sons of God. Religion says only God can forgive sins and you are not God. Jesus said, "I ascend to my Father, and your Father, my God, and your God" (John 20:17).

When John the Baptist stood in the Jordan River, the crossover, with Jesus, he had religion standing on the side. John could have discussed the issue of the Messiah with them, but instead he chose to hear the Father's voice baring record that Jesus is the Son of God, and seeing the Holy Spirit descending and remaining on Him, the symbol of peace (John 1:32-34).

Jesus said in Luke 7:28, "Among those that are born of women there is not a greater prophet than John the Baptist." John was considered greater than all the many patriarchs of old testament because he saw God (Matt.5:8), and he was a peacemaker (Matt. 5:9).

The kingdom of God will be built by the peacemakers that forgive sins. To hold no man's sins against them.

Let there be peace on earth. To think and speak as my Father. Let peace begin in me. I have to die to my own natural mind, my opinion, and the opinion of others in order to operate and obey my Father's mind, the mind of Christ, that has the power to make peace on this earth. As they see me let them see you, Father.

May God bless you with this message of His Word.

CHAPTER 19

COUNTING THE OMER

*Moses said, "This is the thing which the Lord commanded, **Fill an omer of it to be kept for your generations; that they may see the bread** wherewith I have fed you in the wilderness, when I brought you forth from the land of Egypt. 'And Moses said unto Aaron, "Take a pot, and put an omer full of manna therein, and lay it up before the Lord, to be kept for your generations"* (Exodus 16:32-33).

*"And **you shall count unto you** from the morrow after the Sabbath, from the day that **you** brought the sheaf of the wave offering; seven Sabbaths shall be complete: Even unto the morrow after the seventh Sabbath shall **you number fifty days**; and **you shall offer a new meat** offering unto the Lord"* (Lev.23:15-16).

This period is known as the **Counting of the Omer**. An omer is a unit of measure. On the second day of Passover, in the days of the Temple, an omer of barley was cut down and brought to the Temple as an offering.

Jesus the Bread of Life (John 6)

25 When they found him on the other side of the lake, they asked him, "Rabbi, when did you get here?"

[26]Jesus answered, "Very truly I tell you, you are looking for me, not because you saw the signs I performed but because you ate the loaves and had your fill.

[27]Do not work for food that spoils, but for food that endures to eternal life, which the Son of Man will give you. For on him God the Father has placed his seal of approval."

[28]Then they asked him, "What must we do to do the works God requires?"

[29]Jesus answered, "The work of God is this: to believe in the one he has sent."

[30]So they asked him, "What sign then will you give that we may see it and believe you?

What will you do?

[31]Our ancestors ate the manna in the wilderness; as it is written: "He gave them bread from heaven to eat."

[32]Jesus said to them, "Very truly I tell you, it is not Moses who has given you the bread from heaven, but it is my Father who gives you the true bread from heaven.

[33]For the bread of God is the bread that comes down from heaven and gives life to the world."

[34]"Sir," they said, "always give us this bread."

*[35]Then Jesus declared, "**I am*** **(the finish of the count)** ***the bread*** **(supernatural)** ***of life**. Whoever comes to me will never go hungry,and whoever believes in me will never be thirsty.*

[36]But as I told you, you have seen me and still you do not believe.

[37]All those the Father gives me will come to me, and whoever comes to me I will never drive away.

38*For I have come down from heaven not to do my will but to do the will of him who sent me.*

39*And this is the will of him who sent me that I shall lose none of all those he has given me,* ***but raise them up at the last day*** **(Resurrection Day)**.

40*For my Father's will is that everyone who looks to the Son and believes in him shall have* ***eternal life*** **(God Life, I AM),** ***and I will raise them up at the last day*** **(Resurrection Day).***"*

Why was it important to count the days from the bringing of the omer until Shavuot? It has to do with harvest, and bringing of the omer was the first fruit harvesting of the new grain crop. Why is this important to Christians? Jesus Christ is the first fruit, but notice this verse is plural. *"But now is Christ risen from the dead, and become the firstfruits of them that slept"* (1 Corinthians 15:20). *"Of his own will begat he us with the word of truth, that we should be a kind of firstfruits of his creatures"* (James 1:18).

The preparation of counting omer was not considered a hardship to God's children, but a desire and passion. One of the most beautiful images of Shavuot, or Pentecost, is that of the marriage between the Messiah, the groom, and Israel, the bride. Counting the omer would be a period of courtship.

I believe there are hidden treasures in our Christ life that the church has yet to discover which are found in counting the omer. The Messianic branch of the Christian faith knows about this personal blessing opportunity linked between Pesach or Passover, which commemorates the Exodus, and Shavuot, which commemorates the giving of the Torah and God's Spirit. They are reminded that the redemption from slavery was not complete until they received the Torah (God's Word). They are also reminded that without God's Spirit they cannot keep the Torah. The Red Sea Passover brought out the separation of Truth of who we are from the world which the Temple diagram is the outer court. Jesus died once and for all. The Jordan River Passover experience testifies ones discipleship and trust in the Lord as a priest separating the many parts of HIS body to personally cross over in one's own free will in order to come together with one voice according to the Lord causing the walls of Jericho (death and hell) to fall.

Unfortunately, there is still something of the believer's inheritance of the Kingdom of God we are to bring into this world because we have yet to manifest raising the dead as Jesus did. In Hebrews 6:1-6 we read,

"Therefore let us move beyond the elementary teachings about Christ and be taken forward to maturity, not laying again the foundation of repentance from acts that lead to death, and of faith in God,

2 instruction about cleansing rites, the laying on of hands, the resurrection of the dead, and eternal judgment.

3 And God permitting, we will do so.

4 It is impossible for those who have once been enlightened, who have tasted the heavenly gift, who have shared in the Holy Spirit,

5 who have tasted the goodness of the word of God and the powers of the coming age

6 and who have fallen away, to be brought back to repentance. ***To their loss they are crucifying the Son of God all over again and subjecting him to public disgrace."***

This Passover season that we have recently celebrated I found very unique. I enjoy using two calendars for my everyday life, one that marks Christian holidays, and the other that marks Jewish holidays. I noticed this year that on Monday, March 25, 2013, the Jewish calendar was celebrating Passover Eve. The other calendar would be celebrating Passover on Friday, March 29, 2013. Then on March 27, 2013, from the Jewish calendar would be Resurrection Day, but on the Christian calendar it was Sunday, March 31, 2013.

I had a conversation with Father God and asked Him which calendar was more accurate, and did I miss the Resurrection by not celebrating it on the proper day? The response I received from Father with a humorous voice was, "I AM the RESURRECTION NOW."

I started chuckling inside because the question I was really asking was coming from observing the feast of the Lord. The Children of God were required to come to Jerusalem three times a year to celebrate Passover, Shavuot, and Tabernacles. I simply wanted to honor this according to the proper observation and celebration commanded. But then I heard Jesus say, "I AM the RESURRECTION LIFE NOW." Ok, why was that necessary Jesus for you to tell me that? Holy Spirit teach me TRUTH in the midst of this time situation of the calendars?

I was first taken to 2 Kings 13:14-21where Elisha shows up after 50 years of being silent. He knows his time on the earth is about the end, and his concern is that he carries a blessing of a double portion, but he has no heir to pass on this anointing. When the king of Israel cries out "My father, my father..." Elisha knows that this is his heir, for these were the words spoken by himself when he received the mantle of Elijah:

When Elisha became sick with the illness of which he was to die, Joash the king of Israel came down to him and wept over him and said, "My father, my father, the chariots of Israel and its horsemen!

[15]*Elisha said to him, "Take a bow and arrows. So he took a bow and arrows.*
[16]*Then he said to the king of Israel, "Put your hand on the bow. And he put his hand on it, then Elisha laid his hands on the king's hands* (transfer opportunity of the anointing Elisha had).

[17]*He said, "Open the window toward the east* (going forward in time)*, and he opened it. Then Elisha said, "Shoot! And he shot. And he said, "The Lord's arrow of victory, even the arrow of victory over Aram; for you will defeat the Arameans at Aphek until you have destroyed them.*

[18]*Then he said, "Take the arrows, and he took them. And he said to the king of Israel, "Strike the ground, and he struck it three times and stopped* (he only took care of himself, not the position he held as king).

[19]*So the man of God was angry with him and said, "You should have struck five or six times* (the number of the beast of man, antichrist spirit), *then you would have struck Aram* (ALL your enemies) *until you would have destroyed it. But now you shall strike Aram only three times.*

[20]*Elisha died, and they buried him. Now the bands of the Moabites* (seducers of TRUTH) *would invade the land in the spring of the year.*

[21]*As they were burying a man, behold, they saw* (were fearful) *a marauding band; and they cast* (threw) *the man into the grave of Elisha. And when* ***the man*** *touched the bones* (DNA) *of Elisha he revived and stood up on his feet.* THE BRIDE is the body of this one new man, CHRIST, whom Jesus is the HEAD (Isaiah 61).

The Holy Spirit shared with me that when we are born again we enter into our new creation birthed out of Tabernacles, not Passover. It is in the oneness of God that He knew us before we were conceived in our mother's womb (Jer. 1:5). Before Passover the CHILDREN of GOD are in bondage and slavery or ignorance and darkness, but they are the CHILDREN of GOD, they just don't know the fullness of what that is all about. After Jesus died once and for ALL, the state of MAN was in ignorance and darkness whether Jew or Gentile.

We go through seasons of development, training, and discipline that have placed boundaries for us to abide in this world as babies and children. We come to Passover; we now have the ability to crossover from those growing up in the world's boundaries to unveil our personal identity with Jesus Christ that is set apart from the world's patterns. This would be like a bar mitzvah or the puberty years. Jesus has washed our feet making us all clean (John 13:8-10).

From this point in time we are to begin counting the omer, but the only thing we know of why we count the omer is from what we were taught as children, yet our bodies begin to process things differently than they did as a child. Out of our belly begins to flow rivers of living water that are cleansed by our heart and our heart begins to speak with an authority that produces life or death. We war within ourselves as the Shavuot experience takes us back to oneness with the Father in Tabernacles studying and learning how to put on the mind of Christ.

What we have is a MAN, male and female, that was born into Tabernacles, created in the image of the Father, had their feet washed by Jesus to prepare them for their Passover into LIFE, stirred the creative organs that reproduce bringing LIGHT out of darkness, Shavuot. Then giving the new creation LIFE the Father's Torah. The MAN spends time in oneness Tabernacle with the Father to become a son to do the Father's business where the heart and mind of MAN (male and female) are in unity with Christ.

It is now the time for the bride to make herself ready!

This year, the first Passover was for the Old Testament, Messianic believers in Yeshua. The second Passover is for the church of the Lord Jesus Christ. They both have a celebration of the Resurrection of Jesus/Yeshua from death, hell, and the grave, so now what?

Jesus could have had His glorious ascension to the Father and sent the Holy Spirit immediately saying, "That's it, and I'm done. I did my part, take over now Holy Spirit, but we know that He didn't do this. Instead, after He completed His personal work of restoration, He continued to appear for 40 days after Passover to over 500 people as the RESURRECTION LIFE of CHRIST while they were counting the omer. Why did Jesus need to appear and teach as the RESURRECTION LIFE?

We are one in Christ coming through Passover in preparation for Pentecost. This is the time Christ taught the disciples AS the Resurrection Life, the finished work of God for 40 days. They then waited for 10 days until they received the Holy Spirit. The disciples did not have a clue of what it would look like when Jesus told them to wait in Jerusalem for the Holy Spirit which was a gift to them from the Father, but they would have noticed the pattern found in counting the omer. Unlike the English language, every Hebrew letter had a numeric value application which we find in Psalm 119. They would have known that this was day forty when Jesus ascended and that on day 50 was the giving of the Torah which

Jesus said He came to fulfill. *"For verily I say unto you, Till heaven and earth pass, one* ***jot*** *or one* ***tittle*** *shall in no wise pass from the law, till all be fulfilled"* (Matthew 5:18).

It is no coincidence that this occurred during the season of counting the omer for 49 days and then Jubilee where everything was restored.

My life verse is 1 John 4:17, *"As He is, so am I in this world today."* It is the apostolic window the Lord has given me to edify and build up the body of Christ in the unity of HIS faith. I share my nuggets to help unite the body. I do not hold a position of understanding or having the fullness of revelation on counting the omer given to me alone. I believe this connects with the bride's (male and female MAN) responsibility to making themselves ready, shedding off their old identity in their mind, and being prepared for consummating the personal marriage with the Beloved as one identity. Each number has a meaning that builds upon the number 7 = rest in GOD.

Again, this is a personal preparation of intimacy. Each bride of Christ only gets to be a bride for one day, and then she/he (MAN) is a wife. The Holy Spirit has given me a WORD, a seed of Resurrection LIFE identity as I have been counting the omer. I am sharing my WORDS as tools, but what the Holy Spirit teaches you and prepares you for is to transform YOU into His image by renewing your mind.

Earth awaits the outpouring of the Holy Spirit in us to bring unity and healing.

It begins with supernatural, unconditional LOVE, "for God so loved you, that He gave..." (John 3:16). This releases the supernatural LIGHT wave of JOY that brings atmospheric change. When the Resurrection LIFE is with you there can be no sorrow. The list at the end are WORDS and Scriptures that the Holy Spirit has given me for the WORD to become flesh in me. I would hear the voice of my Beloved Jesus say, "I AM_______, and then I had to say the same, "I AM_______. Be ready for battle with religions, cultures, and customs, creating your own Battle of Armageddon between your ears.

I believe the 10 days between the assencion and Pentecost has a connection with the parable of the 10 virgins that Jesus talked about in Matthew 25. The number 10 denotes Divine order where Divinity has responsibility to MAN, and MAN has responsibility toward GOD.

The bride must make herself ready with oil in her **own** lamp. The earth is ready for the outpouring of the Holy Spirit in us as it was with the first disciples, uniting together in one accord around the world, but the preparation includes counting the omer as being in Resurrection Life. Each counting will unveil riches and glory of Christ in you that you were not aware of before. *"The word of the Lord was unto them precept upon precept, precept upon precept; line upon line, line upon line; here a little, and there a little; that they might go, and fall backward, and be broken, and snared, and taken"* (Isaiah 28:13).

Below are the words and Scriptures the Holy Spirit gave me. I share these as tools to encourage personal intimacy for yourself between Jesus Christ as the Resurrection Life today. Your words and Scriptures will probably be different, but have a basic foundation that is built on knowing the Father as LIFE, LOVE, LIGHT, and NOW through the Resurrection Life and Power of Jesus Christ.

Count all other issues minor compared to the intimacy of knowing the power of HIS Resurrection (Phil. 3:8, 10). This year in 2013, Pentecost will be celebrated beginning on May 14, 2013 to May 17, 2013 depending on the calendar. Never before in history has MAN had the opportunity as we have today to come together in one accord as one body/bride ready for the Bridegroom to come. Most of the organized church will miss this wedding union Jubilee celebration. Remember it is a personal preparation as a first fruits company, not a child of God, a son of God, or a disciple of Christ celebration, but a BRIDE.

"And I heard as it were the voice of a great multitude, and as the voice of many waters, and as the voice of mighty thunderings, saying, Hallelujah: for the Lord God Almighty reigns" (Revelation 19:6).

"The Spirit and the bride say, 'Come.' And let the one who hears say, 'Come.' And let the one who is thirsty come; let the one who wishes take the water of life without cost" (Revelation 22:17).

CHAPTER 20

COUNTING THE OMER: I AM...

*D*ay One

One in Christ (Col. 1:27)

Day Two

Testimony & witness (1 John 4:17)

Day Three

Resurrection Life (2 Corinth. 5:17)

Day Four

Universal completion (Psalm 18:30)

Day 5

Grace (Zech. 4:7)

Day 6

Created in my Father's image (Gen. 1:26-27, 2 Corinth. 5:18, 2 Corinth 6:17-18)

Day 7

Sabbath rest in Elohim (Gen. 2:1-2, Mark 2:27-28)

Day 8

Seer of dreams & visions (Acts 2:17)

Day 9

Birthing creation life (John 5:19-20)

Day 10

Perfect order (Matt. 5:48, Luke 6:40)

Day 11

Equal & Co-heir (John 17:23, Romans 8:17)

Day 12

Ruling & Reigning (Eph. 2:6, Eph. 1:10)

Day 13

Resurrection, redemption, & restoration (1 Thes. 5:23)

Day 14

Deliverance (Isaiah 54:14)

Day 15

Peace & joy (Rom. 15:13, Is. 55:12)

Day 16

Love & obedience (Deut. 11:8-32)

Day 17

Victory (Joshua 24:3-13, Ezek. 16:6-14)

Day 18

Personal revelation as one with the Triune (Matt. 18:20)

Day 19

Faith Heb. 11, John 10:16, Gal. 5:22-23)

Day 20

Redemption & Justice (Rev. 5:9)

Day 21

In Christ (Rom. 12, Phil. 2:5, 2 Tim. 3:2-5)

Day 22

Light (1 Thes. 5:5)

Day 23

Redeemed & Resurrected from death & hell (2 Corinth. 5)

Day 24

Priest (Rev. 5:10)

Day 25

Forgiveness (Eph. 1:7)

Day 26

Gospel (Col. 1:11)

Day 27

Truth (1 John 4)

Day 28

Christ in me (Col. 1, 2 Corinth. 11:10)

Day 29

Holy Ones (Col. 1:22, 1 Peter 1:15, 1 Peter 2:9, Num. 16:21)

Day 30

Blood (Col. 1:14)

Day 31

Family, offspring (Ezek. 37:25, Ps. 45:16-17)

Day 32

Fellowship covenant (Matt. 26:28)

Day 33

Scattered remnant promise (Acts 16:31, Prov. 17:6)

Day 34

Naming the promise (Ps. 89:3, 36)

Day 35

Hope (1 Corinth. 13:13, Rom. 8:23-24)

Day 36

Wholeness (Acts 9:34)

Day 37

Chosen One in Love (Rom. 8:1)

Day 38

Freedom (Isaiah 61)

Day 39

Healed (Jeremiah 30:17, Ps. 122:18)

Day 40
Finished, overcomer (John 19:30, 1 John 5:4)

The next 10 days are the waiting numbers and WORDS of the Beloved to come to you in the fullness of intimacy, bringing forth in your flesh the oneness of CHRIST in you and HOPE is consummated with the Lamb of God. Let the identity of Christ in you be released in the fullness of the cup He has given to you, so together the earth will be manifesting the glory of the Lord in one accord.

CHAPTER 21

THE POWER OF THE HOLY SPIRIT IN YOU

"*Then the same day at evening being the first day of the week, when the doors were shut where the disciples were assembled for fear of the Jews came Jesus and stood in the midst, and saith unto them, Peace be unto (into) you*" (John 20:19).

Let's ponder some issues taking place at this time. "Evening" speaks of the day that you are in as coming to a close. Either things are completed or they don't seem as clear as they should if light were shining on the subject. Since the disciples were in fear, which is an emotion reflecting the unknown, we can assume that they were in a state of confusion not understanding the fullness of all that had taken place. A "closed door" speaks of having no hope and full of fear. The "first day" speaks of a new age or a new beginning. "In the midst" refers to in the very center or the heart of the issue. The "Jews" are a type and shadow of religious dominance.

At this time the disciples did not understand the implication of the resurrection of Jesus. They did not know a relationship with God as their Father. Even though they had been a part of performed miracles of healing, and raising the dead before the crucifixion as found in Matt. 10, Mark 6, and Luke 9 and 10, they had not received the Holy Spirit. What did they really receive that was different from what they had before? Why did they fear the religious leaders but not the Roman soldiers? Could there have been something supernatural that the soldiers didn't care about but would have a great impact on religion as they knew it? What they received was the ability to manifest peace (wholeness). **Peacemakers are the children of God.**

Jesus gave a sermon we call the Beatitudes found in Matthew chapter 5. The order in which he gave the blessings reflects the pattern of a Christian's development to maturity. One blessing builds upon the other.

Beginning with verse 3 in Matt. 5, "*blessed are the poor in spirit, for theirs is the kingdom of heaven,*" is not instruction to have a "mousy" personality that others can walk all over, nor is it a reason to be financially poor. Being poor in spirit is a door opener to hunger for more of the Holy Spirit's presence. To mourn is a door opener for the comfort of the Father's presence. To be meek is an opportunity to inherit the earth; the creations of God.

Each of these three characteristics deals with self identity: poor, mournful, and meek. Each brings a desire to hunger and thirst for the presence of the Holy Spirit and to be filled with righteousness. That is why there is a blessing. If your cup is full to overflowing then you now have something to give away and there are no more "pity-parties" for self-need. To be filled with the Holy Spirit produces fruit of blessings. When you have the fruit of the Spirit, blessings can be given away to others that are in need. The summation of the fruit found in Galatians 5:22 are all at the mercy seat of God. We can now obtain mercy because there is now mercy to give. Matt. 7:2 tells us that how you judge others is how you will be judged. Being merciful brings forth a pure heart. A pure heart sees God. People with mercy see God everywhere they look. With a pure heart full of mercy you become a peacemaker. A peacemaker is a child of God. Luke 6:36 says, "*Be ye therefore merciful, as your Father also is merciful.*" We have now gone through the Beatitudes.

God is calling his children to follow in the path as His firstborn, Jesus, to be able to declare as Jesus did, "*He that has seen me hath seen the Father*"

(John 14:9). The Beatitudes end with blessings to the children of God for righteousness' sake. Righteousness comes forth out of the order of Melchizedek, the King of Peace, verses the order of the Law of Moses, religion, which uses the word of God with legalism versus love.

A peacemaker is one that makes peace. Most of the church today is waiting to get peace someday when the Lord returns. We have so much sickness, disease, worry, anxiety, and death in the body of Christ today because the church is not eating from the Tree of Life, but from the Tree of Knowledge of Good and Evil. Jesus hung on that tree and destroyed it, but man's imagination has continued to give place to it. We, as Christians, keep trying to justify its existence by mixing God's word with emotionalism, insecurity, doubt, and not really believing that God meant what He said. We feel we have to see results before believing the truth of God's Word. (Sounds like the attitude of the disciple Thomas whom we often critique).

Peace is made by the Holy Spirit. It is the creative power of the Spirit of God. Adam used his own power of emotionalism and sensuality instead of relying on God's Word. We are not talking about a book called the Bible, but the identity that Adam was created in. **Only the Holy Spirit can give the power to create peace in the midst of darkness.** When Jesus declared peace to the disciples in John 20 he breathed on them, giving them the ability to create peace, which is the identity of being a Son of God.

Let's shift gears a little and talk about Melchizedek who was King of Salem (peace) and the priest of the "Most High God." He is a major mystery to most scholars because he has no lineage, and it was not possible in the Old Testament for one to be a king, priest, and prophet (Hebrews 7).

This king appears to Abram before the time when God created a new covenant with Abram. Abram's name changes in Chapter 17. Melchizedek is the king of peace; his kingdom is the kingdom of peace. He is also referred to as the king of righteousness in Hebrews 7:2. When he met Abram in Genesis 14, it was after the slaughter of the kings stated in Hebrews 7:1. Melchizedek brought him bread and wine, and blessed Abram.

How can we apply what is really going on here other than a lesson in history? If Melchizedek was the king, the highest rank possible carrying all power and authority over the kingdom of peace and righteousness, who are these other kings that were slaughtered? They represented anything that opposed God: the kings of fear, selfishness, depression, sickness, hunger, anger, greed, pride, etc.

God instilled an order for life to come forth in all of His creations. It takes a seed to be planted in darkness (womb, soil) first, and then, with the right amount of water (word), and Light (Son of God, mind of Christ), there is growth.

Melchizedek brought the soil of peace to Abram with his presence. Then he gave him bread and wine which is the type and shadow of the covenant exchange Jesus gave his disciples with his body and his blood. This meeting that Abram had with Melchizedek in Genesis chapter 14 prepared the soil and planted the seed for the covenant exchange of Abram and God. It also was the soil Abram needed in order to see God as declared in Matthew 5 (face to face as the child of God). The King of Peace prepared the way.

Jesus was born as the prince of peace as predicted by Isaiah. A prince is not a king, but one going through training to become a king. A prince has power, but not all power and authority until his training is over and he is crowned king. In Hebrews 6 and 7 we see that Jesus was the prince under the order of Melchizedek. In Matt 5:17, Jesus tells us that he did not come to destroy the law or the prophets, but to fulfill them. In order to completely fulfill the kingship of the Mosaic Law, the order of Melchizedek had to be established as the kingdom of peace and righteousness. When Jesus fulfilled all the requirements of Passover; exchanged his body and blood; placed the Word of God (Jesus) in the very depth of hell and the grave; and resurrected from the dead as the Son of Man, he then had all power and all authority as stated in Matthew 28:18. He went from being a prince to King of kings, the King of peace. The cross was the crossover of power. The same king that came to Abram to do away with the whole lineage of the kingdom of darkness came to the world on resurrection morning to save the world and declare peace to the sons of God, the lineage of Adam (Luke 3).

This is the wisdom of the "New Age," the church or body of Christ, established 2,000 years ago by the disciples when they received the power of the Holy Spirit. This creativity to be peacemakers and build the Kingdom of God had been established. Jesus finished it all at Calvary. The kingdom of God is in the power of peace.

Prophets today who declare judgment and destruction are not prophets of God working under the power of the Holy Spirit. All "religious prophets" are opposed to the creative power of peace. Instead, they try to blow up the earth with God's Word. Satan tries to encourage this mindset to get rid of the inheritance, the children of God (Matt. 5:5), before they discover their true identity and power. God created the earth by His Word. If He were to destroy the earth as some have prophesied He would be destroying His son Jesus who is the Word (John 1).

Jesus said, "*Peace be into you*" (John 20). He restored the peacemaking power that man had lost by giving us the Holy Spirit. The Holy Spirit was given to make peace. Our mouths are conditioned to glorify the works of natural man versus declaring the works of God. When sweet and sour come out of our mouths, we are incorporating the Kingdom of God and the kingdom of Satan. This violates our identity in Christ; a Christ one; a child of God. We must choose whose kingdom will be manifested, for the temple of God is to be a declaration of peace.

How do we make peace? Not by acknowledging the works of the devil, but by holding no man's sins against them.

We must believe by faith that God gave us the capability to forgive sins by the power of His Holy Spirit in us according to John 20:21-23. Keep in mind that Jesus was persecuted for forgiving sins in Luke 5:20-21. Religion will persecute those that are peacemakers, because to establish peace we must know our identity and power as sons of God. Religion says only God can forgive sins and you are not God. Jesus said, "*I ascend to my Father, and your Father, my God, and your God*" (John 20:17).

When John the Baptist stood in the Jordan River, the crossover, with Jesus he had religion standing on the side. John could have discussed the issue of the Messiah with religion, but instead he chose to hear the Father's voice. The voice declared Jesus as the Son of God, and he saw the Holy Spirit descending and on Him which is the symbol of peace (John 1:32-34).

Jesus said in Luke 7:28, "*Among those that are born of women there is not a greater prophet than John the Baptist.*" John was considered greater than all the many patriarchs of Old Testament because he saw God (Matt.5:8), and because he was a peacemaker (Matt. 5:9).

The kingdom of God will be built by the peacemakers that forgive sins, holding no man's sins against them. If Jesus holds no sin against us, we have no right to hold sin against another.

Let there be peace on earth; to think and speak like our Father. Let peace begin in me. I will die to my own natural mind, my opinion, and the opinion of others in order to obey my Father's mind, the mind of Christ, which has the power to make peace on this earth. As they see me let them see you, Father. Amen.

CHAPTER 22

THE SEASON OF TABERNACLE ONENESS

"Thanks be to God, Who in Christ always leads us in triumph [as trophies of Christ's victory] and through us spreads and makes evident the fragrance of the knowledge of God everywhere, for we are the sweet fragrance of Christ [which exhales] unto God" (2 Corinthians 2:14-15a AMP).

These words of Paul are describing an atmosphere that goes before us as a parade for a victory celebration because we are manifesting the glory of His presence in the world. He goes on to say, *"For we are not as many, which corrupt the word of God: but as of sincerity, but as of God, in the sight of God speak we in Christ"* (verse 17).

Notice Paul's words, *"as of God, in the sight of God."* This is not the position of a Christian that knows about God as a sinner saved by grace. It is not the wisdom of a Christian that fellowships with Christ having the ability to pray in tongues. These positions are stepping stones of preparation of the bride, but have yet to encounter the experience of oneness with Christ as the beloved bridegroom.

The position that Paul is referring to is an experience that has already taken place by faith in Christ Jesus. This is a position of one that knows what it means to come boldly to the throne of God in the Holy of Holies. We no longer are coming to our Father as children with needs, but entering His presence as a prepared bride for her beloved bridegroom.

This is a position where God fellowships in intimate union to impregnate His seed with His own image and kind. His Holy Spirit quickens our spirit as one (1 Cor. 15:45). This experience requires a total surrender and death of the identity we had of yesterday (Gal. 2:20). The womb of His bride, His church, is to be the place where rivers of living water flows (John 7:38) to the heart of circumcision (Deut. 30:6), then released by the mouth of His body (Matt. 15:8) filling the earth with His glory (Hab. 2:14).

This is a position where the alter of sacrifice is not only removing our sins, but taking the blood covenant exchange of Jesus Christ as a bride shedding our old name and nature. We have prepared ourselves as His spotless bride to enter into the Holy of Holies with the willingness to consummate the marriage with the Lamb of God. This is a personal experience that each member of His body must encounter. It is a Tabernacle experience of oneness.

Then corporately as one body, as His beloved wife, we exit the Holy of Holies with the testimony of blood covenant on our sheets and His fragrance of love upon on our hearts. The bride of Christ is only a bride for one day. After the marriage has been consummated by the Lamb of God, the church is the wife of Christ Jesus carrying His seed to reproduce His Kind. We have a responsibility to be His ambassador as king and priest reigning on the earth (Rev. 5:10).

When we are seen by the world, coming out through the veil, exiting the inner court, we have a new name and new nature in I AM as a new creation in Christ Jesus (2 Cor. 5:17). We have a responsibility while in our natural body to, *"Be fruitful, and multiply, and replenish the earth, and subdue it"* (Gen. 1:28). As His church/wife, we have the ability to carry His seed, the Word of God, in our inner most being to grow and develop so that in the fullness of time, birthing takes place releasing into the atmosphere HIS WORD from our heart and filling the earth with God Kind. In this manner, "The Word was made flesh, and dwelt among men, (and we beheld his glory, the glory as of the only begotten of the Father) full of grace and truth" (John 1:14). *"Behold the handmaid of the Lord; be it unto me according to thy word"* (Luke 1:38).

"The [Holy] Spirit and the bride (the church, the true Christians) say, Come!" (Rev. 22:17 AMP).

"The Spirit of God (Elohim, Christ) was moving (hovering, brooding) over the face of the waters (His beloved bride). And God said, Let there be light (Let there BE ME); and there was light" (Gen. 1:2b-3).

"This is the revelation of Jesus Christ [His unveiling of the divine mysteries]" (Rev. 1:1) *"I am the Alpha and the Omega, the First and the Last"* (Rev. 1:11 AMP).

As she leaves the Holy of Holies, she passes by the Alter of Incense clothed with the sweet fragrance of the Lord, *"For God so loved, He gave...while we were still in darkness and sin"* (John 3:16, Romans 5:8). Her radiance of life is filled with the glory of her beloved. *"Now the Lord is the Spirit, and where the Spirit of the Lord is, there is liberty (emancipation from bondage, freedom).* ***And all of us, as with unveiled face, [because we] continued to behold [in the Word of God] as in a mirror the glory of the Lord, are constantly being transfigured into His very own image in ever increasing splendor and from one degree of glory to another;*** *[for this comes] from the Lord [Who is] the Spirit"* (2 Corinthians 3:17-18 AMP).

"The earth is the LORD's, and the fullness thereof; the world, and they that dwell therein" (Psalm 24:1). We as His body have a responsibility to fill the earth with the glory of the Lord that all creation groans to see manifested.

It takes the position of being in Christ, one with Him as the head (Jesus Christ, Eph. 4:15) united with His body (the church, Romans 12:5) so that Christ is manifested in the earth as all and in all (Col. 3:11). *"For all who are led* (gathered together in oneness in the Holy of Holies) *by the Spirit of God are sons of God"* (Romans 8:14).

"For He has made known to us the mystery (secret) of His will (of His plan, of His purpose). [And it is this:] In accordance with His good pleasure (His merciful intention) which He had previously purposed and set forth in Him, [He planned] for the maturity of the times and the climax of the ages to unify all things and head them up and ***consummate them in Christ****, [both] things in heaven and things on the earth"* (Ephesians 1:9-10 AMP).

"I saw the Lord sitting upon a throne, high and lifted up, and the skirts of His train (His body, His wife) *filled the [most holy part of the] temple... And one cried to another and said, Holy, holy, holy is the Lord of hosts; the whole earth is full of His glory!"* (Isaiah 6:1, 3 AMP).

"The Lord said to me, Say not, I am only a youth (young bride); for you shall go to all to whom I shall send you, and whatever I command you, you shall speak. Be not afraid of them [their faces], for I am with you to deliver you, says the Lord. Then the Lord put forth His hand and touched my mouth. And the Lord said to me, Behold, I have put My words in your mouth. See, I have this day appointed you to the oversight of the nations and of the kingdoms to root out and pull down, to destroy and to overthrow, to build and to plant" (Jeremiah 1:7-10 AMP).

"May grace (God's unmerited favor) and spiritual peace [which means peace with God and harmony, unity, and undisturbedness] be yours from God our Father and from the Lord Jesus Christ. May blessing (praise, laudation, and eulogy) be to the God and Father of our Lord Jesus Christ (the Messiah) ***who has blessed us in Christ with every spiritual (given by the Holy Spirit) blessing in the heavenly realm!*** *Even as [in His love] He chose us [actually picked us out for Himself as His own] in Christ before the foundation of the world, that we are holy (consecrated and set apart for Him) and blameless in His sight, even above reproach, before Him in love"* (Ephesians 1:2-4 AMP).

CHAPTER 23

ARISE AND SHINE FOR YOUR LIGHT HAS COME!

"Arise, shine; for thy light is come, and the glory of the LORD is risen upon thee" (Isaiah 60:1).

"Behold, the bridegroom cometh; go ye out to meet him" (Mathew 25:6).

"And I saw a new heaven and a new earth: for the first heaven and the first earth were passed away; and there was no more sea. And I John saw the holy city, new Jerusalem, coming down from God out of heaven, prepared as a bride adorned for her husband. And I heard a great voice out of heaven saying, Behold, the tabernacle of God is with men, and he will dwell with them, and they shall be his people, and God himself shall be with them, and be their God" (Revelation 21:1-3).

Today is the Resurrection of our Lord and Savior who overcame death, hell, and the grave. He comes in all glory.

"Then shall they see the Son of man coming in a cloud with power and great glory." (Luke 21:27).

I ask you, what is your relationship with the Son of God? Do you know Him in the intimacy of a child's relationship with the Father? Do you know Him as a son doing the Father's business?

These are stages of transformation and growth in our spiritual life as being born again, but the end of the Scriptures in Revelation calls for a relationship with the Son of God as a bride of Christ. Before the church can become a corporate bride, there must be a company of first fruits that have entered into an intimacy relationship with Jesus Christ ready to consummate the marriage of the lamb.

In Matt. 26, when Jesus celebrates the Passover meal with His disciples, He gives them "leavened bread," not unleavened which was tradition. He said, "This was His body." He is the risen Christ that died once and for all. It is not the cross we are to give celebration to, but the resurrected life that is in our midst today. The tomb was found empty in three days. The logical understanding is that there should have been a body with decomposed flesh.

Paul cautions believers not to go back to the old way of understanding, but to discern the Lord's body correctly or else sickness, disease, and death would be our judgment.

Today, we are bone of His bones, and flesh of His flesh. We are "in Christ," the WORD that became flesh and dwelled among men. The end of the book (Rev. 22), tells us that the Spirit and the Bride say COME! It doesn't say, "The Spirit and child of God, or son of God, but the BRIDE."

When a woman gets married, she only marries one man, not a corporate. Just as each person must have a personal experience of knowing Jesus Christ as their savior and redeemer, so also must each person come into the quickening of the spirit to be a bride of Christ as a part of HIS body. Children of God are not produced until the Spirit and the bride have entered into the bridal chamber to consummate the marriage.

The resurrected Jesus Christ is the first fruit of many, patiently waiting for His bride to grow up so that she will be ready to consummate the marriage that took place over 2,000 years ago. He wants His glorious wife to carry within her His seed, so that out of her mouth, His heart is spoken, filling the earth with the glory of the Father as sons of God. God is LOVE. This is the banner that must fill the earth in His identity, character, and nature. God is ALL in ALL. Christ is ALL in ALL.

The end of the book takes us to the beginning where God created man, male and female (both Adam) he created them in HIS IMAGE. God told them to go forth and multiply filling the earth.

"So God created man in his own image, in the image of God created he him; male and female created he them. And God blessed them, and God said unto them, Be fruitful (Fruit of the Holy Spirit), and multiply(speak His Life), and replenish the earth (with god kind), and subdue it (with His banner of Love and Peace): and have dominion over the fish of the sea, and over the fowl of the air, and over every living thing that moveth upon the earth" (Genesis 1:27-28).

Today, we sing unto the Lord a new song! Jesus gave us Isaiah 61 to begin the prophecy, but the bride of Christ brings forth the coming of the Lord of the rest of the chapter including Chapter 62. Isaiah 61 and 62 are the process of the completion that was spoken by Isaiah by faith in Isaiah 60. To understand the heart of the Father we must be willing to come into the unity of His faith as a bride prepared to be a wife (Ephesians 5).

Have you received the new wine transformation of the body and blood of Jesus Christ as the resurrected Life in you? Are you discerning the Lord's body correctly as you celebrate that today we are new creations in Christ Jesus (2 Cor. 5:17)?

CHAPTER 24

A KEY TO TRANSFORMATION: CROSSROADS OF LIFE

*W*hen we read, hear, or see something, we have a choice, a free will, to decide if that information is to be processed and taken within the mind to become a part of the individual or discarded. For example; if a person views a famous painting, do they truly grasp the fullness of what the artist was experiencing when the painting was created? Do they form an opinion of liking or disliking based on what they see without knowing the history of why the artist painted the picture? Or does the viewer simply walk away and several hours later have no recollection that they even saw the painting?

When a person writes, draws or paints a picture, creates a song, creates an art project, etc., these are expressions of the individual's heart. They may not be able to explain why they wrote or created the way they have expressed themselves, and their art, music, writings may not be appealing to others. Nevertheless, it is an expression of what is going on within the individual's heart; an expression of an experience the creator is releasing. The judgments and choices of liking or agreeing with the creator as an outsider trying to grasp the fullness of the creation is irrelevant to the truth of what the heart of the creator is unveiling through the creation. Yet, from the outsider's position, they now have information to process, and with the processing, emanate either acceptance or rejection based on their free will position.

Scripture is the written WORD; the thought of God given form. Mankind are vessels that God used to write the Scriptures as each person experienced a personal encounter with God's thoughts that cannot be questioned of what the vessels were sharing. Only by the Holy Spirit can we experience the depth and life of what is written. Only when the WORD circumcises our heart by personal experience can the truth of God's created identity in us be released to grasp HIS TRUTH. Only then does the "pot" stop questioning the Potter's creation, thus removing the issue of "free-will" to the Potter's hand to release the fullness of being created in His image; Christ in us.

Recently, I was listening to a pastor teach on a familiar passage found in Paul's letter to Corinth in 2 Corinthians 4:17 which reads, *"For our light affliction, which is but for a moment, works for us a far more exceeding and eternal weight of glory."*

The message was wonderful, practical, and relevant for releasing a word of encouragement to the congregation during a time that our world and society is dealing with daily issues of chaos and changes. Basically we were encouraged to persevere during the trials we each were encountering, for as bad as things may appear to be, it won't last long or be a heavy burden in comparison of the rewards we will receive when we enter into our eternal glory in heaven.

It was a good message, but my heart was heavy. I heard that cheerleader from a distance, "Hang in there. Jesus must be returning soon with all the things that are going on in the world."

These trials we encounter today; cancer, diabetes, sudden death of a child, financial wipe out, bankruptcy, foreclosure, poverty, governmental chaos, relationship impurities, mental depressions, etc., the intent was to bring hope, but instead, the heaviness of the burdens and afflictions became heavier.

My thoughts turned inward to hear my Father's voice. "Father...why is it difficult to see joy of receiving heavenly rewards in the midst of these afflictions?"

The Holy Spirit took me to some Scriptures in the Old Testament during the time when Moses was passing the baton of leadership to Joshua to cross the Jordan and conquer the city of Jericho. There is much to consider in these writings that I will leave the reading of the Scriptures to you, but beginning in the book of Deuteronomy, chapter 27, I read that Moses gave a declaration to the elders and the people. They were going to cross the Jordan River and come into the land the Lord God had promised them. However, in order for them to go into the promised land flowing with milk and honey, after they crossed the Jordan River, they had to first set up great stones (whole stones) with the commandments of God's law written upon the stones. These stones are to be a peace offering of rejoicing before the Lord.

From here, the Scriptures talk about the blessings and curses that the children of God would encounter. I have often heard preachers use Deuteronomy 27 and 28 in their sermons to justify a means of what Christians are supposed to being doing or not doing. The decrees found in these chapters are a wonderful foundation to teach children about sowing and reaping consequences, but without the first law of God in their heart to LOVE with their ALL, these chapters become a legalistic approach to our Christian life.

So I asked God, "Ok Father, why have you taken me to these passages?"

"There are many levels of My glory that are being unveiled in My vessels. The basic foundations of dealing with afflictions of this world are within the realm of sowing and reaping. Even though My people know Me through their personal relationship of knowing Jesus Christ as their Savior, the majority of them justify My WORD through the interpretation of the mortal law which functions by what a person sows they will reap; good and evil, right and wrong, doing this produces that, justification and judgment. Often the choices of "good" that are chosen by justification using the Scriptures are not of ME."

"There is a way which seems right unto a man, but the end thereof are the ways of death" (Proverbs 14:12). *"Every way of a man is right in his own eyes: but the LORD ponders the hearts"* (Proverbs 21:2).

I went back to the verse in 2 Corinthians 4:17, *"For our light affliction, which is but for a moment, works for us a far more exceeding and eternal weight of glory."* The words "light affliction" troubled me. How can an affliction be considered "light"? A familiar response people often encounter when afflictions occur to justify a means of what someone is going through is, "Well, be thankful for what you have. It could be worse."

Is that supposed to make a person feel better when they just lost a child in an accident, or the bank is going to foreclose on their home? So do we place a guilt trip on the person because somehow they are having difficulty going through the afflictions in their life? They want to be angry at God instead of counting it all joy.

Light affliction?

*"God is **Light**, and there is no darkness in Him at all"* (1 John 1:5). *"Every good gift and every perfect gift is from above, and cometh down from the Father of **lights**, with whom is no variableness, neither shadow of turning. Of his own will **begat He us with the word of truth**, that we should be a kind of firstfruits of his creatures"* (James 1:17-18).

The word affliction is Strong's #2347. It is used in Matt. 24:21 referring to the great tribulation; in John 16:21 as the anguish of a woman in travail giving birth, and in James 1:27 when children are fatherless and widows have lost their husbands. Does a person in the midst of these afflictions really find comfort when they are told, "Well, be thankful for what you have. Things could be worse?"

God is LIGHT and the Father of light. He begat (Fathered) me by the word (the expression of His thought) of truth (Himself).

In Matthew 13:18-23, we have the parable Jesus shared to his disciples about the sower and seed. The seed is the WORD of God, the expression of the Father's thought being released to produce LIGHT.

The writer of Hebrews tells us, *"The word of God is quick, and powerful, and sharper than any two edged sword, piercing even to the dividing asunder of soul and spirit, and of the joints and marrow, and is a discerner of the thoughts and intents of the heart"* (Hebrews 4:12).

Ezekiel shares with us, *"Ye mountains* (trials of life) *of Israel* (children of God), *hear* (take into your heart) *the word* (seed of life) *of the Lord GOD* (your Father); *Thus saith the Lord GOD to the mountains, and to the hills, to the rivers, and to the valleys; Behold, I, even I, will bring a sword upon you, and I will destroy your high places* (the stones and thorns in our lives)" (Ezekiel 6:3).

Paul also told the church in Corinth, *"In a moment, in the twinkling of an eye, at the last trump: for the trumpet shall sound, and the dead shall be raised incorruptible, and we shall be changed"* (1 Corinthians 15: 52).

So in a moment of time, God sends into our spirit "LET THERE BE LIGHT (Genesis 1)," and the thought of God becomes a word of God made flesh in our natural bodies, and dwells among the thoughts of our carnal man (John 1). Paul shares, *"Even if I should choose to boast, I would not be a fool, because I would be speaking the truth. But I refrain, so no one will think more of me than is warranted by what I do or say, or because of these surpassingly great revelations* (Light of God). *Therefore, in order to keep me from becoming conceited, I was given a thorn in my flesh, a messenger of Satan* (my ego), *to torment me"* (2 Corinthians 12:6-7).

The Apostle John brings this full circle with the Book of Revelation; the unveiling of Christ in you. In the beginning... (Genesis 1:1); in the beginning... (John 1:1); The Revelation of Jesus Christ; Christ in you... and the Spirit and the bride say Come (Rev. 22:17). The word "come" means "to return back to the beginning."

So with all these thoughts, let us read 2 Corinthians 4:17-18, *"For our light affliction, which is but for a moment, works for us a far more exceeding and eternal weight of glory; while we look not at the things which are seen, but at the things which are not seen: for the things which are seen are temporal; but the things which are not seen are eternal."*

God does not cause trials and tribulations to happen, but we must expect that when the Holy Spirit comes into our presence calling forth our spirit and drawing us to our Heavenly Father, trials and afflictions will be encountered. Judgment must begin within us with our own justification. After we have exhausted the sowing and reaping realm we naturally function in, we will come to a crossroad. The words of our mouth and the meditations of our thoughts will have a free will choice to create life or death, blessings or curses.

"For this perishable [part of us] must put on the imperishable [nature], and this mortal [part of us, this nature that is capable of dying] must put on immortality (freedom from death). And when this perishable puts on the imperishable and this that was capable of dying puts on freedom from death, then shall be fulfilled the Scripture that says, Death is swallowed up (utterly vanquished forever) in and unto victory. O death, where is your victory? O death, where is your sting?" (1 Corinthians 15:53-55 AMP).

Your Heavenly Father says to you, *"I call heaven and earth to record this day against you, that I have set before you life and death, blessing and cursing: therefore choose life that both you and your seed may live"* (Deuteronomy 30:19).

Jesus said, *"Peace be unto you: as my Father hath sent me, even so send I you. And when he had said this, he breathed on them, and saith unto them, receive you the Holy Ghost: whose sins you remit* (pardons and bless), *they are remitted* (forgiven and bless) *unto them; and whose sins you retain* (curse), *they are retained* (cursed)*"* (John 20:21-23). *"The word that I have spoken, the same shall judge him in the last day"* (John 12:48).

When "light afflictions" occur, count it all joy in the midst of the trials and tribulations (James 1:2), for your Heavenly Father loves you and is sending His presence to bring transformation into your life, unveiling the life of Christ hidden within His creation in you. The power of His grace and mercy will raise up the resurrected life of Christ in you that releases the eternal power and glory of His presence from the Tree of LIFE into this world that cannot be found from the realm of sowing and reaping.

CHAPTER 25

THE SABBATH REST IN GOD

God said to Moses, "Speak thou also unto the children of Israel, saying, verily my Sabbaths you shall keep: for ***it is a sign between me and you throughout your generations****; that you may know that I am the LORD that does sanctify* (separates/sets apart) *you. You shall keep the Sabbath therefore; for it is holy unto you: every one that defiles it shall surely be put to death: for whosoever doeth any work therein, that soul shall be cut off from among his people"* (Exodus 31:13-14).

As we read these Scriptures in the Old Testament, let us remember that God gave us a blueprint of the Old Testament as a natural statement for what He is doing in the spiritual realm. We read here in Exodus that God is establishing a pattern for the Sabbath Day and the people of God to become one.

"Thus the heavens and the earth were finished, and all the host of them. And on the seventh day God ended His work which He had done; and He rested on the seventh day from all His work which He had done. And God blessed (spoke good of) the seventh day, set it apart as His own, and hallowed it, because on it God rested from all His work which He had created and done. This is the history of the heavens and of the earth when they were created. In the day that the Lord God made the earth and the heavens" (Genesis 2:1-4 AMP).

As the Sabbath is the day of God's rest, so also do the people become the "rest" of God, where God dwells. When God created man in His image, He did so as the last and grandeur creation. He then entered His rest, finishing His work of creation. Man rested with God on this seventh day. Man was celebrating with God the finished work of creation, yet man had done no work in the creation.

When Jesus hung on the cross and declared "IT IS FINISHED" (John 19:30), He was bringing back to God the unity of the Sabbath day as one. The Sabbath is a sign to signify to us that God the Father has set aside a company of people that believe in the finished work of Jesus Christ to BE the resting place, everlasting habitation, of God to dwell. In the "rest" of God, He will bring blessings, sanctification, and a place of knowing His presence is with you wherever you go. This rest is for the whole man—spirit, soul, and body.

Do you rest in God, and does God rest in you? All that is part of the seventh day of creation becomes part of our lives.

Resting in God is not about what God can do for you. When we realize that resting in God means it is finished and it is all about God, then we also begin to personify that righteousness, peace, and joy in the Holy Spirit are in that day of rest; the Sabbath of God.

Jesus Christ died on the cross, was buried, and rose from the grave once and for ALL. The veil into the presence of Almighty God was removed. God did not change, minimizing His Holiness, but because of the Holiness of the blood of Jesus, we have been redeemed and sanctified to come into His place of rest today while in our natural bodies. We do not have to go through a physical death to be one with God. *"As He is, so are we in this world"* (1 John 4:17).

What we do have to realize is that just as there was a first Adam, there is also a last (1 Corinthians 15). We each have a responsibility to enter into the rest of God, but it is not about our individual sanctification. There is only one body/bride/church of the Lord Jesus Christ seated with Him today in heavenly places; the Holy of Holies presence of God. The body of Christ is made of many members/cells which each have the DNA inheritance of Almighty God. Each person's responsibility is to be obedient to the mind of Christ; *"Jesus Christ is the head of the body, the church: who is the beginning, the firstborn from the dead; that in all things he might have the preeminence"* (Col. 1:18).

When the church does not function by the head, Jesus Christ, from which all the body by joints and bands having nourishment ministered, that part of the body will be lacking of the increase of God (Col. 2:19).

"For the kingdom of God is not meat and drink (what you need to sustain your physical body)*; but righteousness, and peace, and joy in the Holy Ghost* (the realm of the Spirit of God)*"* (Romans 14:17).

Resting in God is a place and position that is in this world, but not a part of the world's system. It is illustrated throughout Scripture as a place where eagles fly. Yet most Christians choose to function as chickens (pecking at every little issue); turkeys (gossiping and complaining, but doing nothing); crows (pestering and bullying); hawks (coming in as a thief to steal the joy and peace); and/or buzzards (devouring the dead issues).

Isaiah describes the resting place in God in Chapter 60:

"Arise, shine; for thy light is come, and the glory of the LORD is risen upon thee. For, behold, the darkness shall cover the earth, and gross darkness the people: but the LORD shall arise upon thee, and his glory shall be seen upon thee. And the Gentiles shall come to thy light, and kings to the brightness of thy rising."

The signs of the times are telling us that a major shift is taking place in the heavens. In every dimension there is a shift taking place; politics, homes, economics, cultures, traditions, churches, religions, people's values and beliefs. When we think God is doing very little, it is because He is doing the greatest, but He is moving at such a speed of light that we can't tangibly connect with until after it is finished.

Example, when we fly in a plane twenty-thousand feet above the earth, we are moving through the atmosphere at a very high speed, but it isn't until we land at our destination that we comprehend that we were moving. The plane must slowdown in order to come in for a landing. When God slows down we are then able to comprehend what He has already completed. In the times of our lives when it seems like we are not moving, getting anything accomplished, is when God is moving the fastest if we are resting in Him.

God does not allow us to experience the change until it is done. If He were to suddenly enter our circumstance, we would perish. God is God and only shares His atmospheric space with His identity. When we get ourselves out of the way, He can BE seen. Much of the change that we go through is to get rid of our old mind and way of thinking to allow the presence and rest in God to be in control of His temple/our spirit, soul, and body.

In Genesis 2 we understand that all of heaven and earth were finished including all the hosts of them. What we experience in God within ourselves was already finished, and we are entering into that finished work. There are things that are already done in each of us, but because it is Spirit in us, this finished work of God is too expansive and moving too fast for our natural comprehension until it slows down, yet it is already completed. When our minds comprehend this knowledge, God is resting because it is already done.

"All things work together for good to them that love God, to them who are the called according to his purpose" (Romans 8:28).

We come into the message of salvation, sanctification, sonship, royalty, brideship, and oneness only to come to the fullness that it was already within you because it was already done. God is omnipresent. He cannot "end up" somewhere on the other side when we die to be with the Lord because He is Spirit everywhere. He is as much on this side of our lives while in our natural bodies as we think we will receive after our bodies die.

The Sabbath of God that He set aside as a sign is: GOD and Man.

Everything that is within the blessing of us and God is contained in the Sabbath.

The release of all that God contained in that DAY will begin to flourish. *"This is the day which the LORD hath made; we will rejoice and be glad in it"* (Psalm 118:24). *"Behold, it is come, and it is done, saith the Lord GOD; this is the day whereof I have spoken"* (Ezekiel 39:8).

In Hebrews 4 we read that that God finished the work from the foundation of the world and gave the promise of rest to the people of God, but because of their unbelief, they did not enter into it. *"For we which have believed do enter into rest, as he said, as I have sworn in my wrath, if they shall enter into my rest: although the works were finished from the foundation of the world. For he spoke in a certain place of the seventh day on this wise, And God did rest the seventh day from all his works"* (Hebrews 4:3-4).

Therefore, the promise still remains. Jesus gave us the ability to enter into the rest of God, the DAY of the Lord while in our natural bodies. *"Let us labor therefore to enter into that rest, lest any man fall after the same example of unbelief. For the word of God is quick, and powerful, and sharper than any two edged sword, piercing even to the dividing asunder of soul and spirit, and of the joints and marrow, and is a discerner of the thoughts and intents of the heart"* (Hebrews 4:11-12).

This labor is not working for the Lord, but pressing into His faith.

There remains a promised rest for the people of God today, yet they have still not entered into it (Heb. 4:9-10). We allow ourselves to dwell on being victims to the issues of this world, hardening our hearts to faith and realities we should have in God. We become easy targets to the offenses of the enemy of God, keeping ourselves in a bondage to the frustrations of this world. These things do not belong to the people of God.

All this makes a nice sermon, but most believers in Jesus Christ do not believe what God has spoken and finished. This belief is a position to trust in God as Man did BEFORE the fall. Man's first DAY was God's last DAY. Man awakened in this world into a SABBATH. Paul writes, *"Be not deceived: evil communications corrupt good manners. Awake to righteousness, and sin not; for some have not the knowledge of God: I speak this to your shame.*

But some man will say, how are the dead raised up? And with what body do they come?" (1Corinthians 15:33-35).

This is usually the limitations we ourselves struggle with, trying to figure out how to enter into the rest of God individually instead of as a corporate body. The rest of God is not about the many members, but Christ who is all in all; one body; one man; one church; one SON.

We live today and have our being IN HIM so that HE alone is glorified in our natural bodies. The old man is crucified, and the life we NOW live is by faith in Christ Jesus (Gal. 2:20).

"Wherefore henceforth know we no man after the flesh: yea, though we have known Christ after the flesh, yet now henceforth know we him no more. Therefore if any man be in Christ, he is a new creature: old things are passed away; behold all things are become new. And all things are of God, who hath reconciled us to himself by Jesus Christ, and hath given to us the ministry of reconciliation" (2 Corinthians 5:16-18).

When King David was hungry, he went into the place of the high priest and ate the sacred bread, and then he gave it to his men (1 & 11 Samuel). Are you hungry enough for an intimate relationship with God to eat the body and drink the blood of Christ Jesus?

The first Adam is dead. Yet many believers in Christ are having intimacy with Jesus Christ, the WORD, but allowing the mindset of the old Adam to enter into the bedroom intimacy. Many Christians are committing adultery in the marriage chamber of God when they profess that they are a "sinner saved by grace."

"Let a man [thoroughly] examine himself, and [only when he has done] so should he eat (take within him/herself) *of the bread* (body of the beloved) *and drink* (the life of the beloved) *of the cup. For anyone who eats and drinks without discriminating and recognizing with due appreciation that [it is Christ's] body, eats and drinks a sentence (a verdict of judgment) upon himself* (commits adultery with the covenant marriage of God). *That [careless and unworthy participation] is* ***the reason many of you are weak and sickly,***

***and quite enough of you have fallen into the sleep of death*"** (1 Cor. 11:28-30 AMP).

"Jesus said to them, The Sabbath was made on account and for the sake of man, not man for the Sabbath; So the Son of Man is Lord even of the Sabbath" (Mark 2:27-28).

"The impotent (has no life producing in him) *man answered him, Sir, I have no man* (impotent), *when the water is troubled* (supernatural power of the word of God), *to put me* (make myself whole) *into the pool* (the natural place where healing is found)*: but while I am coming* (make an attempt), *another stepped down before me. Jesus* (the rest of God) *saith unto him, Rise, take up thy bed, and walk. And immediately the man* (in the presence of true REST) *was made whole, and took up his bed, and walked: and on the same day was the Sabbath"* (John 5:7-9).

This is the DAY of THE LORD. Let us rejoice and REST in HIM; the Sabbath of God.

Prophetic Word

"On the evening of that first day of the week, when the disciples were together, with the doors locked for fear of the Jews, Jesus came and stood among them and said, "Peace be with you!" After he said this, he showed them his hands and side. The disciples were overjoyed when they saw the Lord. Again Jesus said, "Peace is with you! As the Father has sent me, I am sending you." And with that he breathed on them and said, "Receive the Holy Spirit. If you forgive anyone his sins, they are forgiven; if you do not forgive them, they are not forgiven." (John 20:19-23 NIV).

Jesus restored the "breath of God" back into man, giving us the ability to create in our Father's image by the thoughts in our heart and the words we speak. Those that have the power of the Holy Spirit ruling in their life have the power of life to overcome death, hell, and the grave.

"[For my determined purpose is] that I may know Him [that I may progressively become more deeply and intimately acquainted with Him, perceiving and

recognizing and understanding the wonders of His Person more strongly and more clearly], and that I may in that same way come to know the power outflowing from His resurrection [[a]which it exerts over believers], and that I may so share His sufferings as to be continually transformed [in spirit into His likeness even] to His death, [in the hope],That if possible I may attain to the [[b]spiritual and moral] resurrection [that lifts me] out from among the dead [even while in the body]." (Phil. 3:10-11 AMP).

"I am about to shake up everything, to turn everything upside down and start over from top to bottom-overthrow governments, destroy foreign powers, dismantle the world of weapons and armaments, throw armies into confusion with their words, so that they end up killing one another. And on that day I will take you as my personal servant and I will set you as a signet ring, the sign of my sovereign presence and authority. I've looked over the field and chosen you for this work." (Hag. 2:21-23 Msg.).

"THE HAND of the Lord was upon me, and He brought me out in the Spirit of the Lord and set me down in the midst of the valley; and it was full of bones. And He caused me to pass round about among them, and behold, there were very many [human bones] in the open valley or plain, and behold, they were very dry. And He said to me, Son of man, can these bones live? And I answered, O Lord God, You know! Again He said to me, Prophesy to these bones and say to them, O you dry bones, hear the word of the Lord. Thus says the Lord God to these bones: Behold, I will cause breath and spirit to enter you, and you shall live; And I will lay sinews upon you and bring up flesh upon you and cover you with skin, and I will put breath and spirit in you, and you [dry bones] shall live; and you shall know, understand, and realize that I am the Lord [the Sovereign Ruler, Who calls forth loyalty and obedient service]. So I prophesied as I was commanded; and as I prophesied, there was a [thundering] noise and behold, a shaking and trembling and a rattling, and the bones came together, bone to its bone. And I looked and behold, there were sinews upon [the bones] and flesh came upon them and skin covered them over, but there was no breath or spirit in them. Then said He to me, Prophesy to the breath

Your thoughts and words create your own atmosphere and destiny.

and spirit, son of man, and say to the breath and spirit, thus says the Lord God: Come from the four winds, O breath and spirit, and breathe upon these slain that they may live. So I prophesied as He commanded me, and the breath and spirit came into [the bones], and they lived and stood up upon their feet, an exceedingly great host. Then He said to me, Son of man, these bones are the whole house of Israel. Behold, they say, our bones are dried up and our hope is lost; we are completely cut off. Therefore prophesy and say to them, Thus says the Lord God: Behold, I will open your graves and cause you to come up out of your graves, O My people; and I will bring you [back home] to the land of Israel. And you shall know that I am the Lord [your Sovereign Ruler], when I have opened your graves and caused you to come up out of your graves, O My people. And I shall put My Spirit in you and you shall live, and I shall place you in your own land. Then you shall know, understand, and realize that I the Lord have spoken it and performed it, says the Lord" (Ezek. 37:1-14 AMP).

The thoughts of your heart and the words you release in the atmosphere will be the great white throne of judgment that you now stand before. *"And I saw a great white throne, and him that sat on it, from whose face the earth and the heaven fled away; and there was found no place for them. And I saw the dead, small and great, stand before God; and the books were opened: and another book was opened, which is the book of life: and the dead were judged out of those things which were written in the books, according to their works"* (Rev. 20:11-12).

"So be merciful (sympathetic, tender, responsive, and compassionate) even as your Father is [all these]. *Judge not* [neither pronouncing judgment nor subjecting to censure], *and you will not be judged; do not condemn and pronounce guilty, and you will not be condemned and pronounced guilty; acquit and forgive and release* (give up resentment, let it drop), *and you will be acquitted and forgiven and released. Give, and* [gifts] *will be given to you; good measure, pressed down, shaken together, and running over, will they pour into* [the pouch formed by] *the bosom* [of your robe and used as a bag]. *For with the measure you deal out* [with the measure you use when you confer benefits on others], *it will be measured back to you"* (Luke 6:36-38 AMP).

"Thus it is written, the first Adam became a living being (an individual personality); *the last Adam* (Christ) *became a life-giving Spirit* [restoring the dead to life]" (1 Cor. 15:45 AMP).

Both male and female were created in the Father's image. Both were given the name ADAM (Gen. 5:1). The Hebrew word for ADAM is spelled "ADHAM." Due to man's ignorance the "heh" letter or the breath of God (the Holy Spirit) was removed until a future time when Jesus redeemed ADAM, breathing LIFE back into him as a Divine creation of God able to do the Father's business.

"The Father said to me, "Prophesy to the breath. Prophesy, son of man. Tell the breath, 'God, the Master, says, Come from the four winds. Come, breath. Breathe on these slain bodies. Breathe life!'" (Ezek. 37:9 Msg).

So I prophesy and declare unto you, *"Arise and shine for your LIGHT has come"* (Isaiah 60:1). Rejoice in the Lord in the midst of your trials for the earth belongs to our Heavenly Father and the fullness of it. His ways are not man's ways. He only has good thoughts for you, filled with abundant life, peace, and joy as long as you remain in His presence, eating from the Tree of Life and not the Tree of Knowledge. With the power of His LIFE in your heart, remove mortality and corruption (1 Cor. 15: 51-55). Our Heavenly Father did not give us a spirit of fear, but of power and of love and of a sound mind. Therefore do not be ashamed of the testimony of our Lord who has saved us and called us with a holy calling, breathing HIS LIFE back into us, not according to our works, but according to His own purpose and grace which was given to us in Christ Jesus before time began. The mystery of our Father's plan has NOW been revealed by the appearing of our Savior Jesus Christ when He rose from the dead. Jesus Christ abolished death and brought life and immortality to light through the gospel at Calvary and has NOW given His resurrected LIFE to HIS body, the church to be manifested in this earth. Let the rivers of living water spring up from your womb, circumcise the hymen of your heart to be released as the WORD made flesh and dwelt among the nations as sons of God, children of the MOST HIGH GOD (Psalm 81:2).

"I *am* with you,' says the LORD of hosts. *According to* the word that I covenanted with you when you came out of Egypt (bondages of this world), so My Spirit remains among you; do not fear! For thus says the LORD of hosts: 'Once more I will shake heaven and earth, the sea and dry land; and I will shake all nations, and they shall come to the Desire of All Nations, and I will fill this temple (Christ in you) with glory,' says the LORD of hosts. 'The silver (redemption) *is* Mine, and the gold (character and nature of ADHAM) *is* Mine,' says the LORD of hosts. 'The glory of this latter temple (Christ in you) shall be greater than the former,' says the LORD of hosts. 'And in this place I will give peace,' says the LORD of hosts."

May the word of the Lord cover you with HIS peace and joy so that your enemies will fight among themselves and scatter, leaving behind the riches of our Heavenly Father that they attempted to steal and destroy.

"There will be weeping and grinding of teeth when you see Abraham and Isaac and Jacob and all the prophets in the kingdom of God, but you yourselves being cast forth (banished, driven away)" (Luke 13:28 AMP).

Today, we live at a time in history with the ability to capture our NOW moment using cameras, videos, and other media resources, bringing our yesterdays to our remembrance of today. Have you ever noticed while looking through photos and reminiscing over the past vacations, birthday parties, or family holidays that we tend to remember those moments with more intensity than when we were actually there? We will often reflect on certain words that were spoken that made us feel good, or the smell of the air as we look at the pictures of the mountains. We can look at our pictures at the beach and hear the seagulls flying nearby, or the waves crashing on the shore.

What is amazing is that at the moment we were actually experiencing the event, we rarely have the intensity of the experience as we are able to recall looking at the pictures. We were just there. So it will be in the Kingdom of God. Today, we have the fullness of His Love, His Life, and the intensity of His presence; yet, it isn't until we move into another day reflecting on the event that we see His presence had always been with us.

Those that have gone before us have the fullness of His presence, yet they cannot share this intensity with others because they too have the fullness of Christ Jesus. True Love must be shared with a servant's heart, unconditionally. For this cause they surround us as a cloud of witnesses to encourage us to grasp the moment NOW, bringing the Kingdom of God into our time and allowing the intensity of the moment to be manifested.

Don't wait until you look back at the pictures to wish that you had captured the moment of the fullness and intensity of God's Love releasing Christ in you into the atmosphere of your time. Take your time to bring the eternal presence of Christ into your day by capturing the moments to give a hug to a stranger, rejoice at the laughter of a child playing in the dirt, blessing the person with peace that is late for an appointment, doing the little things for others that will be appreciated, but they won't know who did them.

God is a consuming fire. His Word, His presence, is a lake of fire. If we allow the consuming fire of His presence to manifest the intensity of the moment, the pictures from our past will be our NOW in the earth taking away the gnashing of teeth of tomorrow. The enemy of God wants to keep you enjoying the good of life instead of capturing the Excellency of His calling that is yours today. The truth that exists, but you are ignorant of, is the domain of antichrist. There will be many Christians gnashing their teeth because they chose complacency of the moment.

Selah.

CHAPTER 26

THE WORDS "EVERLASTING" AND "ETERNAL"

"When Jesus had spoken these things, He lifted up His eyes to heaven and said, Father, the hour has come. Glorify and exalt and honor and magnify Your Son, so that Your Son may glorify and extol and honor and magnify You. [Just as] You have granted Him power and authority over all flesh (all humankind), [now glorify Him] so that He may give eternal life to all whom You have given Him. ***And this is eternal life: [it means] to know (to perceive, recognize, become acquainted with, and understand) You, the only true and real God, and [likewise] to know Him, Jesus [as the] Christ (the Anointed One, the Messiah), Whom You have sent"*** (John 17:1-3 AMP).

Throughout the New Testament, the words "eternal" and "everlasting" are the same Greek word "Aionios" found in the Strong's Concordance as number 166. It means belonging to the time in its duration. Our true God identity, which is constant and abiding within us, not affected by the limitations of time. It is age to age: age abiding life in the midst of time. Eternal (166) belongs to the age or time (165) in its duration. *"I have said, Ye are gods; and* ***all of you*** *are children of the most High"* (Psalm 82:6).

"For we are fellow workmen (joint promoters, laborers together) with and for God; you are God's garden and vineyard and field under cultivation, [you are] God's building" (1 Cor. 3:9 AMP). Paul was writing this to

Corinth explaining who they were today, not someday when they die to go to heaven.

When we understand that our eternal life is our inheritance available NOW, while in our flesh, and not something we obtain when we die, we are challenged with many doctrine teachings that have held us in bondage, keeping us from the fullness of TRUTH within us: Christ in you (Col. 1:27).

"That I may [actually] be found and known as ***in*** *Him, not having any [self-achieved] righteousness that can be called my own, based on my obedience to the Law's demands (ritualistic uprightness and supposed right standing with God thus acquired), but possessing that [genuine righteousness] which comes through faith in Christ (the Anointed One), the [truly] right standing with God, which comes from God by [saving] faith. [For my determined purpose is] that I may* ***know*** *Him [that I may progressively become more deeply and intimately acquainted with Him, perceiving and recognizing and understanding the wonders of His Person more strongly and more clearly], and that I may in that same way come to* ***know*** *the power out flowing from His resurrection [which it exerts over believers], and that I may so share His sufferings as to be continually transformed [in spirit into His likeness even] to His death, [in the hope] That if possible I may attain to the [spiritual and moral] resurrection [that lifts me] out from among the dead [even while in the body]"* (Phil. 3:9-11 AMP).

So why are we not living our lives today as the abundant, eternal, everlasting life of Christ Jesus today while in our natural body?

This "eternal, everlasting" life is found in John 3:16, "For God so loved the world, that gave his begotten Son that whosoever believeth in him not perish, but have **everlasting life**" (The words "he," "only," and "should" are not in the original; these words were added in the translations of history).

We see in this verse "everlasting life" for a believer, but what does this really mean? The word "life" is the Greek word "Zoë" (#2222 in the Strong's) meaning "spirit life." We are told in this verse that believing in

Jesus Christ allows us access to not perishing. So what does "perish" mean? This is the Greek word "apollumi" (Strong's number #622). It is connected throughout the Scriptures with "the destroyer, the antichrist.

Believers in Christ Jesus have been in bondage with an antichrist spirit (doctrines, traditions) bringing "strange fires" to the throne of God; the mercy seat or bridal chamber of "knowing" our Lord and Savior, Jesus Christ.

"He who believes in (has faith in, clings to, relies on) the Son has (now possesses) eternal life. But whoever disobeys (is unbelieving toward, refuses to trust in, disregards, is not subject to) the Son will never see (experience) life" (John 3:36 AMP).

To experience "eternal, everlasting" spirit-filled (Zoë life), a person must:

- Believe that Jesus Christ is the Son of God and that Jesus came to show us our Heavenly Father which makes us a child of God. This is the Gospel of Salvation which allows the anointing of Christ Jesus to be poured upon us. (Outer court of the OT Temple of God).
- From this position we grow up in our Christ (anointed) identity allowing the anointing to be smeared and pressed into our bodies so that we can be transformed into His image. (Middle court of the OT Temple of God).
- Zoë life, eternal life is an inner court experience being with Jesus Christ in an intimate position as His beloved bride. Zoë life (#2222) is the highest and best which Christ is and which he desires to give to us as a husband impregnates his bride with the seed of His identity: THE WORD.

The greatest enemy of God is the mindset of those that are in a position to share Zoë life, but instead, use the Father's identity, THE WORD, and calling themselves "Christ One's" to bring judgment and condemnation to whom God has said is in every way clean (Acts. 10:15). *"Take heed that ye despise not one of these little ones; for I say unto you, That in heaven their angels do always behold the face of my Father which is in heaven"* (Matt. 18:10).

John shares with us in his letters that Zoë life is a reality for us today. He shows us there are different growth and developments of being in Christ: children, sons, and fathers. In 1 John 1:1-5, he writes:

"That which was from the beginning, which we have heard, which we have seen with our eyes, which we have looked upon, and our hands have handled, of the Word of life;(For the life was manifested, and we have seen it, and bear witness, and show unto you that eternal life, which was with the Father, and was manifested unto us;)That which we have seen and heard declare we unto you, that ye also may have fellowship with us: and truly our fellowship is with the Father, and with his Son Jesus Christ. And these things write we unto you, that your joy may be full. This then is the message which we have heard of him, and declare unto you, that God is light, and in him is no darkness at all."

Now, let us re-read these Scriptures removing the words that were not in the original, and writing it in continuation as John wrote:

"Which was from beginning which heard which seen our eyes, which looked upon and our hands handled of the Word life (Zoë); for the life manifested and seen and witness and show you eternal life (Zoë) which was with the Father and manifested us which seen and heard declare you that you also have fellowship with us and truly our fellowship with the Father and with his Son Jesus Christ and these things write you that your joy be full. This then is the messages which heard of him, and declare you, that God is light, and in him is no darkness at all."

Many believers in Christ Jesus must pass through being destroyed or perished (#622 in John 3:16) because they would rather live in the temporary realm of carnality instead of entering into their inheritance of Zoë life today. However, there is also a company of believers in Christ Jesus who stand with Paul to know (intercourse relationship, covenant exchange) the power of His resurrection while in the natural body.

"Take notice! I tell you a mystery (a secret truth, an event decreed by the hidden purpose or counsel of God). We shall not all fall asleep [in death], but we shall all be changed (transformed) in a moment, in the twinkling of an eye, at the [sound of the] last trumpet call. For a trumpet will sound, and the dead [in Christ] will be raised imperishable (free and immune from decay), and we shall be changed (transformed). For this perishable [part of us] must put on the imperishable [nature], and this mortal [part of us, this nature that is capable of dying] must put on immortality (freedom from death). And when this perishable puts on the imperishable and this that was capable of dying puts on freedom from death, then shall be fulfilled the Scripture that says, Death is swallowed up (utterly vanquished forever) in and unto victory" (1 Cor. 15:51-54 AMP).

"I, Jesus, have sent My messenger (angel) to you to witness and to give you assurance of these things for the churches (assemblies). I am the Root (the Source) and the Offspring of David, the radiant and brilliant Morning Star, ***The [Holy] Spirit and the bride (the church, the true Christians) say, Come!*** *And let him who is listening say, Come! And let everyone come who is thirsty [who is painfully conscious of his need of those things by which the soul is refreshed, supported, and strengthened]; and whoever [earnestly] desires to do it, let him come, take, appropriate, and drink the water of Life (Zoë) without cost. I [personally solemnly] warn everyone who listens to the statements of the prophecy [the predictions and the consolations and admonitions pertaining to them] in this book: If anyone shall add anything to them, God will add and lay upon him the plagues (the afflictions and the calamities) that are recorded and described in this book. And if anyone cancels or takes away from the statements of the book of this prophecy [these predictions relating to Christ's kingdom and its speedy triumph, together with the consolations and admonitions or warnings pertaining to them], God will cancel and take away from him his share in the tree of life (Zoë) and in the city of holiness (purity and hallowedness), which are described and promised in this book"* (Rev. 22:16-19 AMP).

Jesus said, "The kingdom of God does not come with your careful observation, 21nor will people say, 'Here it is,' or 'There it is,' because the kingdom of God is within you" (Luke 17:20-21 NIV).

1 John 4:6:

"*We are of God: he that knoweth God* (identify carrying the life of Christ in us as the wife) *heareth us* (out of our mouth flows rivers of living water); *he that is not of God* (has not experienced the intimacy of knowing Jesus Christ as the groom) *heareth not us* (can not be impregnated to bringing forth the fruit of the anointed word). *Hereby know we the Spirit* (Zoë) *of truth* (Christ identity in us), *and the spirit* (bio #979) *of error* (carnality of religion and self)," that has been intertwined to justify the bondage and limitations of Christ in you, the hope of glory.

God's pattern was never for children to produce children. It takes a bride married to the Lamb and consummating the marriage for the body of Christ to become the Word made flesh, going forth and reproducing as God created man in His image, male and female He created them, calling them ADAM. Selah. (Gen. 1:26, Gen. 5:1-2).

What it Means to Follow Jesus
C. T. Studd

If there is no heaven, Christianity is folly: if there is no hell, a Christian is a lunatic, for Christ is a liar: but as Christ is true, then there is a heaven and also a hell, and a million souls a week are rushing to hell, and therefore a Christian must be a heartless and selfish horror if his whole life is not thrown away "to save men from hell," for that is what it means to follow Jesus.

CHAPTER 27

WHEN YOU PRAY

"When you pray, you must not be like the hypocrites, for they love to pray standing in the synagogues and on the corners of the streets, that they may be seen by people. Truly I tell you, they have their reward in full already. But when you pray, go into your [most] private room, and, closing the door, pray to your Father, Who is in secret; and your Father, Who sees in secret, will reward you in the open. And when you pray, do not heap up phrases (multiply words, repeating the same ones over and over) as the Gentiles do, for they think they will be heard for their much speaking. Do not be like them, for your Father knows what you need before you ask Him" (Matthew 6: 5-8 AMP).

Jesus is introducing a system of praying and relationship with God that overrides what the disciples were accustomed to as the pattern to pray. He tells us to go to our most private room and close the door so that no one else will be with you. Maybe this is your bedroom, your closet, or bathroom? Or maybe it is a quiet place among the trees, along the water's edge of the ocean, or even your own backyard garden. Wherever this place is for you, the requirements are that you be alone where you can talk to your Heavenly Father with the freedom of no one hearing you. Your Heavenly Father promises that He will be in this place with you; He will hear you; and He will respond favorably to your words that you've spoken from your heart that will cause a transformation in you when you're among others.

Next, Jesus tells us to NOT pray like most people do by begging, pleading and telling God our needs or someone's needs. Think about this. We are coming in the presence of the Almighty God who knows everything, yet, most of us pray telling Him about our "issues" of what we need or how He needs to handle a situation? Do we really think that God wants us sick, hurt, depressed, angry, victimized, poor, etc.? Do we think that He doesn't see these emotions and issues we are dealing with? So, by telling God our problems are we giving Him information that is new to His ears? Is this secret place that Jesus refers to for us to go to the Father supposed to be like a courtroom, coming before a judge?

Think about the different conversations that go on throughout your house with different people. When outsiders come into your home, do you talk with them in the living room, kitchen, bedroom, closet, or bathroom? The Master's bedroom should be a place of intimacy, not a place to discuss or debate issues of the world. It should be a place that allows a person to let their guard down and feel safe. This is the place that couples come together in the unity of marriage. This is the place where a child will crawl into their parent's bed because the storm outside is scaring them. This is the place where many pillows have absorbed many tears of the heart. This is the place of rest.

The master bedroom in your house should not be a place where household finances are discussed while your spouse is trying to be romantic. It should not be a place of correction when a child is crying and needs comfort and love. The same concept should be understood when we go to our secret place with God. It is NOT a place that God needs to hear our wants or the needs of others via "prayer request."

This is a place where time is not an issue. Everything is God and His identity in you. This is the place that your spirit simply expresses and takes in LOVE, LIFE, LIGHT, PEACE, and a stillness of JOY that no matter what is going on outside the secret place; you know that you know within your spirit that God is in control. We then identify that all things will work together for good because we first loved God, and we are fulfilling the calling of the moment according to His purpose

(Romans 8:28). That calling is for us to seek first the Kingdom of God (where God abided), and his righteousness (his identity, character, and nature); then, all those things that you wanted to pray about to God will be seen from His position and authority where He alone will be glorified through you (Matt. 6:33).

Jesus tells us not to be like others who pray to God. Instead, He tells us to come boldly to the throne of our Father, that secret place where it is just you and God, and you can rest in His presence. Yes He is God Almighty maker of all things. He is also Spirit and the Father of spirits (Heb. 12:9). When we come into His presence as our Father we acknowledge our identity as spirit. We are then able to accept His peace that surpasses all the circumstances and situations we could possibly pray for. Jesus said that God was His Father and our Father, His God and our God (John 20:17), which makes us gods, children of the Most High God (Psalm 82:6).

What goes on behind closed doors between you and the Father is no one else's business. However, when you come out of your secret place, the world should know that you have spent time with Eternity by the fruit that is manifested. You will have been to the third heaven, the Holy of Holies where your Father abides. When you have spent quality time in His presence, He will equip you with His identity, character, and nature to do His business in the world so that He will be glorified. By His Spirit in you, the world will see the work which His presence within you accomplishes: love, joy, peace, patience, kindness, goodness, faithfulness, gentleness, self-control (Gal. 5:22).

Spend time in His rest in your secret place sharing your heart and allowing the Father to surround you with His presences and you will find all of the universe bowing down to Christ in you. They will know you are a Christ One by your LOVE, GRACE, and MERCY that you received while resting in your Father's presence on His throne between the cherubim of our imagination. You will then see the storms of your life calmed, the sickness turned to health, the tears turned to joy, the ashes of death turned to beauty, and the resurrected LIFE of Christ manifested through you.

"We know (understand, recognize, are conscious of, by observation and by experience) and believe (adhere to and put faith in and rely on) the love God cherishes for us. God is love, and he who dwells and continues in love dwells and continues in God, and God dwells and continues in him. In this [union and communion with Him] love is brought to completion and attains perfection with us, that we may have confidence for the day of judgment (life issues/prayer requests) *[with assurance and boldness to face Him], because as He is, so are we in this world. There is no fear in love [dread does not exist], but full-grown (complete, perfect) love turns fear out of doors and expels every trace of terror!"* (1 John 4:16-18 AMP).

God is not forgetful that we need to remind Him of our needs. When we identify our problems in prayer, speaking them out loud for others to hear, instead of speaking what God says, we give place to the world feeding the father of the flesh instead of communing with the Father of spirits (Heb. 12:9). Out of our mouth we are condemned and out of our mouth we are justified. In one breath we bless God, even as our Father, but then we turn and curse men who are made after the similitude of God. We speak out of our hearts both fresh, life giving and edifying words mingled with bitter condemning words, and then blame God for not answering our prayers (James 3:8-12).

God is dealing with each of us to grow up into Sonship and recognize that the trials and tribulations we encounter are to produce faith. God disciplines us to bring us into His holiness to be partakers of the inheritance we have through Jesus Christ. We cannot come into His Holiness except as His kind—spirit. We pray to hear from God, but He can only commune with His kind.

God is God of all, but it is only through Jesus Christ that we have the ability to come to Him as Father. God created man after His KIND. Man was created as Son/Holy Spirit. When man fell from the presence of LIFE and GRACE, he could no longer hear the voice of the Father within the Holy of Holies, but in the garden around him. At the end of the Bible in Revelation chapter one, we come to John's encounter on the Island of Patmos where he is in the SPIRIT hearing the voice of Jesus Christ, the

Alpha and Omega. Then John turns from the direction he was viewing the situation. He now desires to not just hear, but to see the voice. Since he is communing with the voice in the spirit and not in his flesh, John is able to see the voice speaking to him. What he sees is "one like a Son of Man" in the midst of the lampstands. John is communing with His Heavenly Father through Jesus Christ within the temple of God, the body of Christ.

The voice of the Father is coming from within John, yet he does not just hear, but sees as God sees in SPIRIT. John is in a secret place where the Father abides while in his physical body. He sees the truth of his identity by the quickening of his spirit that he is a son of man/God Kind in the midst of the perfection and rest of God's character and nature radiated as LIGHT (Rev. 1:10-13).

Today, we can come boldly to the throne of our Father's grace, the New Jerusalem; His PEACE that surpasses all of our logic, reason, and understanding of things going on in the world. We have been born again (renewed) by the quickening of the LIFE-Giving Spirit of Christ (1 Cor. 15:45). We bear the image of the heavenly, our Father who is in Heaven. It is up to us to change putting on the incorruptible and putting on the immortal of our Father so that the power of disease, depression, suffering, agony, misery, and even death in the body of Christ is removed (1 Cor. 15).

Jesus said, "I am the WAY, THE TRUTH, and the LIFE. No man can come to the Father except by ME. When you know ME, you will know our Heavenly Father" (John 14: 6-7). Jesus took the old way of entering God's presence and nailed it to a cross, crucifying the flesh of all mankind as He cried, "Eloi, Eloi, lama sabachthani" which Mark 15: 34 tells us means "My God, My God, why have You forsaken me?" Jesus died once and for all. Our flesh was crucified when Jesus died. Today, we have been redeemed (body, soul, and spirit) by the blood that was shed by Jesus Christ. Today we are the body of the resurrected Christ Jesus. Therefore, when we pray, our prayers should be addressed to God as Jesus would pray/commune with the Father as He is sitting on the mercy seat in the throne room of God.

Matthew 6:9:

"My Father who is in heaven, hallowed is Your name. Your kingdom has come and Your will is done on earth as it is in heaven…"

I lift up my eyes to heaven and say, Father, the hour has come. Glorify, exalt, honor, and magnify your son (Christ in me), so that Your Son (Jesus Christ) may glorify, extol, honor, and magnify You through me. You have granted Christ power and authority over all flesh, so that Christ Jesus can give Your eternal LIFE to all those whom You have drawn across my path with the manifestation of the fruit of Your Holy Spirit that I have partaken of from the Tree of Life. This pattern of following the firstborn of many brethren is so that as others see me, they see Christ in me, your glory as they hear the words of the SON, my beloved bridegroom, "when you have seen me, you have seen the Father." Let the WORD become flesh in me fulfilling the Scriptures "That they all may be one; as thou, Father in me, and I in thee, that they also may be one in us that they may be made perfect in one…LOVE, LIGHT, LIFE (John 17).

CHAPTER 28

THE FRUIT OF THE HOLY SPIRIT AS WE COUNT THE OMER: THE NUMBER 9

"For the Gentiles (heathen) wish for and crave and diligently seek all these things, and your heavenly Father knows well that you need them all. But seek (aim at and strive after) first of all His kingdom and His righteousness (His way of doing and being right), and then all these things taken together will be given you besides. So do not worry or be anxious about tomorrow, for tomorrow will have worries and anxieties of its own. Sufficient for each day is its own trouble" (Matt. 6:32-34 AMP).

1. Matthew 3:10
   And now also the axe is laid unto the root of the trees: therefore every tree which bringeth not forth **good fruit** is hewn down, and cast into the fire.
2. Matthew 7:18
   A good tree cannot bring forth evil fruit, neither can a corrupt tree bring forth **good fruit**.
3. Matthew 7:19
   Every tree that bringeth not forth **good fruit** is hewn down, and cast into the fire.

4. Luke 3:9
   And now also the axe is laid unto the root of the trees: every tree therefore which bringeth not forth **good fruit** is hewn down, and cast into the fire.
5. Luke 6:43
   For a good tree bringeth not forth corrupt fruit; neither doth a corrupt tree bring forth **good fruit**.

Often we read the Scriptures from a logical understanding, and we miss the real blessing of the WORD that is hidden. Many believers in Christ are searching for answers to the changes that have happened in our past, and what do they mean for our future. Unfortunately, many so called prophets of God are utilizing what the media shares to justify what the WORD says and it brings insecurity and fear to the body of Christ. **Our Heavenly Father is NOT a GOD of confusion.** Below is some thoughts to consider which I pray will cause you to seek first the Kingdom of God and His righteousness, peace, and joy in the Holy Ghost.

Some people see the number nine as judgment, but it also means Divine Completeness from the Lord. It does speak of finality, but finality of what? Significantly it is three times three. It is the number for the fruit of the spirit and it comes after eight, which represents the new birth. Good fruit follows as the result of the tree being made good. The tree (man) is made good in the new birth (8).

We read in Lev. 25:

2 Speak unto the children of Israel, and say unto them, when ye come into the land which I give you, then shall the land keep a Sabbath unto the LORD.

3 Six years thou shalt sow thy field, and six years thou shalt prune thy vineyard, and gather in the fruit thereof;

4 But in the seventh year shall be a Sabbath of rest unto the land, a Sabbath for the LORD: thou shalt neither sow thy field, nor prune thy vineyard.

In the Torah of the Old Testament concerning the Sabbath year and what follows, there is both a picture of the new birth and also the fruit of the spirit. Jesus is our Sabbath.

In the same chapter in Leviticus, we are told what should be eaten in the seventh, eighth, and ninth years.

20 And if ye shall say, What shall we eat the seventh year? Behold, we shall not sow, nor gather in our increase:

21 Then I will command my blessing upon you in the sixth year, and it shall bring forth fruit for three years.

22 And ye shall sow the eighth year, and eat yet of old fruit until the ninth year; until her fruits come in ye shall eat of the old store.

God told the people to eat in the 6th, 7th, and 8th years what was planted in the 6th year. In the 8th year they were to sow again, and in the 9th year they began to eat of the fruit of what was sown in the 8th year. This is a picture of the fruit of the spirit, represented by number nine, which follows the new birth of the number eight.

Now, before you automatically quote the fruit of the Spirit found in Galations 5, I challenge you to do a word study on each word according to the Greek understanding, including cultural versus the English theological study most of us are accustomed to. Within this fruit carry the seeds of LIFE that will bring you to know the power of His resurrection (selah).

<u>Galatians 5:22-23</u>

22 *the But fruit of the Spirit is love, joy, peace, longsuffering, gentleness,*

23 *Meekness, temperance: against such no there is law.*

Fruit/is: 3588 - NT: ho (ho); including the feminine he (hay); and to (to); in all their inflections; the def. article; the (sometimes to be supplied, at others omitted, in English idiom): KJV - the, this, that, one, he, she, it, etc.

Spirit: 2590 - NT: karpos (kar-pos'); probably from the base of NT: 726; fruit (as plucked), literally or figuratively: KJV - fruit.

Love: 4151 - NT: pneuma (pnyoo'-mah); from NT:4154; a current of air, i.e. breath (blast) or a breeze; by analogy or figuratively, a spirit, i.e. (human) the rational soul, (by implication) vital principle, mental disposition, etc., or (superhuman) an angel, demon, or (divine) God, Christ's spirit, the Holy Spirit: KJV - ghost, life, spirit (-ual, -ually), mind. Compare NT: 5590.

Joy: 1510 - NT: eimi (i-mee'); the first person singular present indicative; a prolonged form of a primary and defective verb; I exist (used only when emphatic): KJV - am, have been, it is I, was. See also NT:1488, NT:1498, NT:1511, NT:2258, NT:2071, NT:2070, NT:2075, NT:2076, NT:2468, NT:5600, NT:5607.

Peace: 26: agape (ag-ah'-pay); from NT: 25; love, i.e. affection or benevolence; specially (plural) a love-feast: KJV - (feast of) charity ([-ably]), dear, love.

Long: 5479: chara (khar-ah'); from NT: 5463; cheerfulness, i.e. calm delight: KJV - gladness, greatly, (X be exceeding) joy (-ful, -fully, -fulness, -ous).

* **Suffering**: 1515: eirene (i-ray'-nay); probably from a primary verb eiro (to join); peace (literally or figuratively); by implication, prosperity: KJV - one, peace, quietness, rest, set at one again.

* **Gentleness:** 3115: makrothumia (mak-roth-oo-mee'-ah); from the same as NT: 3116; longanimity, i.e. (objectively) forbearance or (subjectively) fortitude: KJV - longsuffering, patience.

* NT: 5544: chrestotes (khray-stot'-ace); from NT: 5543; usefulness, i.e. moral excellence (in character or demeanor): KJV - gentleness, good (-ness), kindness.

* **Goodness:** 19: agathosune (ag-ath-o-soo'-nay); from NT: 18; goodness, i.e. virtue or beneficence: KJV - goodness.

* **Faith:** 4102: pistis (pis'-tis); from NT: 3982; persuasion, i.e. credence; moral conviction (of religious truth, or the truthfulness of God or a religious teacher), especially reliance upon Christ for salvation; abstractly, constancy in such profession; by extension, the system of religious (Gospel) truth itself: KJV - assurance, belief, believe, faith, fidelity.

* **Meekness**: 4240: prautes (prah-oo'-tace); from NT: 4239; mildness, i.e. (by implication) humility: KJV - meekness.

Temperance: 1466: egkrateia (eng-krat'-i-ah); from NT: 1468; self-control (especially continence): KJV - temperance.

* Expanded teaching can be found in the Lexical Aids of the KJV Hebrew-Greek Study Bible. I encourage those that are seeking more insight to these words than our English comprehension found in Strong to read the Lexical Aids in the back of this Bible.

(Biblesoft's New Exhaustive Strong's Numbers and Concordance with Expanded Greek-Hebrew Dictionary. Copyright © 1994, 2003, 2006 Biblesoft, Inc. and International Bible Translators, Inc.)

CHAPTER 29

THE CLARION CRY: ATTACK THE SPIRIT OF FEAR

We are living at a time in history that is being governed by a spirit of fear. However, throughout history, when the children of God changed their hearts from fear to faith, the tangible substance of things hoped for, the darkness of fear was removed in the presence of LIGHT allowing God's unconditional love and peace to fill the earth which belongs to the Lord. The Kingdom of God is manifested allowing the joy of the Lord to become our strength, removing the Adam and Eve syndrome of judgment and condemnation. He alone is our shepherd ready to pour out everything we need. The Lord is good, giving protection in times of trouble. He knows who trusts in Him, so don't let your hearts be troubled. Allow God to guide you along paths that you did not know and make the darkness become light; the rough ground smooth (Nahum 1:7, John 14:1, Isaiah 42:16, Heb. 11:1, Psalm 24:1).

When a person's steps follow the Lord, God is pleased with his ways. If he stumbles, he will not fall, because the Lord holds our hand. Judge not, so that you will not be judged. We are quick to judge what leadership is, or is not doing, but what about accountability within you? God tells us that judgment begins in the house of God or the body of Christ.

As fathers and mothers, are we being responsible for our children or expecting the government to take care of them? As citizens, are we being responsible for our neighbors and community, or do we expect the community to take care of them?

As co-workers at your job, are you being responsible to do what you have been hired to do with a cheerful heart and a team player, or do you feel your employer owes you something? Are you taking responsibility for your own health by exercising and eating properly, or are you expecting your medicines, doctors, and health insurance to keep your body alive? As a Christian, do others whom God has brought across your path see the love of their Heavenly Father in you that will draw them to the Word, or do they see judgment, condemnation, and separation within the body of Christ, the church? It won't matter who the congress and president is of a country, if the people don't hold themselves accountable to the responsibilities God has given them. (Psalm 37:23-25, Matt. 7:1).

God did not give His people a spirit of fear, but a spirit of power and love and self-control. The Spirit of God within us removes the ability for us to be slaves again to fear allowing us to cry out, "Father." Where God's love is, there is no fear, because God's perfect love drives out fear.

It is insecurity of the unknown that makes a person fear, so love is not made perfect in the person who fears. The people who trust the Lord will become strong again. They will rise up as an eagle in the sky; they will run and not need rest; they will walk and not become tired. God will cover you with his feathers, and under his wings you can hide. His truth will be your shield and protection. You will not fear any danger by night or an arrow during the day. You will not be afraid of diseases that come in the dark or sickness that strikes at noon. At your side one thousand people may die, or even ten thousand right beside you, but you will not be hurt. So we can be sure when we say, "I will not be afraid, because I have an intimate relationship with the Lord who is my helper. People can't do anything to me." Jesus Christ is the same yesterday, today, and forever. (2 Tim.1:7, Romans 8:15-16, 1 John 4:18, Isaiah 40:31, Psalm 91:4-7, Heb. 13: 6,8).

By faith we must believe that nothing bad will happen to you. No disaster will come to your home. He has put his angels in charge of you. They will watch over you wherever you go. The Lord says, "If someone loves me, I will save him." You won't need to be afraid of sudden trouble; you won't fear the ruin that comes to the wicked, because the Lord will keep you safe. He will keep you from being trapped. Even if you walk through a very dark valley, you will not be afraid, because our Heavenly Father is with you. His rod and walking stick will comfort you, preparing a meal for you in front of your enemies. He will pour the joy of the Holy Spirit on your head; filling your cup to overflow, so that you will not judge others, but have an abundance to give to others with the love of our Heavenly Father who supplies you with all of your needs. (Psalm 91, Psalm 23).

Dear brothers and sisters, warn those who do not work for those who work hard make a profit, but those who only talk will be poor. However, you will not succeed by your own strength or power, but by the Spirit of God. We know that in everything God works for the good of those who love him. They are the people he called, because that was his plan.

So don't worry about tomorrow, because tomorrow will have its own worries. Each day has enough trouble of its own. Do not worry about anything, but pray and ask God for everything you need, always giving thanks, and God's peace, which is so great we cannot understand it, will keep your hearts and minds in Christ Jesus. The people that trust in the Lord will return and enter His temple with joy. Their happiness will last forever. They will have joy and gladness, and all sadness and sorrow will be gone far away. Praise the Lord; His mercy endures forever. Amen.

CHAPTER 30

A SENSE OF URGENCY: IT IS TIME TO TAKE THE PROMISED LAND

"At that time the Lord said unto Joshua, make thee sharp knives, and circumcise again the children of Israel the second time. And Joshua made him sharp knives, and circumcised the children of Israel at the hill of the foreskins. And this is the cause why Joshua did circumcise: All the people that came out of Egypt, that were males, even all the men of war, died in the wilderness by the way, after they came out of Egypt. Now all the people that came out were circumcised: but all the people that were born in the wilderness by the way as they came forth out of Egypt, them they had not circumcised. For the children of Israel walked forty years in the wilderness, till all the people that were men of war, which came out of Egypt, were consumed, because they obeyed not the voice of the Lord: unto whom the Lord swore that he would not shew them the land, which the Lord swore unto their fathers that he would give us, a land that flowed with milk and honey. And their children, whom he raised up in their stead, them Joshua circumcised: for they were uncircumcised, because they had not circumcised them by the way." (Joshua 5:2-7).

Today, many people who believe in Jesus Christ as their personal Lord and Savior have experienced what they would consider a "born-again" moment in their life. They have been saved by faith and confessed that Jesus Christ is the only Begotten Son of God. In church history the Scriptures identify this as coming out of death and into a new life in Christ. We celebrate this with baptism and the Passover meal of the bread and blood of Jesus as the Eucharist/communion of oneness in the body of Christ.

This Passover meal is also a recognition of the children of Israel who were in bondage and slavery to the world system of the times upon which God brought death. However, in the midst of one of the greatest stories of world destruction, over 3,000,000 were led by Moses out of Egypt, carrying the wealth of the land as the death angel had passed over them, harming no one.

Moses led them to the Red Sea where the waters parted, and they all walked across to dry land under the guidance of Moses. This amazing story in time demonstrates the magnitude of the personal experience believers encounter when they receive Jesus Christ. The Holy Spirit unveils our true identity as children of God and our birthright position in Christ – in Elohim – when we receive Jesus Christ as the only begotten Son of God. The world may call the Almighty – GOD, but through the Holy Spirit Jesus unveiled Him as our Father.

With this basic level of Christian faith, we recognize that someday when our natural body is worn out, we can have the assurance of being in a place called Heaven where our Heavenly Father – God - resides. Most believers will say they don't know where this place is physically located. Yet, with trillions of believers since Calvary called Christians, we have created images of mansions in the sky, streets of gold, glorified perfect bodies, and total rest while being waited upon by angels. These images have been passed down through history by diverse languages of the scriptures, interpretations of words, cultures, and customs of certain time eras, and those that were in control of the religious system at the time.

When we pause to consider that most of us are not ready to leave our natural bodies and go to an unknown place called heaven, we must consider the question of what does our Heavenly Father expect from us while we are still on the earth in our natural bodies? This is the challenging question – how can one be a child of God in an Egyptian world filled with self-focus, instead of the God of the Bible?

The scripture I opened this teaching with in Joshua chapter 5 is a wonderful path and direction we can apply to our journey into the promised land.

The decree "In the NAME of JESUS" is our birthright. Our blessing is revealed through the Torah when taught by the Holy Spirit released in us by the NAME.

"If the ministry of death, written and engraved on stones, was glorious, so that the children of Israel could not look steadily at the face of Moses because of the glory of his countenance, which glory was passing away, how will the ministry of the Spirit not be more glorious?" (2 Corinthians 3:7-8).

Paul is referring back to the Old Testament; the wisdom of the teachings and instructions of the Father with Moses and the Torah. Since Moses continuously kept the Torah by the Spirit of God, he was blessed with the ability to enter into the Holy of Holies and fellowship with God anytime and not encounter death. The next in line was the High Priest, who could enter only once a year.

On that same concept that separated Moses and Aaron's relationship with God and entering into the Holy of Holies, we have Paul using this illustration to say that because Jesus Christ is our High Priest, we can now enter into the Holy of Holies anytime. However, God did not change the conditions of entering. His WORD was made flesh, but how many of us are being led by the Spirit of God according to HIS WORD?

Paul is unveiling a key when he states, *"You are our epistle, living letters of the Torah, written in our hearts, known and read by all men; clearly you are an epistle of Christ, ministered by us, written not with ink but by the Spirit of the living God, not on tablets of stone but on tablets of flesh, that is, of the heart"* (2 Corinthians 3:2-4).

Jesus Christ is the WORD - the TORAH - made flesh, dwelling among men (John 1:14). He is the Alpha and Omega, the beginning and the end (Revelation 1:8, 11, 21:6, 22:13). He emphasizes His messages to the churches, the many members of His body that IT IS FINISHED (Rev. 21:6, John 19:30).

The WORD that was written on tablets of stone can NOW be written on our hearts. The teachings and instructions of the Father to His children, the blessings on how to obtain the promised land – the earth that belongs to the Lord and the fullness of it is NOW the vision for the bride of Christ, the church, the New Jerusalem.

In Hebrew 8:8-10 we read the Lord saying, *"Because finding fault with them, He says: "Behold, the days are coming, says the Lord, when I will make a new/renewed covenant with the house of Israel and with the house of Judah— not according to the covenant that I made with their fathers in the day when I took them by the hand to lead them out of the land of Egypt; because they did not continue in My covenant, and I disregarded them, says the Lord. For this is the covenant that I will make with the house of Israel after those days, says the Lord: I will put My laws in their mind and write them on their hearts; and I will be their God, and they shall be My people."*

This Scripture is found in the New Testament, which is considered to be for the church, yet God is speaking directly about the House of Israel and the House of Judah, declaring that He will write His Torah on their minds and their hearts. Just before that, we read Paul saying to the converted Gentiles that God would write the TORAH on their hearts. Then we have Jesus speaking to John to address the churches outside of Israel that the WORD – Jesus Christ is finished – the TORAH has been made flesh and is now residing in mankind. *"And I heard a loud voice from heaven saying, "Behold, the tabernacle of God is with men, and He will dwell with/in them, and they shall be His people. God Himself will be with/in them and be their God"* (Revelation 21:3).

There is a great rejoicing in all of Heaven when one person receives Jesus as their personal Savior. The disappointment is when they don't hunger for the fullness of their blessings on the earth. Jesus paid the price of our birthright with His own LIFE. He did this because of His great love and desire for all of His Kind to return to a relationship of oneness with the Father. The birthright is a free gift; however, the way to receive the blessings of the Father is where our free-will option is activated.

To get a better clarity of this, we need to venture back in time to when the Whole House of Israel, all twelve sons/tribes of Jacob were brought out of the land of Egypt to take dominion and authority over the Promised Land that God had already established for them. Here we have one nation that had been in bondage for over 400 years, and NOW they were being taken from the strongholds of bondage and death to life in a land of promise, dreams and visions, with the wealth of Egypt handed to them. We are not talking about a few people here and there, but millions coming together and leaving a land that they were born into as slaves - never knowing there was a world beyond. For several generations the children of God only knew the life of a slave.

That is an amazing event that needs to be remembered as it is filled with details of similar issues we can identify with today.

Being born again is a "Passover" experience we relate to Moses and the children of God crossing the Red Sea, along with the cross of Calvary and the resurrection of Jesus Christ. Our birthright has been established as we are now "new creations in Christ" (2 Corinthians 5:17). However, being a new creation in Christ does not mean that there is a "New Testament people" and the Old Testament has been done away with. It is in the Old Testament where we find our blessings to live life in abundance according to the will of our Heavenly Father. This is where we find the Father's teachings and instructions to train up a child in the way it should go so that as he/she gets older they will not depart from it (Proverbs 22:6).

This training was first introduced to the Hebrew children, not just to the Jewish/Judah tribe at Mt. Sinai when Moses was given the Ten Commandments, fifty days after Passover. This is also the beginning of what is called "the church" in Acts 2. The church was not formed at Passover, but at Pentecost.

After the disciples were "born again" at Passover, they had to go through a wilderness circumcision of their hearts to be able to do the work of the Father that Jesus had commissioned for them to do.

"Speak to the children of Israel, and say to them: 'The feasts of the Lord, which you shall proclaim to be holy convocations, these are My feasts" (Leviticus 23:2).

God told the Hebrew children, all 12 tribes of Israel, that they were to be in Jerusalem three times a year to celebrate the LORD's FEASTS. These three feasts were Passover, Pentecost, and Tabernacles. These were the LORD's, not the Jews'. The celebration was to be honored in Jerusalem. The culture of the times was to travel by foot, which would take a while to get from point A to point B, along with taking time to rest on the Sabbath each week. The preparations for going to Jerusalem for a family was such an ordeal that they would often plan to stay within a day's journey from the city until after the Pentecost celebration, which also required them to be in Jerusalem.

The significance of this is that Jesus told His disciples that He would see them again, after He arose, in the Galilee. *"But after I have been raised, I will go before you to Galilee"* (Matthew 26:32). If you were having a meal with Jesus BEFORE the cross, what would you think He was talking about when He makes the statement that He will be raised and go before you to Galilee?

On foot, a journey to the Galilee from Jerusalem was a 3-4 days' journey through the wilderness along the Jordan River. This statement by Jesus was probably not given much attention about when He would be raised, what He was being raised from, or when this would take place, knowing that they needed to be around the Jerusalem area over the next few months.

"He is not here; for He is risen, as He said. Come, see the place where the Lord lay. And go quickly and ***tell His disciples that He is risen from the dead, and indeed He is going before you into Galilee; there you will see Him. Behold, I have told you****"* (Matthew 28: 6-7). "But go, tell His disciples—and Peter—**that He is going before you into Galilee; there you will see Him, as He said to you**" (Mark 16:17).

The disciples were scared after the crucifixion, hiding in Jerusalem. They had totally forgotten that Jesus had said He would see them again in the Galilee after He had risen. They were aware that it was a long journey to the Galilee, and they would need to be back in Jerusalem within about a month and a half for Pentecost.

They were also supposed to be participating in the counting of the Omer between Passover and Pentecost, going from the barley harvest to the wheat harvest, referred to as "The Feast of Weeks." *"And you shall count for yourselves from the day after the Sabbath, from the day that you brought the sheaf of the wave offering: seven Sabbaths shall be completed"* (Leviticus 23:15). Remember, their survival in this culture depended on the agricultural awareness of planting and harvesting. Going to the Galilee through the wilderness was a great diversion from their survival preparations. If one did not work, they didn't eat. There was no time to chase "what if's," besides, there was the fear of being known by someone that could accuse them of being with Jesus. Panic and fear of the unknown was all around them.

Yet, the hair-size thread of hope was still within them, and ignited when the confirmation to go to the Galilee to see Jesus came by the women. That breath of LIFE is what we each must always keep close to our heart, never giving up on the Father.

Jesus met them at the Galilee in a familiar setting with which they could all identify – fishing. This is how He will meet with us, also. In the process of the disciples needing to return back to Jerusalem, Jesus continued to walk and talk with them AS the RESURRECTION LIFE, not the man Jesus. Each day they would have also been counting the Omer, yet they were now aware of the numeric implication of the WORD; the letters in the Hebrew Torah scroll coming off the pages as LIFE. This journey back from the Galilee to Jerusalem was a journey through the same wilderness where Jesus met Satan and the temptations of man.

"He was seen by Cephas (Peter), then by the twelve. After that He was seen by over five hundred brethren at once, of whom the greater part remained to the present, but some have fallen asleep. After that He was seen by James, then by all the apostles" (1 Corinthians 15:5-7). Jesus took His disciples, along with over 500 people, through a wilderness journey from being born again to being the church with the anointing of the Holy Spirit.

Being the church, the sons of God/bride of Christ, is more than just receiving Jesus as our personal Savior. This is the beginning of turning around from going in the wrong direction and receiving our birthright that was restored by the blood of Jesus. However, Jesus is not going to have intimacy as a husband to His bride if the bride is still a child. He welcomes the children to be trained in the way they should go, but until believers are spiritually mature enough in Christ to literally handle the WORD of God to do the Father's business in the earth, we will not see the return of Jesus Christ for His bride. The bride must make herself ready to carry HIS NAME, HIS NATURE, and HIS CHARACTER in the world so that the unity of the bride – the church – and the groom – Jesus Christ – unveils the one NEW MAN – the LAST ADAM (1 Corinthians 15).

The time is NOW to let go of the old grave clothes of yesterday and to live according to the newness of Christ in you; the hope of glory to the world of bondage and slavery. Circumcision of the heart is a wilderness experience, spending time in intimacy, learning the NAME, the NATURE, and the CHARACTER of Christ in you so that the WORD of God is written on your hearts. Out of the heart the mouth speaks (John 7:38). Our mouth has the ability to produce LIFE or death (Proverbs 18:21). *"The word is very near you, in your mouth and in your heart, that you may do it. "See, I have set before you today life and good, death and evil, in that I command you today to love the Lord your God, to walk in His ways, and to keep His commandments, His statutes, and His judgments, that you may live and multiply; and the Lord your God will bless you in the land which you go to possess"* (Deuteronomy 30:14-17).

"Most assuredly, I say to you, he who believes in Me, the works that I do he will do also; and greater works than these he will do, because I go to My Father" (John 14:12).

CHAPTER 31

PREPARING FOR PASSING OVER DEATH AND ENTERING INTO RESURRECTION LIFE

Exodus 3:13-15, *"Then Moses said to God, "Indeed, when I come to the children of Israel and say to them, "The God of your fathers has sent me to you' and they say to me, what is His name?" what shall I say to them?" And God said to Moses, "I AM WHO I AM." And He said, "Thus you shall say to the children of Israel, "I AM has sent me to you." Moreover, God said to Moses, "Thus you shall say to the children of Israel: "The Lord God of your fathers, the God of Abraham, the God of Isaac, and the God of Jacob, has sent me to you. This is MY name forever and this is MY memorial to all generations."*

The name of God is a noun that moves to a verb - I BE: I will be what I will be, I will become what I will become, and/or I will be whom I will become.

This magnificent name I AM - YHVH- Yahweh, had within the name the ability to free the children of God from slavery, bondage, poverty, and oppression. The name of God not only set the captives free, but also brought the children together, forming one nation after 400 years of being led by another god called Pharaoh. These children of God had lost all hope of returning to the lands of their forefathers. They were just waiting to die to escape the cruelty of the bondage of slavery with a little hope that someday a Messiah would appear to deliver them. They knew they were children of the God of their forefathers, but they didn't know His name that would distinguish Him from the gods of Egypt.

The times and seasons may be different, but the environment conditions are similar today to those during the slavery times of the children of God in Egypt. Today, believers in Jesus Christ know of Him as the Savior who went to the cross, and was resurrected from the dead to open the door for believers in Christ to go to heaven when they die and escape the bondages of this world for a life of glory, unless Jesus returns, and raptures the believers out of the world before they die a physical death. Basically, the hope for the believer is on the other side of death. Many believers remember an old hymnal that says "I'll Fly Away" that has a melody of hope mixed with words led by a spirit of death.

The unveiling of God's name to Moses is the word YAHWEH - YHVH which is made up of three separate phrases/verbs TO BE. With the words: I AM WHO I AM, the repeat of the words "I AM" is saying "I WAS, I AM, and/or I SHALL BE" all at the same moment as eternity into time. A part of each of these forms is combined to form the WORD - YAHWEH.

This name is a revelation and a promise for whatever the people of God needed Him to be: I am, I will be, I will become. Not only did God unveil Himself to Pharaoh and the children of God while they were in slavery, but after they passed over death into resurrection life and freedom, journeying into a territory they had never ventured to before, He became the guide that went before them as a cloud by day and a pillar of fire by night. He was the water they needed out of the rock. He was the bread they needed from heaven. He was their deliverer, provider, substance, healer, counselor, law-giver, military leader, and miracle worker doing wonders they had never seen or heard of by His name.

As we fast forward into the New Testament, we read in Luke 1:31-33 where Mary met the angel Gabriel, *"And behold, you will conceive in your womb and bring forth a Son, and shall call His name Jesus. He will be great, and will be called the Son of the Highest; and the Lord God will give Him the throne of His father David. And He will reign over the house of Jacob forever, and of His kingdom there will be no end."*

"No one has seen God at any time. The only begotten Son, who is in the bosom of the Father, He has declared Him" (John 1:18).

Paul shares with us, *"For in Him, Jesus Christ, dwells all the fullness of the Godhead bodily, and you are complete in Him, who is the head of all principality and power"* (Colossians 2:9-10).

Jesus said, *"All authority has been given to Me in heaven and on earth."* (Matthew 28:18).

Jesus Christ is the personified salvation of YHVH in human flesh. He is the WORD - the Torah, the promise -the covenant, the surety - the payment of sin, the royal majesty of position, the power of all authority, the compassion of the heart of the Father. He is the full unveiling of the unseen God Almighty.

When God came through Jesus Christ, He did not speak as He did through Moses. Moses spoke as the oracles of God. Jesus spoke as God: I AM the Way, I AM the Truth, I AM the Life, I AM the Good Shepherd, I AM the Resurrection, I AM the Door, I AM the bread, I AM the vine, etc. God spoke through Moses as I WILL BE. Jesus speaks as I AM.

Every time Jesus said, "I AM" he would have appeared to be the most egotistical person, a maniac of blasphemy in the culture, taking the name of God to the worst level of sin. He would have been breaking the third commandment, and that would require stoning and death in the Jewish belief. When Jesus proclaims that He is the "I AM," He is saying, "Whoever comes to ME for I AM YHVH in the flesh, I will BE I AM of the Father to them."

In the gospel of John, Jesus spoke the words "I AM" twenty-one times. Why is that important? Because the foundation of who we say Jesus is must become the "I" in our own spirit and heart to bring forth the Kingdom of God manifested in the earth.

If we turn to John 8:58 we read where Jesus has declared himself to the religious leaders while in the temple saying, *"Most assuredly, I say to you before Abraham was, I AM."* The law considered what Jesus said was a crime unto death, so the Jews took up stones to throw at Him. However, Jesus hid Himself and went out of the temple going through the midst of them as He passed by. He did not play hide and seek. Nor did he find a hidden corner, but he was literally not seen by the religious leaders that wanted to stone Him, yet He was in their midst.

We read in the next verse that He sees a blind man from birth. Is this coincidence? Of course not! This is a life lesson for us to ponder and reflect. How often do we know about Jesus, go to a building we call church and sing praises to Him, yet not really comprehend that God goes with us wherever we are, and that God appears as Christ in us?

Jesus told the Jews, *"Therefore I said to you that you will die in your sins; for if you do not believe that I am HE, you will die in your sins"* (John 8:24). Dying in our sins is not about a doctrine of heaven and hell, but about missing the mark of the opportunity for Christ to be formed in us so that the glory of God in us is unveiled in the earth.

"At that day you will know that I in My Father, and you in Me, and I in you. He who has My commandments/Torah and keeps them, it is he who loves Me. And he who loves Me will be loved by My Father, and I will love him and manifest Myself to him" (John14:20-21 NKJV). What day is this? It is the Day of the Lord when He comes in His glory in us. A perpetual, ongoing day that is first unveiled in the individual members/ cells of the body of Christ. Then as these cells unite in Spirit around the world, the body of Christ is unveiled to the kings of this world as King and Lord over all.

The disciples are listening closely to what Jesus is stating to the religious leaders of that time. They know that His proclamation of "I AM" is breaking the third commandment of the Torah, yet, He also says that if you love ME you will keep the commandment/Torah. Can Jesus have it both ways?

As we consider these Scriptures from John's writings, let's take into consideration the time period of these writings. The gospel of John was not written in the same era as the gospel of Matthew, Mark, and Luke. These first three were written between 58-61 AD. John's gospel was written almost a generation after the circulation of the other three's writings. Time-wise John wrote his other letters we know as 1, 2, and 3 John, and the Book of Revelation around the same time that he writes the gospel of John.

John pulls into the ministry of Jesus the "why" factor, and not just the historical wisdom. We can read about Jesus being the Savior, Healer, Redeemer, Provider, etc., but from a historical position, the challenge comes when trying to unveil the relationship between what Jesus did and the question of can He BE this for me today? John unveils the "yes" to that question, but he shows that you have to spiritually die to be spiritually alive in Christ today. Otherwise, you will need to go through a natural death to get your flesh out of the way so that the glory of God may be unveiled, Christ in you, has been within you all the time.

Jesus gets alone to have a prayer conversation with the Father that only John writes as he listens in. In John 17:16 we begin:

"They are not of the world, just as I am not of the world. Sanctify them by Your truth. Your WORD/Torah is truth. As You sent Me into the world, I also have sent them into the world. And for their sakes I sanctify Myself, that they also be sanctified by the truth. I do not pray for these alone, but also for those who will believe in Me through their word/Torah in them: that they all be one, as You, Father in Me, and I in You; that they also may be one in US, that the world may believe that You sent Me. And the glory which You gave Me I have given them, that they BE one just as We are one: I in them, and You in Me; that they BE made perfect in one, and that the world will know that You have sent Me, and have loved them as You have loved Me (John 17:16-23 NKJV).

John 17:21 shares the Oneness of our identity in Christ when Jesus prays:

AS you: YHVH - Jesus

Jesus - YHVH

They - US
Jesus - glory - US - YHVH

The "US" in this verse is first mentioned in Genesis 3:22, "Then the Lord God said, *"Behold, the man has become like one of US, to know good and evil, and now, lest he put out his hand and take also of the tree of life, and eat, and live forever."*

Man was functioning from his soul instead of being led by the Spirit of God. If we do not embrace this prayer of Jesus really decreeing with the Father, we will continue to hang around the Tree of Knowledge of Good and Evil embracing death to the body of Christ. We will die in our sin of missing the mark— still go to Heaven and receive a glorified body, but we will not be able to rule and reign with Him in Heavenly placed in the earth until a company of people around the world unite together as one body in Christ as Paul said, *"For this corruptible must put on incorruption, and this mortal must put on immortality. So when this corruptible has put on incorruption, and this mortal has put on immortality, then shall be brought to pass the saying that is written: "Death is swallowed up in victory"* (1 Corinthians 15:53-54 NKJV).

We have come through church history camping in many realms of doctrines and theology, which served for a season, but we are now at a new season of gathering all the fragments of bread of the body of Christ into twelve baskets, so that none are lost. John shares a story with us in John chapter 6 of Jesus and the disciples involved with feeding 5,000 men during the Passover season with 5 loaves of bread and two fish. When everyone is fed and satisfied, Jesus tells the disciples to *"Gather up the fragments that remain, so that nothing is lost" Therefore they gathered up and filled twelve baskets with the fragments of the five barley loaves which were left over by those who had eaten"* (John 6:12-13).

The number five is identified Biblically with GRACE, and the number 12 is identified with the government of God. Barley is the grain of cleansing/ detoxifying the body. Putting this all together at Passover, crossing over from death to life, Jesus has given the disciples the visual of bringing cleansing to the body of Christ by giving them grace in abundance. Not one person at this time was told they were a sinner, nor to repent. They were fed the miracle working of the grace of God by those that had been with Jesus, and then Jesus tells them to gather them in. In the gathering they had more bread fragments than when they first distributed what Jesus gave them. They had enough for 12 baskets. This is the whole house of Israel, all 12 of Jacob's sons/tribes that were scattered around the world and mixed with the nations of the world.

Jeremiah prophesied in Chapter 51 that the whole house of Israel is one tribe of the Lord's inheritance and would be the "battle-ax and weapons of war" to break the nations of this world in pieces, destroying the kingdoms of man. The great mountain of the religious system that we know of Christianity will be destroyed because of the judgment and separation the church has created taking the word of God/the Torah and using it against the people instead of giving them grace.

The prophet Zechariah releases his nuggets with, "Who are you, O great mountain? Before Zerubbabel you shall become a plain! And he shall bring forth the capstone with shouts of "GRACE, grace to it!" (Zechariah 4:7). Here we have the wisdom of the Tree of Life.

When Jesus took his disciples into the region of Caesarea Philippi, He asked them first, *"Who do men say that I, the Son of Man, am?"* After they answered who the world perceived him to be, He then asked, *"But who do you say that I am?"* Jesus was helping them get clarity of the voices they heard in the world and the religious system of the day, and the voice of the Holy Spirit. Peter responds saying, *"You are the Christ, the Son of the living God"* (Matthew 16:13-16). Just before this scene takes place Jesus had tried to get the disciples to understand the difference between the leaven of bread, and the leaven doctrine of the Pharisees and Sadducees, or the religion of the time in relationship with God.

Jesus responds to Peter saying, *"Blessed are you, Simon Bar-Jonah, for flesh and blood has not revealed this to you, but My Father who is in heaven. And I also say to you that you are Peter, and on this rock I will build My church, and the gates of Hades shall not prevail against it. And I will give you the keys of the kingdom of heaven, and whatever you bind on earth will be bound in heaven, and whatever you loose on earth will be loosed in heaven"* (Matthew 16:17-19).

One more thought I want to bring in, and I will tie everything together.

In Matthew 21, just before the last Passover season when Jesus celebrates with His disciples, we find Jesus hungry. As he comes to a fig tree that had no fruit on it, He curses it, and it instantly withers away. Fig trees begin their season with young leaves in the spring, and produce fruit later. The tree had no ability to produce fruit at this season. Jesus was teaching a lesson to His disciples about hungering for spiritual food, not natural food. Remember when Adam and Eve ate from the Tree of Knowledge of Good and Evil and their eyes were opened to death and their nakedness? They tried to cover themselves with fig leaves.

The identification of the whole house of Israel is the Olive Tree, not the fig tree. Everything Jesus did in the natural was teaching a spiritual implication. He was not saying, "Don't eat figs because they are evil." He is saying, *"When you see the fig tree's branches become tender, and put forth leaves, you know that summer is near"* (Mark 13:28). Translated, when the body of Christ, those that are born again through Passover, take the word of God and create justification and separation to the body because it seems good to the eyes of man, look up, draw near to God so that you can hear what the Spirit is saying, and not the religion of men.

Luke writes that when these things begin to happen, look up and lift up your heads, because your redemption draws near and you will see the Son of Man come in a cloud with power and great glory. Where is the Son of Man? It is Christ in you. What is this cloud? The unity of the body of Christ, the cloud of witnesses of one voice sounding as a loud shofar as was heard by the children of Israel on Mount Sinai.

In closing, our foundation cornerstone is Jesus Christ. Everything of Christianity must have a unity with this foundation alone. It is not about the doctrines and traditions of men. It is not about the issues of the world. It is only about Jesus Christ who is YHVH in the flesh. The capstone is

GRACE. When we know that Christ resides in our heart, and that our mind is the mind of Christ releasing GRACE, the fruit that is developed and birthed from our womb is: Love, joy, peace, longsuffering, kindness, goodness, faithfulness, gentleness, and self-control or temperance. It is in these clusters of fruit found within the body of Christ that we are meshed and stomped together into a great winepress throughout the nations in the world, forming as one the best wine that was served to the people - the blood of Christ that was shed for all mankind.

Grace is not earned, but given through the redemptive quality of the body and blood of Jesus Christ. Grace is not meant to leave us as sinners, but to bring us from death into LIFE with the unveiling of who we are in Christ equipped with the power of His Holy Spirit to set others in bondage free. We do this by identifying with the name and nature of Christ in us, God in us, and together being led by the Spirit of the Lord, we find other parts of His body hungering for unity and oneness.

Ezekiel prophesied in chapter 37, bones coming together, then flesh, then the Spirit of the Lord entering into the body and uniting two branches into one to form a new nation, the Kingdom of God in the earth in every country. This is the whole house of Israel. The Jews are in the land of Israel, but Israel is not all Jews. The Jews were only identified with the tribe of Judah and Benjamin. The other sons of Israel were scattered around the world, and today we find the Lord calling them together by the Spirit through Christ Jesus. Not a particular denomination or theological foundation, but simply by knowing Jesus Christ personally, and allowing the Spirit of the Lord to teach us through the Bible unveiling the risen Christ in us, just as it was with the two disciples on the road to Emmaus.

"I will deliver them from all their dwelling places in which they have sinned, and will cleanse them. Then they shall be My people, and I will be their God. David My servant will be king over them, and they will all have one shepherd, Jesus Christ; they will also walk in My judgments and observe My statutes, and do them (My Torah). Then they shall dwell in the land that I have given to Jacob My servant, where your fathers dwelt; and they shall dwell there, they, their children, and their children's children, forever; and My servant David

will be their prince forever. Moreover, I will make a covenant of peace with them, and it will be an everlasting covenant with them; I will establish them and multiply them, and I will set My sanctuary (God's dwelling place) in their midst forevermore. My tabernacle with be with them; indeed, I will be their God, and they shall be My people. The nations also will know that I, the Lord, sanctify the whole house of Israel, when My sanctuary is in their midst forevermore" (Ezekiel 37:23-28 NKJV).

"Now I saw a new heaven and a new earth, for the first heaven and the first earth had passed away. Also there was no more sea (confusion in the body of Christ). Then I, John, saw the holy city, New Jerusalem, coming down out of heaven from God, prepared as a bride adorned for her husband. And I heard a loud voice from heaven saying, "Behold, the tabernacle of God is in men, and He will dwell in them, and they shall BE His people (His I AM). God Himself will be in them, their NAME" (Revelation 21:1-3).

As the kingdoms of this world filled with logic, reason, and self-focus increase, so shall the coming of the Lord, Christ in us be unveiled in the earth as a New Jerusalem adorned as a bride, and filled with the Spirit of the Lord in wisdom and knowledge of the teachings and instructions of Moses to rule with Christ from the heavens on earth.

The Son of Man, Jesus Christ will have a place, a body to lay His head, and rest together in the Sabbath of God (Luke 9:58, Colossians 1:18, Genesis 2:1-2).

"As He is, so are we today in this world" (1 John 4:17).

CHAPTER 32

WEARING THE PRIESTLY GARMENT IN THE LIFE OF OTHERS

"Now take Aaron your brother, and his sons with him, from among the children of Israel that he may minister to ME as priest, Aaron and Aaron's sons: Nadab, ABihu, Eleazar, and Ithamar. And you shall make holy garments for Aaron your brother, for glory and for beauty" (Exodus 28:1-2).

Verse 4: *"And these are the garments which they shall make: a breastplate, an ephod, a robe, a skillfully woven tunic, a turban, and a sash. So they shall make holy garments for Aaron you brother and his sons that he may minister to Me as a priest."*

We are a royal priesthood, a holy nation. What do our garments look like? Are we putting on the royal garments of the high priest? Are we unveiling Jesus Christ in us to others, so that the glory of the Lord in them that had been hidden can now be seen?

Moses was told by God to clothe his brother and his brother's sons for the job they would be doing to honor and serve the Lord.

Many times individuals of the body of Christ are not functioning in their purpose and calling on the earth because they have yet to meet a believer in Christ that has clothed them with their royal garments of glory. Instead, we are busy telling them how to change their ways to be a better Christian.

The responsibility of those that are mature in Christ is to not wrestle against flesh and blood, but against principalities, against powers, against the rulers of the darkness of this age, against spiritual hosts of wickedness in the heavenly places.

Stand in your identity: Christ carries the ephod. The government is on his shoulders. He bears our names the names of all the children of God since the beginning of time. The Father is looking to raise up sons that are ready to do the Father's business in the earth, putting on the priest's garment that Paul shares in Ephesians 6:

- Put on the sash around their waist of truth
- Breastplate of righteousness/faith/judgment of God among the tribes over our heart
- The gospel of peace is your tunic/clothing/shoes
- Helmet of Salvation/sword of the Spirit/word of God - turban, the mind of Christ.
- Praying always with all prayer and supplication in the SPIRIT - ROBE
- Being watchful to this end with all perseverance and supplication for all the saints.

The gospel of peace is the tunic, but it begins with the feet. The path that was walked before needs to be cleansed and restored by Christ in us. Jesus showed us the humbleness of service of the high priest by washing the feet of his disciples (John 13:14). As our Lord and teacher, we must follow the example by holding no man's sin against him. The path of where he was must be cleansed by the blood of Jesus and the washing of the word of God. Who is doing the cleansing? Jesus did it for us while we were in darkness and sin consciousness before we even knew we were sinners and apart from God. We did not go searching for Jesus, but He sent His Holy Spirit to come search for us. God did this through those that have gone before us spiritually. It may not be an immediate person we know, but it did happen all the way back to the root, over 2,000 years ago with Jesus Christ praying and redeeming you and me before we were conceived in our mother's womb.

Peter wanted Jesus to wash every part of him, but Jesus said, *"He who is bathed needs only to wash his feet, but is completely clean; and you are clean, but not all of you"* (John 13:10). **Jesus has cleansed all mankind**. God judges no man, but gave all judgment to the Son (John 5:22-23). When we wash our feet and the feet of others, we illustrate the repentance of turning from the wrong path of darkness to the path that is lit up by the Holy Spirit. The darkness we saw of the outer garments becomes lit up with the glory of God.

The greatness and vastness of the love of God was poured out when Jesus breathed on the disciples and said, *"Peace to you! As the Father has sent Me, I also send you: And when He had said this, He breathed on them, and said to them, Receive the Holy Spirit. If you forgive the sins of any, they are forgiven them; if you retain the sins of any, they are retained"* (John 20:21-23).

When we focus our heart and thoughts on the things of the world, we are held in bondage to that system as the children of God were slaves in Egypt. The world system does not know or have a personal relationship with God as bloodline family. There are many religions in the world that worship God, but there really is only one God, and only through Jesus Christ can we know an intimate relationship with God as our Father and carry His name to do His business on the earth as Jesus decreed.

The prophet Isaiah wrote, *"My people went down at first into Egypt to dwell there; then the Assyrian oppressed them without cause. Now therefore, what have I here, says the Lord, "That My people are taken away for nothing? Those who rule over them make them wail," says the Lord, and My name is blasphemed continually every day. Therefore, My people shall know My name: Therefore, they shall know in that day that I AM He who speaks; BEHOLD, it is I"* (Isaiah 52:4-6).

Isaiah establishes the condition of the world situation, but then the scene is changed when God's name "I AM" is unveiled.

"How beautiful upon the mountains are the feet of him who brings good news, who proclaims peace, who brings glad tidings of good things, who proclaims salvation, who says to Zion, your God reigns! Your watchmen shall lift up their voices, with their voices they shall sing together; for they shall see eye to eye when the Lord brings back Zion. Break forth into joy, sing together, you waste places of Jerusalem! For the Lord has comforted His people, He has redeemed Jerusalem. The Lord has made bare His holy arm in the eyes of all the nations; and all the bends of the earth shall see the salvation of our God" (Isaiah 52:7-10).

When we wash the feet of others, by counting no sin against them but bringing the cleansing, anointing presence of Christ in us through the Love of God, we must move forward by faith that we are the WORD, the living epistle of truth and righteousness in their midst that redeems, not judges. When the presence of Christ radiates through us, through our eyes and heart, the darkness must leave.

Do not take it personally if you try to bring the love of God to others and even if you are truly not judging their lifestyle, they are very uncomfortable with you being around them. It isn't you, but the Holy Spirit in you that has met their familiar spirit holding them captive in their lifestyle. The greatest stronghold on mankind is the religious spirit among believers; those who know Jesus Christ as their personal savior, but then justify their righteousness by what the world does.

The universal language of God is the Love of God that He gave to the world - all mankind - while we were all in darkness and ignorant of the truth behind His teachings and instructions He gave to Moses. Before Jesus came into the world, no man had the ability to keep the purity and holiness of a relationship with God in intimacy and oneness for which mankind was created in the beginning.

Mankind was resting with God in the seventh day when all the heavens and the earth, and all the hosts of them were finished. Then when the Lord God formed man from the dust of the ground and breathed into his nostrils the breath of life, man became a living being. We then had a form placed on the image of God, and the Spirit of God in the form of man. Woman was inside of the form of man and together they were called Adam (Genesis 5:1). In this eternal moment mankind communed with God in oneness. The "I" that was spoken from mankind was the name of God "I AM." As long as mankind stayed away from the Tree of Knowledge, there was oneness with God. To gain refreshing intimacy with God, mankind could eat the fruit of the Tree of Life.

The fruit of the Tree of Life is the fruit of the Holy Spirit which Paul shares in his letter to the Galatians. *"The fruit of the Spirit is love, joy, peace, longsuffering, kindness, goodness, faithfulness, gentleness, and self-control. Against such there is no law (no boundary of right or wrong). When we are Christ's and live in the Spirit, our flesh of logic and reason to justify is not in existence"* (Galatians 5:22-25).

God gave Adam the responsibility to name all of the beasts in the field and the birds in the air. The names Adam spoke are still in existence today. The names that Adam gave created a "kind" of species putting a form on that name. A bear is a bear, a lion is a lion, a snake is a snake, etc. With the name, he gave the ability to reproduce its own kind. However, Adam did not have the ability to create his kind, another god by speaking it into existence the way he did with the beasts. Adam's helpmate was already in him - the Holy Spirit. God Almighty had to put Adam to sleep, to death, in order to awaken him to resurrection life of the truth that was already in him. When the Spirit of God is in us, we have the ability to be the manifestation of Christ in the earth. The "I" we speak is not the old man, but the new creation we now are as Christ in us, the glory of God.

Now here is wisdom; did you ever wonder how a serpent got in the garden of man's residence? How comfortable are we when we see beasts of the field inside our home? Adam was to name the beasts of the field, not bring them into his home. Adam was looking into the world system for a helpmate, not in his garden. How often do we bring the world into our home, our sanctuary through our intellect and reasoning instead of by the Spirit of God?

We read in Genesis 2:24-25 that the man and woman were both naked, not ashamed, and they were joined together as one flesh. So who gave the serpent the ability to speak a language the woman could understand, and where is the man while this is taking place? There is no historical documentation that a serpent could ever literally speak a language using words that mankind could understand.

The woman is now in the garden where there are two trees in the midst. Where is the man? He is with her. When the man was told NOT to eat from the Tree of Knowledge where was the woman? Inside of man. Man was given the wisdom NOT to eat from the Tree of Knowledge while woman was still inside him, and before he was given the ability to name the beasts of the field. This is one of those enlightening moments to ponder so we don't end up repeating the same thing that man did.

God is a loving Father who already knew before Genesis 1:1 that a deceptive spirit would enter into the hearts of men. It is why Jesus Christ is the lamb slain BEFORE the foundations of the world, before He was conceived in the womb of Mary, and before He entered into the world as a baby in a manger.

We are told not to grieve the Holy Spirit. What does this mean? (Ephesians 4:30).

"Let him who stole steal no longer, but rather let him labor, working with his hands what is good, that he may have something to give him who has need. Let no corrupt word proceed out of your mouth, but what is good for necessary edification, that it may impart grace to the hearers. And do not grieve the Holy Spirit of God by whom you were sealed for the day of redemption. Let all bitterness, wrath, anger, clamor, and evil speaking be put away from you, with all malice. And be kind to one another, tenderhearted, forgiving one another, even as God in Christ forgave you. Therefore, be imitators of God as dear children. And walk in love, as Christ also has loved us and gave himself for us as an offering and a sacrifice to God for a sweet-smelling aroma" (Ephesians 4:28-32, 5:1-2).

Just as God brought the beasts of the field for Adam to name, so in like manner we have the same ability to name the beasts, but it does not mean they are to be the helpmate to man. Many of the beasts in creation have a place in the universal design of God, but there was also to be discernment in the naming by the character and nature of what was presented. A fox has a spirit nature that belongs to a fox, not a god-kind. A snake has a spirit nature of a snake, not a god-kind. God caused a separation/death to Adam's exposure of what he had just named, totally removing the potential consciousness of identifying with any of the beasts he had just named. God brought forth the helpmate that was already created in him.

The logic to this is that Adam should have been able to recognize his helpmate with him, bone of his bone and flesh of his flesh, versus the difference between a beast of the field and the "god kind" that belongs in the garden as he is with her next to the Tree of Knowledge. If that is not clear enough, remember Adam was already told which trees he could eat from and the one tree he could not.

Now we have both the man and the woman hanging around the Tree of the Knowledge of the world instead of a relationship with Christ, the Tree of Life. Remember, both trees are in the garden and both trees have fruit on them. Along with male and female Adam hanging around the Tree of Knowledge together, we also have from the field a serpent that has found his way into their home – garden - and knows how to speak their language. Remember, this man and woman are not gentile/pagans/non-believers. They are created in the image of their Father God.

Does the man say, "Woman, get away from that tree?" Does he speak to the serpent and say something like, "I gave you form, and with that form I did not give you the ability to speak, so be quiet?" No because there is a hidden thought going on in the man when he created words that were not created from his image as a God kind. This is why the man is also hanging around the Tree with the woman, and the voice she is talking to is the accuser of the brethren of her own husband.

He created the atmosphere and brought it into the garden where now the woman considers the familiar spirit as the voice of god, her husband who said, *"We may eat the fruit of the trees of the garden; but of the fruit of the tree which is in the midst of the garden, god (husband) has said, 'You shall not eat it, nor shall you touch it, lest you die. For GOD knows that in the day you eat of it your eyes will be opened, and you will be like God, knowing good and evil. So when the woman saw that the tree was good for food, that it was pleasant to the eyes, and a tree desirable to make one wise, she took of its fruit and ate. She also gave to her husband with her, and he ate"* (Genesis 3:2-6).

Why did man eat also? Was he not created in the form of LOVE? Why did he not throw the fruit down, get the serpent out of the house, and then turn to the Father and request guidance and instructions for healing from death given by the gift of a helpmate God had created for him? God came and addressed Adam asking, "Where are you?" He did not address the woman. God already knew what had happened, giving the man the opportunity to humble himself by giving his life for the woman who was his helpmate.

God says to man, *"Have you eaten from the tree of which I commanded you that you should not eat?"* (Genesis 3:11). God is not asking the woman because He had not spoken this command to her, but to Adam while she was still in seed form inside of man. Man had the ability to be the nurturing side of God carrying a seed called woman. When the seed was developed and woman was taken out of man, it is the imagery today of women birthing a baby they have carried in their womb. That baby is bone and flesh of women. God placed the seed of His kind in man with the blessing to be fruitful and multiply, filling the earth and subduing it, having dominion over the fish of the sea, over the birds of the air, and over every living thing that moves on the earth (Genesis 1:28). Adam gave birth to a woman that he did not give his life for as the mother side of God's image would have done.

When a mother sees her children doing something they should not be doing, she will do everything she can to help them get on the right path to reaching the full potential of who they were created to be. A child carried in the womb has the mother's blood life feeding and supporting it. The life of the flesh is in the blood. The blood life remembers via the DNA of who your father and mother are. Adam carried the baby woman in the womb. Woman was birthed as the helpmate to man; the two are one.

God addresses Adam about eating of the Tree of Knowledge, giving him the opportunity to reconcile the situation. If he had said anything in essence of, "It's my fault; I did not take responsibility for the gift you gave me; I didn't truly give her love and protections; I let her hang around the wrong tree, and I allowed another voice into our home that was not your voice, etc." Any of these "I" situations would have been an act of repentance turning the situation around.

However, what did the man say to God in response to His question? "Then the man said, *"The woman whom YOU gave to be with me, she gave me of the tree, and I ate"* (Genesis 3:12). Basically, it is like saying, "It is your fault, God, because the woman you gave me made me eat." So God goes along with the conversation and speaks to the woman who passes the blame on to the accuser of the brethren coming from the serpent. Now notice that God does not ask the serpent to defend himself. He simply speaks to the unfamiliar voice that does not belong in His presence and curses it to the ground the dust where man was formed from the earth.

How often do we justify the Adam and Eve syndrome in relationships - he made me do this, she made me do that? How often do we place blame on a "devil"? The accuser of the brethren is a lion roaming around to devour. This lion comes from the tribe of Judah that carries the blessings and leads the children of God with praise in their heart. Jesus Christ is the foundational rock that has declared our birthright as children of God, but He also gave us our inheritance of heavenly blessings to be poured out upon all the earth to set the captives free.

Jesus Christ has raised up a nation of kings and priests in the earth to His God and Father and to our God and Father to release His glory and dominion over all the earth from every tribe of Israel around the world to rule and reign now with Him. *"And from Jesus Christ, who is the faithful witness, and the first begotten of the dead, and the prince of the kings of the earth. Unto him that loved us, and washed us from our sins in his own blood, and hath made us kings and priests unto God and his Father; to him be glory and dominion for ever and ever. Amen. Behold, he cometh with clouds; and every eye shall see him, and they also which pierced him: and all kindred of the earth shall wail because of him. Even so, Amen"* (Rev. 1:5-7).

The children of Israel were vulnerable to become slaves to the world system of Egypt because they did not know their true position and authority they carried in the earth. Instead of speaking as the oracles of the Father, they allowed the kings and kingdoms of the world to dominate and control their atmosphere instead of taking authority by the power of Christ in them as the children of the Most High God.

How often do we use the word "I" in our everyday conversation, yet the heart of the matter of our "I" is not releasing the voice of God in us, but the voice of our own self. As new creations in Christ Jesus, we are to be dead to self and alive in Christ. Christ is one body with many members. When we see others not following a path that reflects the edification and form of God in the earth, we have the responsibility to cover them in Christ as Jesus Christ did for us. This requires carrying your cross daily and being willing to wash the feet of others, as we stand in the gap in intercessory prayer. Our hearts have a fullness of love when we see others not living their life to their full potential of their Heavenly Father's creation in them.

God holds no man's sin against him, but has given all judgment unto the Son. Today, God sees all mankind through the filter of Christ who shed His blood and paid the penalty of death that came upon mankind by the accuser of the brethren's words, created by a god-kind that had the head knowledge of justice, but not the heart of the Father.

*"I said, you are gods, and all of you are children of the Most High. But you shall die like men, and fall like one of the princes (instead of reigning like kings and priests). Arise O God (Christ in you), judge the earth; for you shall inherit all nations" (*Psalm 82:6-8).

CHAPTER 33

WHAT WAS MAN'S REAL NAME?

*I*f we ponder the time period of Moses and the children of God in the wilderness, we can gain an understanding of the ways of God that go beyond childhood stories like the "Prince of Egypt." During the time of the wilderness experience there were three to four million people that could have crossed over into the Promised Land, but only two, which walked in the ways of God entered in (Joshua and Caleb). A whole generation went through the tabernacle experience with the rituals and priesthood ordained by God, yet it took the death of that mindset to be able to cross over (Selah).

Now, let's consider the scriptural definition of death. Death is separation from God. If the temple of God has light, life, and love then there is no death. Moses knew God as a burning bush that was consumed by the fire, but not destroyed. He knew God as the tree of Life that didn't die. He built a tabernacle designed by God for man to enter and have relationship with Light. The Holy of Holies was the place in which man could become one with the light. Moses demonstrated this for us and didn't limit the potential of having this relationship with God to himself. On the mount of transfiguration Moses appears as the light with Elijah and Jesus.

The opposite of the tree of life is the tree of the knowledge of good and evil. Whether it is the knowledge of good or the knowledge of evil, the fruit of this tree will still bring death. The generation that died in the wilderness was practicing their faithfulness to religion and the priesthood. They kept order and lived in a practical way, but this didn't take them into the Promised Land. Interestingly, however is that the priesthood was not supposed to come near death or anyone unclean. Today, we have big churches that are handing the people of God over to "death," and they think that this is the way they are supposed to go. It is the natural way, but it isn't God's way of entering into His presence. He cannot come near death.

In 2 Timothy 1:9-10 we are told that death was abolished and that the gospel was given to teach us life and immortality. Much of the body of Christ has been out of order in the preaching of the gospel. The purpose of the gospel is to show us our inheritance today, not someday after we die and get to heaven. We are not to be preaching healing, prosperity, etc., but these things should be seen as signs and wonders, not leading. We have filled our minds with the tree of knowledge calling it good versus recognizing that His mind is our mind, which should be manifesting the tree of life. People do get healed in our churches today, but then they get sick again which causes them to go from healing to healing and eventually dying. We are teaching surface Christianity and not the gospel. If we would teach the gospel those things would follow, but instead the church has been running after the manifestations of miracles. The church has been following after the little veins in the body instead of what controls the whole body, the mind of Christ.

Let's go back to the beginning when these two trees were introduced in scripture. The tree of knowledge is not the tree that the woman was referring to in the midst of the garden when she was talking to the serpent. Genesis 2:9 says that the tree of life is in the midst. In Genesis 3:3, the woman has been taught by Adam (the god image she knows) that the tree of knowledge is in the midst. I refer to Adam as the god she identifies with because the word "touch" has been added to what the Father God said about the tree of knowledge. He never used the word touch in Gen. 2:17. The word "touch" could only have come from a being that could create words. The serpent couldn't create but could only imitate that which was already created.

When Adam named all living creatures as told in Gen. 2:19-20, he gave himself the name Adam, meaning "man + kind." He took the nature of which he was (as he did with every living creature) and gave himself a natural name and identity. The problem with this is that he was created a "god-being" to live a supernatural life without limitation. He was created in the image, likeness, and kind of his Father and Creator God. You can't separate your name/nature from Light, Life, and Love expecting to still have the power and authority of the Creator. Adam did not lose the seed of his eternal identity when he gave himself the name Adam, but he did lose the power to bring forth the unconditional love and eternal life of the Father. Adam introduced the limitations of time when he separated himself (his name) from the eternal or spirit life.

God did not call Adam by the name Adam until he created it for himself. Before Gen. 2:19 God called him "man" and Eve was called "woman" for she came out of man, and the man saw himself, the form of god when he looked at her. The woman also knew the man as god in a form and was one with him. When the man spoke, it was the voice of god on the earth to her, but it was not Father God. In Genesis chapter 3, the serpent questioned the woman, and she answered in truth as she knew it by repeating the information the god (Adam) had told her.

If we go to Col. 1:15-17 we read, *"who is the image of the invisible God, the firstborn of every creature: for by him were all things created that are in heaven, and that are in earth, visible and invisible, whether they be thrones, or dominions, or principalities, or powers: all things were created by him, and for him: and he is before all things, and by him all things consist."* Adam could have named mankind as: Light Beings, Love Beings, Word Beings, Eternal Beings, or Sons of God to give man distinction when naming all the other creatures of the earth. Instead, he brought the eternal, infinite power and authority that Father God gave him into a limited realm of time on the earth. Instead of maintaining unity and oneness with the eternal; the realms of spirit, soul, and body were separated (veiled) bringing mortality into existence.

If we look into a few Hebrew words, we will have a better understanding. The Hebrew word "Adon" means master, lord, owner, ruler, commander.

God gave man the blessing to *"be fruitful, and multiply, and replenish the earth and subdue it: and have dominion over the fish of the sea, and over the fowl of the air, and over every living thing that moveth upon the earth"* (Genesis 1:28).

Man's responsibility was to produce more "god-kind" or heavenly beings on the earth. By taking dominion over every living thing that moved upon the earth, the man would be IN the earth realm, but not OF the earth. "Adon" was the position or title Father God gave him. He was already the lord of the Lord, master of the Master, creator of the Creator. He was the son of God (Luke 3:38) being placed on the earth to do the Father's business. However, "Adon" was not his identity nature/name. Man was his name, and he was made in God's image and His likeness. There is a difference between a person's job title or position and who they are. For example, I carry the title Reverend/teacher as the job that I do, but this is not who I am. I am a Christ-One or son of God doing the work under that title. It may seem like a fine line, but the difference changed everything in man's life for he then walked in the natural sense realm once separated from the eternal mindset of the Father. The manifestation of sin and death (anything which is not of faith) came forth following this event.

How many times do we see people retire from a job position that they have done for so many years, and they seem to lose their identity after retiring because that position was all they connected to in defining their life? How many times do we ask someone about themselves and their answer has something to do with the type of job they do. We don't hear answers like "I'm a USA citizen, or a Christian, but we hear answers like "I am a construction worker, a nurse, a lawyer, a teacher, etc." We, like the first son of God, need to realize that God sees us as His children first. He is primarily a Father and He has responsibilities for us, but our identity as His loved-one, His son/daughter comes first.

The Hebrew word "Adamah," translated as "earth" is derived from the underlying root "Adam." Even though this word means "earth" it is not the word used for the planet earth, which is "Erets." This word "Adamah" is used in Gen. 2:7, 9 as the body of the first Adam that has the breath of God in it. The form that God created from the ground had the ability to support water and food. It had the ability to multiply and produce fruit over the entire planet. Keep in mind that God is Spirit and His kind is spirit so when we use words like water, food, and fruit we are talking spiritual, not natural. The man had a responsibility to bring forth the "word" of God through a form that had the breath of God in the natural realm. His food was Life, Love, and Light that would produce the fruit of the Holy Spirit as found in Galatians 5:22 on the earth, *"But the fruit of the Spirit is love, joy, peace, longsuffering, gentleness, goodness, faith, meekness, and temperance."* The Holy Spirit was brought forth out of the man as the "help meet." The woman was the manifestation of the man's innermost being to be multiplied as a family of "god-kind."

When the man named all living things in Father God's image with the "Adon" position, he also gave himself a distinction of identity, separate from the one he already had. He went from being "Adon" over the earth to being "Adam." The word "Adam" means "red" and is generally used to denote the human race and its characteristic nature in contrast to God in heaven. It is used in the collective sense of all mankind, not just one man or one woman. However, God does not use the word "human" anywhere in scripture. This is a word that has been created by man, not God.

God gave the man "Adon," a position, authority, and power to do the Father's business as the Father on the earth. The man took the Father's business and made it his identity when he gave himself the name "Adam." Jesus came to restore the family of God **through the Life of the flesh**, which is in the blood (Deut.12: 23). Jesus showed us the pattern to follow in doing the Father's business in Gen. 1:28 (having dominion over the earth and replenishing it with His image), "god-kind," as sons of God. This is why God (Jesus) had to come in the flesh and His blood was necessary. He had to identify with the blood of Adam as the second Adam (Adam even meaning "red") to transform Adam's (our) flesh and blood life into spirit life by the light of His life and love. We are transformed into His image through revelation knowledge (tree of Life) and the light which Jesus, Moses, and Elijah displayed will be made manifest in us.

Jesus tells us in John 5:30 that, *"I can of mine own self do nothing: as I hear, I judge: and my judgment is just; because I seek not mine own will, but the will of the Father which hath sent me."*

In John 5:22 we read, *"For the Father judgeth no man, but hath committed all judgment unto the Son."*

The Father's will was completed on the cross 2,000 years ago when Jesus said, *"It is Finished"* in John 19:30. The word "finished" is the Greek word "Omega." Jesus said he is the Alpha and Omega (Rev 1:8), which tells us that when he said it is finished, he took us back to the beginning of Genesis 1:1 and John 1:1. Time does not exist with the things of God.

When Jesus came to do the Father's will, he completed what Peter wrote in 2 Peter 3:9, *"The Lord is not slack concerning his promise, as some men count slackness; but is longsuffering to us-ward, not willing that any should perish, but that all should come to repentance."* The word "repentance" used here is the Greek word "metanoia" which means to change or alter of one's mind. In other words, stop eating off the tree of the knowledge of good and evil, and begin to eat off the tree of life, being heavenly minded versus earthly minded.

Many theologians use the word "repentance" as the Greek word "metanoeo" meaning to repent with regret accompanied by a true change of heart. This word includes emotionalism, and God is not interested in emotional responses. God is Spirit, and the Holy Spirit in us is our true identity, not our feelings or emotions.

These two words take us back to the beginning of this teaching where the word "touch" is used by the woman in Genesis 3:3. Even though Jesus was crucified on the tree of the knowledge of good and evil, and He has given us a new mind; emotions and feelings will try to draw us back to the old way of thinking and acting. It is by Christ Jesus, our tree of Life, that we can, by the faith of the Son of God, manifest His life, which is eternal. His life and immortality will work through us so that the finished work of Jesus Christ can be seen on the earth (2 Tim. 1:10).

As we walk by faith, believing that we are who God says we are, we will do the Father's business by being Sons of God. I Corinthians 15:53 tells us, *"For this corruptible must put on incorruption, and this mortal must put on immortality. So when this corruptible shall have put on incorruption, and this mortal shall have put on immortality, and then shall be brought to pass the saying that is written, Death is swallowed up in victory."*

Paul is referring to us as the corruptible and the mortal that must put on incorruption and immortality. Jesus has already finished the process for us. Now, we must take hold of what has already been done. This is not a someday in the future verse, but TODAY. Today is the day of salvation; today we are with Him in paradise.

CHAPTER 34

THE POWER IN HIS NAME: BEGINS WITH REST

*H*ave you ever wondered why God took so much time in Scripture to put the names of generations in the Bible? As I was studying the book of Genesis, I came to Chapter 10, which records the generations of the sons of Noah. As I went down the list, trying to pronounce each name, I asked the Lord "why is this in here, and what do these names mean to me and my relationship with Him that He would consider it necessary for me to know this information?"

The first thing that was brought to my attention by the Holy Spirit was that these were the people that were saved from the judgment of God! They came AFTER the flood. Noah's sons and the seeds of the future generations were not destroyed. The next thing that I became aware of, was that only Noah truly believed in what God was doing. He did not know what rain or flooding was all about, or how it would cause all the people to perish except whom was in the Ark, but he believed God and obeyed. Noah brought his sons and their wives with him into the safety of the Ark, but Scripture does not tell us that they believed also. They may have thought they were following a crazy old man who had been building this huge boat for 100 years while he declares that rain is coming and everyone will be wiped out.

So what was the personality and character of the generations of people that here brought into the Promised Land after the flood without experiencing death? I believe we can grasp some wisdom by the names that are given to us in this chapter in Genesis. This information is not exhaustive, but to be used as nuggets of revelation to stir a hunger to dig deeper into some Biblical truths that God has for us.

Noah - rest
Shem - honor, dust, outer court of the tabernacle, children in Christ
Ham - hot, sand, middle court, Pentecostal, spirit filled believers
Japheth - open, stars, inner court understanding, crossing over, transformation
Japheth's sons:
Gomer - complete, perfect
Magog - land of God
Madai - middle land
Javan - hot and active
Tubal - you shall be bought
Meshech - drawing or fishing out
Tiras - desire
Gomer's sons:
Ashkenaz - man sprinkled with fire
Riphath - spoken for by the word
Togarmah - you will break her (the soul's control)
Javan's sons:
Elishah - God of the coming one
Tarshish - yellow jasper, precious stone, character of gold
Kittim - someone who is tough and stands firm, tough love
Dodanim - leader, overcomes

I would like to point out that Scripture does not mention in the genealogy of Noah the other sons of Japheth. I do not believe we can assume that there were no male children born to the other sons, but that there was a reason by God for us to know the ones that are spoken of to give us wisdom that carries a revelation for us today.

Scripture does tell us in verse 5 of Chapter 10 that Japheth's children and grandchildren formed the isles of the Gentiles, yet his genealogy represents the inner court of the Tabernacle of God. This inner court is recognized throughout Scripture of where God resides, the Most Holy place that exists. This is something to think about, declaring that the Gentile's land is the Most Holy place!

To continue on with names...

Ham's sons:
Cush - black
Mizraim - land of Egypt, worldly, dual minded, against God
Phut - a bow as a weapon, not a covenant of peace
Canaan - land or the lowest, low degree of people, people of little worth or value
Cush's sons:
Seba - you drink
Havilah - circular
Sabtah - striking, old age
Raamah - a mane on a horse running in the wind
Sabtechah - to cause wounding
Nimrod - rebellion, hunter, mighty in the earth
Raamah's sons:
Sheba - the number seven, oath, covenant
Dedan - judge in the low country
Mizraim's sons:
Ludim - strife
Anamim - affliction of the waters
Lehabim - flames
Naphtuhim - opening, Egyptian tribe, confusion
Pathrusim - region of the south, comfort place, complacent
Casluhim - fortified
Philistim - rolling in the dust, enjoying the earthly things
Caphtorim - island shaped like a crown, isolated, separated, self focused
Canaan's sons:
Sidon - catching fish

Heth - terror (Hetites)
Jebusite - religious spirit
Amorite - spirit of pride
Girgasite - lying spirit
Hivite - violence
Arkite - gnawing at something
Sinite - bush with thorns
Arvadite - "I shall break loose", rebellion at the maximum
Zemarite - double fleece of wool, insecurity
Hamathite - walled, a religious mind that can't be changed, not teachable

Again, we note that not all of Ham's sons' families are mentioned. Ham's genealogy represents the middle court of the Tabernacle of God. Many Christians refer to this as a place of Pentecost, being spirit-filled, mature in Christ, etc. In Old Testament times, it was the Holy place where only the Levitical priesthood was allowed to enter. If Ham's genealogy is a type and shadow of the personalities and characters that reflects the middle court, we need to re-evaluate our own judgmental views of what God calls good and righteous and what we do!

Scripture informs us in Genesis 10:10 that the beginning of the kingdom of Babel (confusion), Erech (rebellion), Accad (subtle), Calneh (fortress), in the land of Shinar (2 rivers, doubleminded) came from the genealogy of Ham. Out of this land of the middle court mindset also came the city of Ashur (happy, success), Nineveh (pagan gods), Rehoboth (center of city focus, self-centered), Calah (maturity), and Resen (bridle of a horse, control).

Moving into the outer court of the Tabernacle of God, we have the genealogy of Shem:

Elam - eternity, distant
Asshur - happy, successful
Arphaxad - doesn't want the milk of the mother
Lud - strideful
Aram - exhausted, prideful
Aram's sons:

Uz - council of words, knows everything in his mind
Hul - circle, keeps going over the same thing, can't make decisions
Gether - fear of unknown
Mash - drawing out, draining
Arphaaxad's son:
Salah - sprout
Salah's son:
Eber - region beyond
Eber's sons:
Peleg - division, earthquake
Joktan - small, little
Joktan's sons:
Almodad - not measured (the outer court is not measured)
Sheleph - extracted or drawn forth
Hazarmaveth - village of death
Jerah - new moon
Hadoram - noble honor
Uzal - I shall be flooded
Diklah - palm grows
Obal - stripped bare
Abimael - father is God
Sheba - oath or covenant
Ophir - reduced to ashes
Havilah - circular
Jobab - hatred, howling like a dog

Scripture informs us that Shem's families dwelled from Mesha (freedom, eternity) to Sephar (numbered, time) of a mount of the east (new beginnings).

This chapter ends by repeating that these are the families of the sons of Noah. They came out of the seed that Noah produced, and they came after the flood. Even though this chapter does not continue on with the genealogy of the man named Eber, it is continued in the next chapter. From his lineage we find the man called Abraham that God said ALL families of the earth would be blessed through.

The ways of God are foolishness to the natural man's understanding. We can not interpret God's word with boundaries that most people may be able to fit into, yet leave some people. God uses the word ALL throughout Scripture in the context of ALL. His Tabernacle, or dwelling place, includes all 3 courts, as well as, what is outside the courts. When the High Priest went into the Holy of Holies once a year, the sins were forgiven for ALL the people, not just the ones inside the courts, and not just the ones that were aware of what the High Priest was doing.

Most people have at least two names. The last name gives identity to their natural heritage. The first name gives identity to their place and position of their God identity for His glory. Few people would consider naming a child Lazarus which means "no hope," but God had a plan of taking "no hope" and resurrecting life to him for ALL generations to witness that the power of the WORD creates LIFE or DEATH.

It is God's will that no one should perish, but ALL come into the kingdom of God. When we put limitations and conditions on people's lives of what they should or shouldn't be doing based on how we have interpreted God's word, we may be hindering the unity and development of the body of Christ that is not suppose to be manifested for generations to come. There is the realm of life where what we sow we will reap. It doesn't take being a Christian to justify the laws of God and the consequences of the law. Being born again, born from above, means that today we live in the age of the Dispensation of GRACE where the law cannot go. Because of the amazing GRACE and LOVE God bestowed on us while we were in the pit of ignorance and hell, we now have that same power and authority to release to others.

Jesus Christ is the head of the WHOLE body. He died for the sins of the world. Our belief or unbelief does not change the fact of what He did. Our belief is supposed to bring unity in working with Him to bring forth the manifestation of His coming. However, those that do not believe have just as significant a part in what God is doing for the whole body. God allows the rain and sun to bless the righteous and the unrighteous. It is the responsibility of the Holy Spirit to draw all men to the Father, not ours.

Our responsibility as believers is for non-believers to see Jesus in us (the character and nature of our Heavenly Father), so that the whole earth will be filled with His glory.

With all the diversity and uniqueness in the body of Christ, the testimony of this message is to enter into His gates with praise and thanksgiving. Each of us has a song in our heart waiting to be released into the atmosphere that gives praises unto God. It is the beginning of any fine musical piece. Then comes the REST. The REST is not the end of the song, but determines how the song is to be continued. If our desire is to come into His presence into the Holy of Holies and stay there resting with Him in heavenly places, we will die. Our Heavenly Father's ways are new every morning and are meant to be released in the earth, bringing others to the Father. Resting with our Beloved Savior and Lord Jesus Christ is not the end of the song, but the opportunity to arise and shine for our LIGHT has COME.

And the Spirit and the Bride say come (Rev. 22:17).

CHAPTER 35

DESTINY: ASK FOR CHANGE IN THE SEASON OF CHANGE

"Cause My people to remember where I have been with them, so they will see me in where I am taking them."

We must begin with a song in our hearts, the shofar of the voice of the Lord is blowing.

Psalm 81:

Sing aloud unto God our strength: make a joyful noise unto the God of Jacob.

Take a psalm, and bring hither the timbre, the pleasant harp with the psaltery.

Blow up the trumpet in the new moon, in the time appointed, on our solemn feast day.

For this was a statute for Israel, and a law of the God of Jacob.

This he ordained in Joseph for a testimony, when he went out through the land of Egypt: where I heard a language that I understood not.

I removed his shoulder from the burden: his hands were delivered from the pots.

Thou called in trouble, and I delivered thee; I answered thee in the secret place of thunder: I proved thee at the waters of Meribah (troubles). Selah.

Hear, O my people, and I will testify unto thee: O Israel, if thou wilt hearken unto me;

There shall no strange god be in thee; neither shalt thou worship any strange god.

I am the LORD thy God, which brought thee out of the land of Egypt: open thy mouth wide, and I will fill it.

We are told in 1 Chronicles 12:32, *"The men of Issachar, knew what to do for Israel because they had understanding of the times and season."*

Zech. 10:1 says, *"ASK OF the Lord rain in the time of the latter or spring rain. It is the Lord Who makes lightnings which usher in the rain and give men showers, and grass to everyone in the field."*

Daniel tells us in Chapter 2, *"Blessed be the name of God for ever and ever: for wisdom and might are his: And he changes the times and the seasons: he removes kings, and sets up kings: he gives wisdom unto the wise, and knowledge to them that know understanding: He reveals the deep and secret things: he knows what is in the darkness, and the light dwells with him."*

Prov. 25:2 says, *"It is the glory of God to conceal a thing: but the honor of kings is to search out a matter."*

Today, we live in a universe of WORDS. Words alone have the power to produce life or death anywhere in the world in a moment, in a twinkling of an eye, or a click of a button.

Words create; they have the ability to produce. They can cause a heart to leap, or they can cause sadness and sorrow. Someone can give you a report that will make you happy, or make you sad.

Words have the power and ability to carry energy to penetrate into the patterns of our thinking, releasing chemicals into our body that gradually affect every cell of our body, creating life or death.

Words can carry faith, happiness, and joy, but they can also cause depression, sickness, and disease.

Out of our mouth we are judged by the words we say. They are clothed thoughts that are identified by what is inside of us when we speak them.

"Man does not live on bread alone but on every word that comes from the mouth of the LORD" (Deut. 8:3).

"Heaven and earth shall pass away: but my words shall not pass away" (Mark 13:31).

A parent can speak a word over their children, and that word has the ability to form the destiny of their life. When a parent names their children, there is a word taking form. Scripture shows us that naming a child creates an identity.

In Genesis 35:18 after Rachel gave birth to her second son, the Scripture tells us that she named her son one name, but Jacob changed it to another. *"As her soul was departing, for she died, she called his name Ben-oni [son of my sorrow]; but his father called him Benjamin [son of the right hand]."*

WE are entering the season where the earth is controlled by the WORDS of our mouth. These words have the ability to travel around the world in a twinkle of the eye, a click off the button, and instantly we can cause unity or destruction in the hearts of men (John1:1-16):

1 *In the beginning was the Word* (Christ), *and the Word* (Christ) *was with God, and the Word* (Christ) *was God.*

2 *The same was in the beginning with God.*

3 *All things were made by him; and without him was not anything made that was made.*

4 *In him was life; and the life was the light of men.*

5 *And the light shines in darkness; and the darkness comprehended it not.*

6 *There was a man sent from God, whose name was John.*

7 *The same came for a witness, to bear witness of the Light that all men through him might believe.*

8 *He was not that Light, but was sent to bear witness of that Light.*

9 *That was the true Light, which lights every man that cometh into the world.*

10 *He was in the world, and the world was made by him, and the world knew him not.*

11 *He came unto his own, and his own received him not.*

12 *But as many as received him, to them gave he power to become the sons of God, even to them that believe on his name:*

13 *Which were born, not of blood, nor of the will of the flesh, nor of the will of man, but of God.*

14 *And the Word* (Christ) *was made flesh, and dwelt among us, (and we beheld his glory, the glory as of the only begotten of the Father,) full of grace and truth.*

15 *John* (Love) *bare witness of him, and cried, saying, this was he of whom I spoke, He that cometh after me is preferred before me: for he was before me.*

16 *And of his fullness have all we received, and grace for grace.*

While we are in the midst of change in the valley of darkness, death, ignorance, sickness, job loss, financial issues, or even our unknowns, the Lord has already prepared a table before us while our enemies are all around us. He desires to unveil to us that we are God's favored with all spiritual blessings of Heaven today. However, without partaking of the blessing, eating the food the Lord has prepared for you, you cannot be transformed into the fullness of the blessing that is at hand. If you are dehydrated and there is a gallon of water in front of you, until you drink the water, your body will stay dehydrated.

The WORD must be internalized to bring forth transformation. Just talking about it doesn't make things happen. *"Just as the body without the spirit is dead, so faith without works is dead also"* (James 2:26). *"Without faith it is impossible to please him: for he that cometh to God must believe that he is, and that he rewards them that diligently seek him"* (Hebrew 11:6).

The WORD of God tells us that on this table set before us we have been served:

Double portion blessings, abundance of harvest blessings, restoration of lost years blessings, miracles, signs, and wonders, the presence of God in our midst blessings, deliverance of sickness, affliction, and poverty blessings, unity of family and legacy blessings. We have blessings that we are a child of the King, a son of God, and a bride of Christ. Today, we are the heir of the Great I AM made in our Heavenly Father's image. We are the salt of the earth and a light of the world. We are an ambassador of love, a winner, a champion. We are more than conquerors, and no weapon formed against us shall prosper. We are inseparable from God's love because we are the temple of God. We are each a unique master piece of God's handiwork.

This is the table the Lord has Prepared for us to partake of which will prepare us for where He is taking us in our tomorrows. But, how do we get to this place to have the assurance of where He is taking us? We may be eating the goodness of the Lord, but do we really know what we are eating, or are we asking, "What is it?" Are we eating manna or the bread of LIFE?

Before a banqueting table is set, there is a lot of behind the scene preparation that begins with visions and thoughts. Those that have prepared a feast for the holiday family gathering have put in a lot of love, time, and thought to make that moment of togetherness special, even though it may only last a fraction of the amount of time that went into the preparation. We may see ourselves now as only surviving as Jonathan's son Mephibosheth did calling himself a "dead dog," but when he was summoned before King David, God had already prepared the way for him to sit at the King's table, not just to survive, but to thrive, receiving back what had been stolen because he was a king's son (2 Sam. 9).

Let's take a look at how our Heavenly Father has been preparing High Places as one prepares a prince for this time and hour to rule and reign as kings and priests unto the Lord.

The Lord's shofar was heard the very first time at Mt. Sinai with all Israel present in giving of the Torah. Today, we celebrate this time as when the church was formed and the Holy Spirit came upon the believers all in one accord; they sounded as the voice of the Lord being released in the upper room. Matt. 24:27-28, *"For just as the lightning (power) comes from the east (the turmoil) and shines and is seen as far as the west, so will the coming (Parousia, to be present, to be at hand) of the Son of Man within the midst. For wherever there is a fallen body (a mountain collapsing), there the eagles will flock together declaring it is finished."*

The Gospel of Jesus Christ is the power of reconciliation, speaking to the darkness of this world as the light of the world breaking the bondage around each mountain and setting the captives free. We each have a key to unlock the mysteries of Heaven, and every key is necessary for the fullness to be manifested. No one person has all the keys. We each need to find our key and unlock the door before us, because until you use your key, someone else may not be able to unlock their door.

In Matthew 16 we read in the Message translation a conversation Jesus is having with His disciples about His identity: "*When Jesus arrived in the villages of Caesarea Philippi, he asked his disciples, 'What are people saying about who the Son of Man is?' They replied, 'Some think he is John the Baptizer, some say Elijah, some Jeremiah or one of the other prophets.' He pressed them, 'And how about you? Who do you say I am?'*

Simon Peter said, 'You're the Christ, the Messiah, the Son of the living God.' Jesus came back, 'God bless you, Simon, son of Jonah! You didn't get that answer out of books or from teachers. My Father in heaven, God himself, let you in on this secret of who I really am. And now I'm going to tell you who you are, really are. You are Peter, a rock. This is the rock on which I will put together my church, a church so expansive with energy that not even the gates of hell will be able to keep it out. And that's not all. You will have complete and free access to God's kingdom, keys to open any and every door: no more barriers between heaven and earth, earth and heaven. A yes on earth is yes in heaven. A no on earth is no in heaven.'"

We were taught that every good promise in the word, the Bible, is ours. God is not going to keep us in darkness. Christians have the ability to set the spiritual climate in their area by the WORD released from their mouth and the meditations from their heart if they are acceptable and in right order with the Son of God.

Living victorious is recognizing that one season is ending and a new season is struggling to be born. Our minds have to change from the way our Christian walk was before in order to function in our full anointing. The body of Christ would be coming into seven spheres or seven mountains that would be our responsibility to be the head and not the tail: Business, education, family, media, art, and religion.

Friends don't know the keys of the master's house, but family does.

We are in new times and new seasons. We must discipline ourselves to think the way of God which is New Covenant. Within the hardness that is found from last season, there is still a river of life to bring forth a new season; however, the debris of yesterday can put a block to our blessing of life today.

What stirs our passions will help us find our personal key that God will use to unlock the doors of His mysteries to His Kingdom now. We are connected to 3 tribes as a foundation of our spiritual roots that we must each analyze within our hearts:

Judah - the tribe of praise. The Apostolic tribe that leads forth with praise, filling the atmosphere with song, both singing to Him, but also we need to come to a oneness of hearing that same song in our heart being sung by His Spirit in us to us.

Zebulon - braking old patterns with a willingness to seek something new and unusual. Keep in mind that Our Heavenly Father's ways are new every morning.

Issachar - new times and seasons are accompanied with the sound of the prophetic. If we are hearing the same message of our relationship with the Father as we did last year or the year before, we are forming a religion and not a relationship of oneness to do the Father's business.

God used these three tribes to lead the whole house of Israel into a battle that was already won through the praises of His people. The WORD of our Heavenly Father has spoken our potential, but we have to decide what is holding us back from manifesting what He has decreed in our lives.

1. Are we hanging on to the past even though the WORD tells us we are a chosen generation, a new creature, all things are past?
2. Are we repeating the cycle of the way we use to do things? Is your life manifesting the blessings of God today in greater abundance than you were a few years ago, a year ago, six months ago? Do you have a testimony that says, "Look what the Lord has done" that is fresh, not many years ago, but new?
3. How do we see ourselves? What do we see ourselves accomplishing? Are we surviving or thriving even though we are surrounded by enemies in business, finance, health, family, government, media, and/or education? What is holding you back from eating what the Lord has prepared for you?

4. Do you allow other's views to hinder your potential? Are you honoring God with what you have, so He can take the small things and transform them into His greatness?

In Exodus 19:5-6 we read: *"Now therefore, if you will obey My voice in truth and keep My covenant, then you shall be My own peculiar possession and treasure from among and above all peoples; for all the earth is Mine. And you shall be to Me a kingdom of priests, a holy nation [consecrated, set apart to the worship of God]. These are the words you shall speak to the Israelites."*

God wants us to understand the language of God, having the mind of Christ. We have the ability to know all things. Our mission is not just to make it into heaven, but to manifest what God designed for us to do now. It takes God to love God.

Hebrew 6:1-5 AMP says, *"THEREFORE LET us go on and get past the elementary stage in the teachings and doctrine of Christ (the Messiah), advancing steadily toward the completeness and perfection that belong to spiritual maturity. Let us not again be laying the foundation of repentance and abandonment of dead works (dead formalism) and of the faith [by which you turned] to God, With teachings about purifying, the laying on of hands, the resurrection from the dead, and eternal judgment and punishment. [These are all matters of which you should have been fully aware long, long ago.] If indeed God permits, we will [now] proceed [to advanced teaching]. For it is impossible [to restore and bring again to repentance] those who have been once for all enlightened, who have consciously tasted the heavenly gift and have become sharers of the Holy Spirit, And have felt how good the Word of God is and the mighty powers of the age and world to come."*

Isaiah 61:5-6, *"Aliens shall stand [ready] and feed your flocks, and foreigners shall be your plowmen and your vinedressers. But you shall be called the priests of the Lord; people will speak of you as the ministers of our God. You shall eat the wealth of the nations, and the glory [once that of your captors] shall be yours."*

We were born at such a time as this to make a footprint in the earth that will never be erased. We are heirs to the KING, as kings and priest with the ability to draw a line in the power of Jesus's name bringing God's Kingdom into manifestation on this earth. It was decreed that we would obtain Kingdom living, God's laws of economics, God's supernatural increase, and God's authority would flow with fresh anointing in the fields we are in. God wants us to get to the place in our heart to unveil His purpose of why we were conceived at this time in history.

Our key timing is with the Hebrew Calendar and the Feast of the Lord. We have been in seed time and now we are in harvest time. The kingdoms of this world must be engaged with the kingdom of God in us as salt and light. It is the Holy Spirit and the blood of Jesus Christ that makes a way for us to crossover from yesterday's season, but we must also be discerners that the enemy will also try to cross over by utilizing our emotions.

In the position of being priests, the souls of our feet must step into the high waters of the unknown of our future in order to have the ability to feed others from a kingship position. Every place that God will send us, He has already gone, but we must bring the authority of our position and right to see the unveiling. Once we prepare ourselves as a bride of Christ to be one with Him, and an ambassador of the Lord to represent His power and authority in a foreign land, we will be ready to step into the high waters (Joshua 3:13, Josh. 1:2, Acts. 16:6). We have to trust 100% in Him that He will part the waters of our red sea with no compromising the position we hold.

I encourage you to be watchful of the spirit of antichrist, also known as anti-anointing. This spirit tries to keep the church of Jesus Christ bound, denying the Kingdom manifest in the natural on the earth. We each have a marketplace ministry defined by our everyday paths of life's journey, not just the church building. Every assignment from God has a sphere where God wants us to take the territory for His Kingdom.

We are in a mercy season where Jesus wants us to understand the culture with the relationship of the Father influencing the world with His glory, not with guilt or condemnation religion.

We are in a phase of conversion. We have received the invitation from God (heavenly realm) to bring heaven's power and authority, activating eternity into the midst of time. We are moving in the power of the eternal while in our natural body.

When we do our gifting of what God calls us to do in this season, then things are attracted to us. Depression is the harassment of hell to pressure the conversion of our giftedness to express our glory in God. Our battle is not with the world, but within ourselves of where God is taking us. The enemy knows this and is trying to keep us from the blessing. We battle with the territory God has placed us in that the enemy is trying to possess and keep us from dominion and power in our sphere to work for the Lord.

We do not wrestle with present circumstances but the barrier of what we are about to occupy. Jesus wrestled with Satan, the (master-ego), for 40 days. "If you are..." will be the antichrist voice that whispers in your ear.

Our first battle is within ourselves. We must gain sphere authority of where we are at. Whatever we bow the knee to on the way to the top, we will have to confront when we get there. It is not just what we do in worship, but what we become.

In our conversion, be prepared to be out of control in many areas. Your gift will attract blessing, but also hassle. If God's favor is on the gift, then there is peace, so don't chase after validation. For every level of depth of the sphere we are to take authority over, we will encounter a process to deal with between self and God's identity in us. There are seven major powers of influences in the world. They are: arts, politics, education, media, economics, entertainments, and religion.

Smaller territorial areas that feed these are: race, cultural, gender, and age.

Jesus gave the disciples the keys to pray to the Father with these words, *"Pray, therefore, like this: Our Father Who is in heaven, hallowed (kept holy) be Your name. Your kingdom come, your will be done on earth as it is in heaven."*

If you were to write your own obituaries, would God bless you with the satisfaction that you finished the purpose for your life? Could we describe ourselves the way God sees us that would be a blessing to Him. When God speaks over us, He is putting demands on Himself to be manifested. We take the Lord's name in vain when we counter His WORD that is in us with our own words that are contradictory to His.

Living in the will of God is to let go of the old while the new is struggling to emerge. Our fight is for the future, closing the gap between heaven and earth. Every mountain has a history, but we each have a personal history that must be redeemed back to God.

God seeds the bride of Christ, the womb of Adam. The body carries the seed until the time of birth to release the LIFE as rivers of living water, circumcised by the heart and spoken into our sphere to take the mountain that God wants us to take. **We will know by the passion and desire He gives us what our mountain is. We will function and conquer in LOVE, not works.**

Jesus has already won every mountain. A person with faith having a personal intimacy with Christ will cause intimidation to Satan, forcing the enemy to flee. Caleb took the land without firing one shot or arrow.

Today, we are raised up and seated in places of authority because we are in Christ (Col. 1:27).

Isaiah 33:5-6 declaring, *"There is a Kingdom invasion taking place now with revelation, wisdom, and words that no other generation has heard. The Kingdom of Heaven is an eternal realm, not just in our mind and not some place we are going. It is the alpha and omega. The Kingdom of God is: Christ in you, righteousness, peace, and joy. There is pressure in us as this kingdom merges with the kingdom of the world."*

God does not need us on the other side in the invisible realm of heaven. The Kingdom of God is being released in the earth, and we are caught in the middle. As God brings the Kingdom of Heaven into our atmosphere, the Kingdom of God (Christ in us) will exist. *"The last enemy that shall be destroyed is death. For he hath put all things under his feet. But when he saith all things are put under him, it is manifest that he is accepted, which did put all things under him. And when all things shall be subdued unto him, then shall the Son also himself be subject unto him that put all things under him, that God may be all in all"* (1 Cor. 15:26-28).

We have the power an authority to claim Christ's love and perfection here and NOW.

When our voices release the WORD, we are as a pregnant wife of Christ, giving LIFE to the Life in our belly. Revelation 12 talks about this hour. Our words have the ability to bring Heaven/eternity into time. We have great responsibility for those in a weaker position. If we glorify God from the top of the mountain, not just when we are in the valley of the shadow of death, the anointed blessing will flow off of us to those in the valley.

The number 666 is the invasion mode into evil where evil is having its final manifestation. We can stop the momentum of hell by our anointing and favor we have with God. The anointing is the carrier, and the favor is the impression we leave of the assignment given. We are in a season of apostolic reformation, bringing in the Kingdom of Heaven through the Kingdom of God, Christ in you.

We have the ability to clean the terrain, diseases, negative issues, and anything that does not line up with the identity of God's presence. We can detoxify our environment by bringing in peace, prayer, and intercession, but it must have the heartbeat of the Father's love and compassion.

All failure is insufficient understanding of the revelation, missing keys, and/or insufficient flowing of the anointing.

This Passover season, we are reminded of the great significance of the Blood Life given to us by Jesus Christ when He died and rose again. This blood is in us, and as the body of Christ, we are bone of His bone and flesh of His flesh. We are all, together, new creations in Christ Jesus, and that the life that we now live in our body is the Life of Christ. All things are new, and all things are of God. We learned that the blood remembers, so that when something tries to attack us we can lift up His authority in us saying, "STOP" for the blood of Jesus carries within it the remembrance that the issue has already been cleansed and redeemed, and that no weapon trying to form against us can prosper.

With this season of the Lord's Feast and the preparations we spent so much time and energy, let us also be learning about our gifting's that Paul wrote about in Romans 12:2-11:

"Do not be conformed to this world (this age), [fashioned after and adapted to its external, superficial customs], but be transformed (changed) by the [entire] renewal of your mind [by its new ideals and its new attitude], so that you may prove [for yourselves] what is the good and acceptable and perfect will of God, even the thing which is good and acceptable and perfect [in His sight for you].

For by the grace (unmerited favor of God) given to me I warn everyone among you not to estimate and think of himself more highly than he ought [not to have an exaggerated opinion of his own importance], but to rate his ability with sober judgment, each according to the degree of faith apportioned by God to him.

For as in one physical body we have many parts (organs, members) and all of these parts do not have the same function or use,

So we, numerous as we are, are one body in Christ (the Messiah) and individually we are parts one of another [mutually dependent on one another].

Having gifts (faculties, talents, qualities) that differ according to the grace given us, let us use them: [He whose gift is] prophecy, [let him prophesy] according to the proportion of his faith;

[He whose gift is] practical service, let him give himself to serving; he who teaches, to his teaching;

He who exhorts (encourages), to his exhortation; he who contributes (giver), let him do it in simplicity and liberality; he who gives aid and superintends (ruler), with zeal and singleness of mind; he who does acts of mercy, with genuine cheerfulness and joyful eagerness.

[Let your] love be sincere (a real thing); hate what is evil [loathe all ungodliness, turn in horror from wickedness], but hold fast to that which is good.

Love one another with brotherly affection [as members of one family], giving precedence and showing honor to one another.

Never lag in zeal and in earnest endeavor; be aglow and burning with the Spirit, serving the Lord.

With each of these gifts, we learned their foundational principles, the demonic strongholds, the root iniquity, the essential virtues, the curses on the birthright, and the blessings needed for effectiveness and unity to the body of Christ. Again, we were encouraged to function in our gifting in the marketplaces of the mountain the Lord has positioned us to take: government, business, education, family, media, arts & entertainment, and religion.

We must learn the relationship differences of being a slave, a servant, a friend, a child, and a son of the Most High God. Slaves, servants, and friends may have very close relationships with God, but not as Father. A child of God needs to be taken care of, always looking out for themselves and their needs. They know God as Father, but their focus is what God can do for them.

The maturity of moving from being a child of God into being a son of God prepares us to do the business of our Heavenly Father on this earth. Sons are given keys to unlock the mysteries of God (Prov. 25:2). We also learned that a "sonship" relationship allows us to become brides of oneness.

At Pentecost, we are encouraged to partake of the new wine, the new outlook, with a new song in our hearts, confessing boldly of who I AM with a new prayer, new strategies, new life styles, new identity, new language, and new relationships. God is shifting the circumstances of our life to fit

His Divine plan for today to be manifested in this world. We have been birthed into time for such a time as this.

The manifestation of this process begins with functioning in agape love instead of phileo love. Phileo love will deny agape love when the going gets rough. It comes from the Tree of Knowledge and is the best that can be offered. It has a basis of Eros connection. Agape love comes from the Tree of Life. A key difference between the two is conditional or unconditional. A oneness, covenant love with Christ instead of a follower of Christ. We learned that in Christ there is no condemnation. *"THEREFORE, [there is] now no condemnation (no adjudging guilty of wrong) for those who are in Christ Jesus, who live [and] walk not after the dictates of the flesh, but after the dictates of the Spirit. For the law of the Spirit of life [which is] in Christ Jesus [the law of our new being] has freed me from the law of sin and of death"* (Romans 8:1-2).

God speaks His WORD through us and it is placed in time. In the fullness of time, that truth becomes known, setting the captive free. When we accept the fact that God cannot lie and His WORD will not return void, we accept that His promises must come to past. The blessings of God are looking for us because God has already sent them. When all "hell" is breaking loose, we must stand by faith that it is just a matter of time that His promises will be manifested. It is time to position ourselves for the revelation of what has been spoken bringing LIGHT to our mind, quickening our spirit to bring forth resurrection life from within. We must awaken what has been asleep. Our prayer should be as the prayer that Jesus prayed to the Father in John 17. Not what God can do for us, but doing the Father's business as a son in Christ Jesus.

God wants us to trust Him so completely that we don't even know that we are being tried. Jesus is the firstborn who received the double portion which He then gave to us. We are God's dream, and what He will do in our Life because of His love and desire that He has for us. God so loved us, He gave us His son; while we were still in darkness, He declared the end from the beginning. **Our job is to own the dream**

in our heart before it comes to manifestation. We have to conceive the dream first before giving birth.

With these tools and revelation we have: identify our vision, declare a mission statement that God has given, be convinced of who you are in God, establish a plan (short and long term), develop a routine, practice consistently, measure results (are you moving in faith more than fear?) take your mountain and give glory to God over the process and journey, not just the victory.

We are not dealing with the sin of commission because we are in the season of grace and mercy; however, because of fear, complacency, doubt, and insecurities we can fail to do what we are supposed to do, giving Satan a legal right by our own actions. The sin of omission is the failure to activate the promises of God with authority. This must be dealt with as we approach the fall feasts.

God has made us accepted in the beloved as joint heirs with Jesus Christ. We are throne worthy with His power and authority. From a Sonship level of maturity, we must enter a relationship of Oneness gathering together in oneness as a consuming fire, complete, Holy, Life giving identity in Christ Jesus. This is a marriage relationship of intimacy of consummation.

The preparation for this is as a bride of Christ so that on the Day of Atonement we enter into the Holy of Holies in oneness. We have been told of our oneness as being favored of God by the WORD of our beloved. We have partaken of the banqueting table being transformed in His image as we have been eating of the Lamb (I AM). We have fellowshipped in a Tabernacle experience of oneness to now enter into the world all together new.

A bride is only a bride for a day, and then she becomes a wife with the anticipation of carrying the seed of her beloved to give birth to a son. The Word is made flesh and dwells among men. Our security is not in what we do, but being in Him.

Romans 8:31-39:

- God is for me, I am favored.
- He freely gives us all things, lacking nothing.
- He is our defense attorney against the accuser.
- There is now no condemnation. Again, we are favored.
- Nothing can separate us from God's love.
- In all the tribulations, we are more than conquers.

Jesus told religion: *"I assure you, most solemnly I tell you, he who believes in Me [who adheres to, trusts in, relies on, and has faith in Me] has (now possesses) eternal life. I am the Bread of Life [that gives life—the Living Bread]. Your forefathers ate the manna in the wilderness, and [yet] they died. [But] this is the Bread that comes down from heaven, so that [any] one may eat of it and never die. I [Myself] am this Living Bread that came down from heaven. If anyone eats of this Bread, he will live forever; and also the Bread that I shall give for the life of the world is My flesh (body)"* (John 6:47-51). The consummation of oneness allows His life to be released through us.

Psalm 23: Are we eating from His table and drinking the blood of the Lamb?

- On this table we have the dish.
- You are beyond condemnation.
- You are perfect.
- You belong to the King and are heir to the throne of God.
- You have immediate access to His Holy presence.
- You are part of His royal priesthood.
- You are always surrounded by His presence.
- Your inheritance will never perish and is always complete in all things.
- You have every spiritual blessing now that can be released from the Kingdom of Heaven into this world according to the power and authority of Christ in you.

- You are perfect, a winner, a champion, victorious, loved, excellent, praiseworthy, pure, righteous, and created in the image of the great I AM.

So where do we go from here? What is our destiny?

To take the preparations that we have experienced this past year and out of His rest, His Holy presence with the Father's blessings to, *"Be fruitful, multiply, and fill the earth, and subdue it [using all its vast resources in the service of God and man]; and have dominion over the fish of the sea, the birds of the air, and over every living creature that moves upon the earth."* (Gen. 1:26).

"For God, who commanded the light to shine out of darkness, hath shined in our hearts, to give the light of the knowledge of the glory of God in the face of Jesus Christ" (2 Cor. 4:6).

"Then in the Spirit He conveyed us away to a vast and lofty mountain and exhibited to us the holy (hallowed, consecrated) city of Jerusalem descending out of heaven from God, Clothed in God's glory [in all its splendor and radiance]. The luster of it resembled a rare and most precious jewel, like jasper, shining clear as crystal" (Rev. 21:10-12).

"For in the year that King Uzziah died (strongholds of the world), I saw the Lord sitting upon a throne, high and lifted up, and the skirts of His train (the bridal veil of His beloved) filled the most holy part of the temple. And in this place the Spirit and the bride say, come. Let him that hears say, Come. And let him that is thirsty come. And whosoever will, let him take the water of life freely" (Isaiah 6:1-2, Rev. 22:17).

Our destiny is not about us, but a oneness in Him, so together, every breath fills the temple singing "Holy, holy, holy is the Lord of hosts; so that the whole earth is full of His glory!"

For the LORD said unto Joshua, *"This day have I rolled away the reproach of Egypt from off you"* (Joshua 5:9).

"For we are God's masterpiece. He has created us anew in Christ Jesus, so we can do the good things he planned for us long ago" (Eph. 2:10 lv).

"For we are a chosen people. WE are royal priests, a holy nation, God's very own possession. As a result, we each can show others the goodness of God, for he called us out of the darkness into his wonderful light" (1 Peter 2:9).

"For as He is, so are we in this world" (1 John 4:17).

CHAPTER 36

THE LATTER RAINS POUR FORTH, JUBILEE IS NOW

Our call of God brings us into salvation, our purpose on this earth, life and intimacy with HIM, and our likeness of HIM. However, it also brings us to the cross, into persecution, rejection, and separation of the things of this world. Hebrew 12:2 says, *"Looking unto Jesus the author and finisher of our faith; who* ***for the joy*** *that was set before him endured the cross, despising the shame, and is set down at the right hand of the throne of God."* **The wealth and abundance of this inheritance is here for us now.**

The hope of the calling is on the other side of the cross. However, if we lose sight of the joy we will not be able to endure the cross that is set before us to go through and BE the resurrected Christ today while in our natural body that God has called us to move and function in on this earth (Philippians 3:11). Most Christians today are walking in compromise, grieving the Holy Spirit in them, and not in the renewed power and authority that was given to the body of Christ at Pentecost over 2,000 years ago. Today, the Spirit of God is moving around the world and calling forth a company of people to arise and shine for your LIGHT has come. The bridegroom calls. The trumpet is sounding!

We are to KNOW the hope of our calling no matter what the difficulty is, never losing sight of the joy of the LORD that is in our midst and gives us the strength to BE the LIGHT of the world, as HE is (John 4:17).

Paul shares this message to the church in Ephesus 1 when he writes:

1. God gave us all spiritual blessings from heaven in Christ in us.
2. God ordained this before the foundation of the world that we are HOLY and blameless before HIM in love, HIS love.
3. We are accepted in the beloved, Christ Jesus as one in HIM.
4. We have total redemption in HIS blood, filled with the abundance of HIS grace and mercy
5. He has abounded toward us all wisdom, power, and authority that was given to Jesus Christ through the Holy Spirit.

"That in the dispensation of the fullness of times he might gather together in one all things in Christ, both which are in heaven, and which are on earth; even in him: In whom also we have obtained an inheritance, being predestinated according to the purpose of him who worked all things after the counsel of his own will: That we should be to the praise of his glory, who first trusted in Christ."

Believers are not getting punished for sin because of the blood of Jesus Christ cleansing us from all unrighteousness is a completeness within itself that most Christians rest in until they die to go on the other side to be with the Lord, never realizing that the fullness of the redemption of the cross was to experience spirit, soul, and body of Christ's resurrection Life on this side of death. He gave us the same power and authority that raised Jesus from death, hell, and the grave to be released in our natural bodies.

A key for this to be seen in manifestation and glory is when a company of people put aside their own agenda of glory, and bring to the alter what the Lord has given to them alone, no titles, no positions, no gifts, no doctrines, no traditions, no politics, no gender issues, no racial issues, no cultural issues, no financial or education issues, or anything else that would separate the body from the love of God only. We must recognize the unique creation of our God identity that is necessary for the whole body to come together in the unity of HIS faith in Christ Jesus. Some will be likened to a big toe and another to the hairs on the head, but both need one another.

Let us say "yes" to God allowing Him to have HIS way in each of us so that we can rule and reign with HIM now.

"Let the eyes of your understanding being enlightened; that ye may know what is the hope of his calling, and what the riches of the glory of HIS inheritance in the saints, And what is the exceeding greatness of his power to us-ward who believe, according to the working of his mighty power, Which he wrought in Christ, when he raised him from the dead, and set him at his own right hand in the heavenly places..." (Ephesians 1:18).

GOD has an inheritance in YOU, and His calling in you is to unveil HIS inheritance!

Whatever our circumstance is right now, if we are setting the joy of the LORD before us, we should see it as IMPOSSIBLE to have fear, worry, insecurity, or fret over the temporary issues the world is dealing with. Paul is writing his letter to BELIEVERS in CHRIST, not unbelievers. If this is not our position while going through trials and tribulations, we are miles away from the truth that we are GOD's delight and we are not tapping into HIS inheritance that is available to us now.

You are HIS inheritance, FILLED with richness, glory, and power because you have the HOLY Spirit in you. It is this same power that raised Jesus from the dead!

"And what is the exceeding greatness of his power to us-ward who believe, according to the working of his mighty power, Which he wrought in Christ, when he raised him from the dead, and set him at his own right hand in the heavenly places, Far above all principality, and power, and might, and dominion, and every name that is named, not only in this world, but also in that which is to come" (Ephesians 1:19-21).

When we acknowledged that Jesus Christ saved us from sin, we too were raised from the dead. We too are today seated with HIM in heavenly places above EVERY power and principality and dominion in this world. There is no greater power anywhere than the power of the HOLY Spirit who lives in the believer!

He put all things under HIS feet... your feet are HIS. This is dynamos power, earth shattering, and mountain moving power that is beyond measurement. Jesus made this power available for every believer and there is not a devil in the world that has greater power over the power of the Holy Spirit in you. Grieve not the Holy Spirit today.

The solution to every world issue is to know who you are in Christ. When God is walking with you in the cool of the day and He calls your name, do not hide behind a situation, a title, a denomination or doctrine. Simply let HIM hear HIS name in you... here I AM.

God fellowships with His own...I AM that I AM...

EPILOGUE

Christ comes in the voice of the archangel...YOU!

"For the Lord himself shall descend from heaven with a shout, with the voice of the archangel, and with the trump of God: and the dead in Christ shall rise first" (1 Thessalonians 4:16).

Christ comes in the voice of the chief messenger:

"And there was war in heaven: Michael and his angels fought against the dragon; and the dragon fought and his angels, and prevailed not; neither was their place found any more in heaven" (Revelation 12:7-8).

Michael means, "One like god."

Christ comes in the message using YOU as the messenger. He comes in the voice **in you** that is witnessed by the written word and the Holy Spirit unveiling **Christ in you** (Col. 1:27).

He comes in the shout, the command; His sound that brings the revelation of God (Christ identity) in you. The Word is flesh and dwells in and among us, and we beheld His glory. We are the glory of the Father (John 1:14).

Truth is not "what" which Pilate asked Jesus, but Truth is Christ. "I am the way, the truth, and the life" (John 14:6).

We waste the Lord's time to minister truth if the Spirit and Life of God are not in us. Jesus said let the dead bury the dead. There are many Christians that are dead in Christ waiting for the coming of the Lord to raise them up.

Once His Word and Spirit quicken our flesh and spirit by a relationship of intimacy (intercourse consummation) understanding, a covenant exchange takes place that cannot be separated. Our voice becomes His voice; our Spirit is His Spirit. We are the righteousness of Christ. We are bone of His bones and flesh of His flesh. We are married to HIM as our beloved, ready to go into the world as the LIGHT of the world. We are pregnant with the seed of God (His WORD) to produce LIFE.

"And God blessed them, and God said unto them, Be fruitful, and multiply, and replenish the earth, and subdue it" (Genesis 1:28).

Unless Christ descends in the voice, in the revelation of awakening us to Truth, we are as dead men walking, waiting to be risen. When He comes in the power of His authority and the command of His voice in us, the dead in Christ will be raised. There are many professional preachers that are dead in Christ.

When we hear the WORD, we cannot live on yesterday's diet—manna. **God's ways are new every morning**.

It is time for the church (the bride) of the Lord Jesus Christ to consummate the marriage of the LAMB that took place over 2,000 years ago when Jesus Christ rose from the dead.

"And Mary said to the angel, How can this be, since I have no [intimacy with any man as a] husband? Then the angel said to her, The Holy Spirit will come upon (in) *you, and the power of the Most High will overshadow* (the natural way of conception) *you [like a shining cloud]; and so the holy (pure, sinless) Thing (Offspring) which shall be born of you* (the WORD in you) *will be called the Son of God"* (Luke 1:34-35 AMP).

Christ is both male and female (Genesis 1:27). For over 2,000 years, the voice of Christ has been spoken through the male understanding and interpretation of the ways of God. It takes the female vessel of Christ to understand what it means to be the bride of Christ, and a wife carrying the seed of God to bring forth sons of God filling the earth with His IMAGE.

"Let us rejoice and shout for joy [exulting and triumphant]! Let us celebrate and ascribe to Him glory and honor, for the marriage of the Lamb [at last] has come, and His bride has prepared herself" (Revelation 12:7 AMP).

"I, Jesus, have sent My messenger (angel) to you to witness and to give you assurance of these things for the churches (assemblies). I am the Root (the Source) and the Offspring of David, the radiant and brilliant Morning Star. The [Holy] Spirit and the bride (the church, the true Christians) say, Come! And let him who is listening say, Come! And let everyone come who is thirsty [who is painfully conscious of his need of those things by which the soul is refreshed, supported, and strengthened]; and whoever [earnestly] desires to do it, let him come, take, appropriate, and drink the water of Life without cost" (Revelation 22: 16-17 AMP).

- It was the voice of the Lord that spoke at Sinai and shook the earth.
- It was His voice that said to the dead man, Lazarus, come forth.
- It was His voice that said to the widow's son to arise.
- It was His voice as the prince of peace that calmed the stormy seas.
- It was His voice that cried out it is finished, and it has been finished ever since Jesus hung on the cross.
- It was His voice that ripped the veil in two, and now we can go into the most Holy Place because of Christ in us.
- It was His voice that came from above and caused the dead to be raised.

The dead shall hear the voice of the Son of God, and shall live.

Christ is still descending in every dark place in our lives by the power of His WORD unveiling Christ in us, His body and His flesh. He is piercing and dividing us by the sword of truth, reaching into every joint and marrow where His blood is turning water into wine by discerning the thoughts and intents of our hearts.

He became flesh and dwelled IN and among US. *"And the Word (Christ) became flesh (human, incarnate) and tabernacled (fixed His tent of flesh, lived awhile) among us"* (John 1:14 AMP).

SHARING JESUS THROUGH LOVE

*I*nterfaith Chapel Service

The service began with the music "The Rose" being sung by Cecilia. I had, sitting on the alter at the front, a vase with two open red roses and a small empty bowl. Here are the words to the song:

Some say love, it is a river
that drowns the tender reed.
Some say love, it is a razor
that leaves your soul to bleed.
Some say love, it is a hunger,
an endless aching need.
I say love, it is a flower,
and you its only seed.

Welcome to the Interfaith Chapel Service.

Today, we have entered a season that is universally celebrated around the world as the opportunity to share the love in our heart with others. It is a celebration that crosses the boundaries of religions, cultures, customs, genders, ages, races, and nationalities. Even though there are many flowers in creation, this season of expressing ones love is often shared through roses. Why roses?

Carolyn Huffman, the author of *Meditations on a Rose Garden*, wrote, *"Although many of us may never wrestle with roses, we all are destined to wrestle with life as we wrestle with finding truth, love, and acceptance.*

The promises of God can be discovered in the beauty of a rose and in the reality of life."

Often we use the word "love" with vagueness and sentimentality. We give place to love as some rare and mystical event, when in fact it is our natural state of being. God so loved, He gave Himself, His Life. In doing this He opened up the opportunity for us to be able to give that unconditional love to others. When we love, we see things in other people that are hidden deep within. We see beneath the surface, to the qualities, which make that person special and unique. To see with loving eyes is to know inner beauty. To be loved is to be seen, and known as we are known to no other. One who loves us unconditionally gives us a unique gift, a piece of ourselves that has been hidden by pain, low self-esteem, and insecurities.

We, who love, can look at another's life and say, "I touched his life," or I touched her life", just as an artist might say "I touched this canvas." Those brushstrokes in the corner of this magnificent mural, those are mine. I was a part of this life, and it is a part of me like two threads crossing in different directions, yet weaving one tapestry together." The secret of unconditional love is emerged when one has a relationship with the Divine love of God. It is the emergence of the larger self. It is the finding of one's life by losing it. It is the greatest commandment given:

"Love the Lord your God with all your heart, with all your soul, and with your entire mind." (Deut. 6:5-6). When the ALL becomes you, then you can love your neighbor as yourself, as God has loved you (Mark 12:31).

While love is our natural state of being, it takes life's challenges, just as growing a rose bush, to come to a state of producing the fruit of a rose that can be given away to bless others. *"Every way of a man is right in his own eyes, but it is God who weight the heart of the issue"* (Proverbs 21:2).

The presence of giving one's life for another is the greatest gift one can give. Just as the foundation of planting a rose bush must be in good soil, so the foundation of the soil of our heart must be good soil. The good soil we receive from God comes from the Tree of Life, and is unconditionally found on the mercy seat of grace. When the conditions are right, **Love sprouts forth by the drawing of the SON and the watering of love by the seed sower.** This watering and sun life is patient and kind to the newborn seed. It does not receive pride or arrogance or unbecoming actions that would produce weeds in the soil. The sower's love protects the new growth from windstorms and heavy rains. This love from the sower watches carefully for wild growths that need gentle pruning, as he or she bears the personal burden of caring for the rose bush.

In the Message Translation of Scripture, the Apostle Paul tells us, "If I speak with human eloquence and angelic ecstasy but don't love, I'm nothing but the creaking of a rusty gate. If I speak God's Word with power, revealing all his mysteries and making everything plain as day, and if I have faith that says to a mountain, 'Jump,' and it jumps, but I don't love, I'm nothing. If I give everything I own to the poor and even go to the stake to be burned as a martyr, but I don't love, I've gotten nowhere. So, no matter what I say, what I believe, and what I do, I'm bankrupt without love."

Love never gives up.

Love cares more for others than for self.
Love doesn't want what it doesn't have.
Love doesn't strut.
It doesn't have a swelled head.
Love doesn't force itself on others and isn't always "me first."
Love doesn't fly off the handle or keep score of the sins of others.
Love doesn't revel when others grovel.
Love takes pleasure in the flowering of truth; it puts up with anything, and trusts God always.
Love always looks for the best.
It never looks back, but keeps going to the end. Love never dies. (1 Cor. 13:1-8)

As our rose bush grows, life's thorns and hurdles are encountered along the way, yet as grace and mercy are feed by the vine of life and watered with the drawing of the warmth of the SON's love, the fruit of the rose bush is formed. Paul tells us in 2 Corinthians Chapter 12 there were three different times he encountered thorns in his flesh, painful circumstances that on his own, he could not remove. But each time it was God's grace and mercy that allowed forgiveness to override the issue and love to flow freely.

Then suddenly the essence of glory buds opens and releases the sweet fragrance of a new life: Within this life are the ingredients of Love, joy, peace, longsuffering, kindness, goodness, faith, humbleness, and self-control. One Life, One Spirit, One Fruit, One Love, One Rose. When this Rose has released the fullness of its life, it sends a message that says, "Take my body, my petals that have been broken for you. Now you have a part of my love to give away."

Paul continues to tell us that "We don't yet see things clearly. We're squinting in a fog, peering through a mist. But it won't be long before the weather clears and the sun shines bright! We will then see it all as clearly as God sees us, knowing him directly just as he knows us! But for now, until that completeness, we have three things to do to lead us toward that consummation: Trust steadily in God, hope unswervingly, love extravagantly. And the best of the three is love" (1 Cor. 13:12-13).

I close this service with a very familiar song that is often played at funerals. Even though we may be in the midst of struggles and death, the spirit in the song has the ability to release to our spirit God's grace and love. Please listen to the words of Amazing Grace sung by Cecilia to the back drop of the voice of killer whales. I encourage you as you leave to take a petal of love that has been given to you and pass it on to another that needs the hope of unconditional love today.

May God's grace and mercy be the foundation of Light that guides your path.

(While the music played, I went to the two roses and removed the petals placing them in the bowl. I turned to the congregation carrying the bowl in front of me as an offering to them and I walked to the back of the room placing the bowl by the door for the people to take a petal as they left the chapel.)

Music: Traditional, Lyrics: John Newton

Amazing grace! How sweet the sound
That saved a soul like me!
I once was lost, but now am found;
Was blind, but now I see.

'Twas grace that taught my heart to fear,
And grace my fears relieved;
How precious did that grace appear
The hour I first believed.

Through many dangers, toils and snares,
I have already come;
It was grace that brought me safe thus far,
And grace will lead me home.

When the song was over, there was a beautiful moment of silence in the chapel that you could have heard a pin drop. I was the last to leave the chapel. All the rose petals were gone...

We celebrate Passover with the bread and wine, the fragmented body and poured out blood of Jesus Christ that paid the penalty of death because God, our Heavenly Father loves you.

THE PRAYER OF JESUS CHRIST

During one of my many quiet times I was having with Father, He told me to read the prayer that Jesus prayed in John 17. After much meditation on these Scriptures, He then told me to make this prayer my prayer. This opened a whole different realm of understanding my responsibility as a son of God. Afterwards, He told me to share what the Holy Spirit revealed to me. As I was writing I found myself wanting to justify with other Scriptures where this personal implication could be found. Father told me to stop justifying and just to write what His Spirit had revealed. This is wisdom given to those that have ears to hear what the Spirit of God is saying to the sons of God.

John 17:13-26 KJV:

"And now come I (one that is mature in Christ) *to thee* (Father); *and these things I speak* (the power of the word and authority coming from within me that you gave me) *in the world* (ignorance, imagination, and darkness), *that they* (your children) *might have my joy* (manifestation of the fruits of the Holy Spirit) *fulfilled in themselves."*

"I have given them thy word (unconditional love, mercy, forgiveness, and grace); *and the world* (carnal mind) *hath hated them* (natural understanding demands justification), *because they are not of the world* (only God-kind can release the unconditional realm) *even as I* (Son of God) *am not of the world."*

"I pray (intercede) *not that thou* (Father) *shouldest take them* (your children) *out of the world* (separate from ignorance and darkness of a relationship with God as Father), *but that thou* (Father) *shouldest keep them* (anointed

ones, children) *from the evil* (being double-minded with understanding who they are in Christ.)"

"They (mankind) *are not of the world* (antichrist spirit), *even as I* (my life in Christ) *am not of the world* (ignorance to truth)."

"Sanctify (immerse, anoint, cloth) *them through thy truth* (reality that Christ in them is the hope of glory): *thy word* (identifying with the Father's character and nature) *is truth* (as Jesus Christ is, so are we in this world)."

"As thou hast sent me (it was your unconditional love that drew me into understanding that I am your son being equipped to do my Father's business) *into the world* (those that are living in judgment and condemnation), *even so have I* (interceded with unconditional love to all you have brought across my path) *also sent them* (your word will not return void) *into the world* (the ignorance and confusion of who they are)."

"And for their sakes (unity of the body of Christ) *I sanctify* (immerse and cloth holding no man's sins against him) *myself* (Christ identity*) that they also might be sanctified* (walking in Christ identity) *through the truth* (I see all mankind as born again, sanctified, and righteous because I sit in a heavenly place, seeing them as my Father sees them today, even though they may not believe or understand the greatness of His love and mercy that He has bestowed to each person)."

"Neither pray I for these alone (those that have been a direct part of my life), *but for them* (all mankind) *also which shall believe* (every knee will bow and every tongue will confess that Jesus Christ is Lord) *on me* (Christ identity) *through their word* (out of the heart the mouth speaks. Their Christ identity will become real to them.)"

"That they all (mankind) *may be one* (it is the Father's will that no one will perish or else the cross wasn't enough); *as thou, Father, art in me* (I have the DNA of my dad), *and I in thee* (the character and nature*), that they also may be one in us* (come to the understanding of their true identity of being a Christ-One with Jesus as the head of the body): *that the world may*

believe that thou hast sent me (we have the mind of Christ to be the king, lord, and ambassador for the head of the body; Christ Jesus)."

"*And the glory* (sonship) *which thou* (Father) *gavest me* (Christ-One) *I have given them* (there is no condemnation in Christ Jesus. I count no man's sins against him); *that they* (those that are brought across my life) *may be one* (come to the understanding of Christ in you), *even as we are one* (the life I now live in the flesh, I live by the faith of the Son of God.)"

"*I* (Christ-one) *in them* (mankind) *and thou* (identity and character of the Father) *in me* (Christ-one), *that they* (all) *may* (already completed) *be made perfect* (transformed to manifest unconditional love life, and light) *in one* (their true identity in God in one body of Christ); *and that the world* (ignorance and imagination of our natural mind) *may know* (intimacy of covenant exchange) *that thou hast sent me* (Christ-One), *and hast loved them* (unconditionally), *as thou* (Father) *hast loved me* (we are sons of God)."

"*Father, I will* (my identity in you) *that they* (those that are brought across my path) *also, whom thou hast given me, be with me* (heavenly understanding while in the flesh) *where I am* (mind of Christ) *that they may behold my glory* (doing the Father's business with His authority and power as a son of God), *which thou hast given me* (those I am to disciple): *for thou lovedst me* (unconditionally) *before the foundation of the world* (before time; before ignorance and darkness were created by Adam; before I was conceived in my mother's womb)."

"*O righteous Father, the world* (natural understanding) *hath not known thee* (your ways of justice*); but I* (Christ-One) *have known thee* (covenant exchange understanding), *and these* (those you have brought across my path) *have known that thou* (Father) *hast sent me* (I am in this world, but not of it.)"

"*And I* (Christ-One) *have declared unto them thy name* (you are their Father, creator of all), *and will declare it* (manifesting your character and nature); *that the love* (unconditional) *where with thou* (Father) *hast loved me* (you gave your life) *may be in them* (they have your DNA), *and I* (Christ-one) *in them* (together we are one body of Christ with Jesus as the head.)"

May this prayer be heard and understood with the mind of Christ and the wisdom of God.

FATHER'S LOVE LETTER

By Bryan Adams

My Child…

You may not know me, but I know everything about you…Psalm 139:1
I know when you sit down and when you rise up…Psalm 139:2
I am familiar with all your ways…Psalm 139:3
Even the very hairs on your head are numbered…Matthew 10:29-31
For you were made in my image…Genesis 1:27
In me you live and move and have your being…Acts 17:28
For you are my offspring…Acts 17:28
I knew you even before you were conceived…Jeremiah 1:4-5
I chose you when I planned creation…Ephesians 1:11-12
You were not a mistake, for all your days are written in my book…Psalm 139:15-16

I determined the exact time of your birth and where you would live… Acts 17:26

You are fearfully and wonderfully made…Psalm 139:14
I knit you together in your mother's womb…Psalm 139:13
And brought you forth on the day you were born…Psalm 71:6
I have been misrepresented by those who don't know me…John 8:41-44
I am not distant and angry, but am the complete expression of love…1 John 4:16
And it is my desire to lavish my love on you…1 John 3:1
Simply because you are my child and I am your father…1 John 3:1

I offer you more than your earthly father ever could…Matthew 7:11
For I am the perfect father…Matthew 5:48
Every good gift that you receive comes from my hand…James 1:17

For I am your provider and I meet all your needs…Matthew 6:31-33
My plan for your future has always been filled with hope…Jeremiah 29:11
Because I love you with an everlasting love…Jeremiah 31:3
My thoughts toward you are countless as the sand on the seashore…Psalm 139:17-18
And I rejoice over you with singing…Zephaniah 3:17
I will never stop doing good to you…Jeremiah 32:40
For you are my treasured possession…Exodus 19:5
I desire to establish you with all my heart and all my soul…Jeremiah 32:41
And I want to show you great and marvelous things…Jeremiah 33:3
If you seek me with all your heart, you will find me…Deuteronomy 4:29
Delight in me and I will give you the desires of your heart…Psalm 37:4
For it is I who gave you those desires…Philippians 2:13
I am able to do more for you than you could possibly imagine… Ephesians 3:20
For I am your greatest encourager…2 Thessalonians 2:16-17
I am also the Father who comforts you in all your troubles…2 Corinthians 1:3-4
When you are brokenhearted, I am close to you…Psalm 34:18
As a shepherd carries a lamb, I have carried you close to my heart… Isaiah 40:11
One day I will wipe away every tear from your eyes…Revelation 21:3-4
And I'll take away all the pain you have suffered on this earth… Revelation 21:3-4
I am your Father, and I love you even as I love my son, Jesus…John 17:23
For in Jesus, my love for you is revealed…John 17:26
He is the exact representation of my being…Hebrews 1:3
He came to demonstrate that I am for you, not against you…Romans 8:31
And to tell you that I am not counting your sins…2 Corinthians 5:18-19
Jesus died so that you and I could be reconciled…2 Corinthians 5:18-19
His death was the ultimate expression of my love for you…1 John 4:10

I gave up everything I loved that I might gain your love…Romans 8:31-32
If you receive the gift of my son Jesus, you receive me…1 John 2:23
And nothing will ever separate you from my love again…Romans 8:38-39
Come home and I'll throw the biggest party heaven has ever seen…Luke 15:7
I have always been Father, and will always be Father…Ephesians 3:14-15
My question is…Will you be my child?…John 1:12-13
I am waiting for you…Luke 15:11-32

Love,

Your Dad, Almighty God

APPENDIX

IDENTITY IN HIM

TODAY, I AM the righteousness of God in Christ Jesus! 2 Corinthians 5:21

TODAY, I AM Blessed with ALL Spiritual blessings in heavenly places! Ephesians 1:3

TODAY, I AM born again by the word of God! 1 Peter 23:1

TODAY, I AM redeemed by the blood! Ephesians 1:7

TODAY, I AM complete in Jesus! Colossians 2:9-10

TODAY, I AM not a sinner. ALL sin identity has been nailed to the cross! Colossians 2:14

TODAY, I AM sealed with the HOLY SPIRIT! Ephesians 1:13

TODAY, I rule and reign in the name of Jesus! Romans 5:17

TODAY, I AM more than a conqueror! I take dominion! Romans 8:37, Genesis 1:28

TODAY, I AM able to do ALL things through CHRIST who strengthens me! Philippians 4:13

TODAY, I AM strengthened in ALL might by His glorious power! Colossians 1: 9-10

TODAY, I AM able to command the powers of darkness in the name of Jesus! Mark 16:17

TODAY, I AM triumphant in Jesus' name! His word never returns void! I come boldly before the throne of grace receiving unconditional mercy and love. 2 Corinthians 2:14, Isaiah 55:11, Hebrews 4:16

When I know the name of God, I become the duplicate of that name manifesting those attributes and apprehending that character which the name denotes. This signifies the active presence of His glory: And the WORD BECAME FLESH!

SCRIPTURE REFERENCES

The following are Scriptures that will be an encouragement for you to step out of your comfort zone of traditional teachings on Christianity. As I began my research, the word "ALL" began to stand out bringing me to ask the Father, if "all" really meant "ALL." The Holy Spirit challenged me with the question, "How big is your faith to want to believe that "all" really means "ALL"? The extent of your faith is what will determine "ALL" in your life. It was then that the Lord reminded me that, *"I could do ALL things through Christ which strengthened me"* (Philippians 4:13)

These Scriptures have been taken from the King James Version of the Bible. The parenthesis are mine, along with capitalizing the word "ALL" to help you reconsider the way you may have been interpreting our Father's love letters in the past.

"Which was the son of Enos, which was the son of Seth, which was the son of Adam, which was the Son of God." (Luke 3:38)

"In the day that God created man, in the likeness (image) *of God* (himself) *made he him: Male and female* (both Adam) *created he them; and blessed them, and called their name Adam, in the day when they were created."* (Genesis 5:1-2)

"And in thee shall ALL families of the earth be blessed." (Genesis 12:3)

"The Lord is gracious, and full of compassion; slow to anger, and of great mercy. The Lord is good to ALL: and his tender mercies are over ALL his works. ALL thy works shall praise thee, O Lord; and thy saints shall bless thee." (Psalm 145:8-10)

"For since by man came death, by man came also the resurrection of the dead. For as in Adam ALL die, even so in Christ shall ALL be made alive."

(I Corinthians 15:21-22)

"For it is God which worketh in you both to will and to do of his good pleasure." (Philippians 2:13)

"Do ALL things without murmurings and disputing: That ye may be blameless and harmless, the sons of God, without rebuke, in the midst of a crooked and perverse nation, among whom ye shine as lights in the world." (Philippians 2:14-15)

"Let this mind be in you, which was also in Christ Jesus: Who, being in the form of God, thought it not robbery to be equal with God." (Philippians 2:5-6)

"For the Father judgeth no man, but hath committed all judgment unto the Son." (John 5:22)

"Verily, verily, I say unto you, the Son can do nothing of himself, but what he seeth the Father do: for what things so ever he doeth, these also doeth the Son likewise." (John 5:19)

"ALL things were made by him; and without him was not any thing made that was made. In him was life: and the life was the light of men." (John 1:3-4)

"But as many as received him to them gave he power to become the sons of God, even to them that believe on him name." (John 1:12)

"Jesus saith unto them, 'My meat is to do the will of him that sent me, and to finish his work.'" (John 4:34)

"The Lord is not slack concerning his promise, as some men count slackness; but is longsuffering to us-ward, not willing that any should perish, but that ALL should come to repentance." (2 Peter 3:9)

"Not by the works of righteousness which we have done, but according to his mercy he saved us, by the washing of regeneration, and renewing of the Holy Ghost; which he shed on us abundantly through Jesus Christ our Savior; that being justified by his grace, we should be made heirs according to the hope of eternal life." (Titus 3: 5-7)

"Therefore as by the offense of one judgment came upon ALL men to condemnation; even so by the righteousness of one the free gift came upon ALL men unto justification of life." (Romans 5:18)

"There is therefore now no condemnation to them which are in Christ Jesus who walk not after the flesh, but after the Spirit." (Romans 8:1)

"For I am persuaded, that neither death, nor life, nor angels, nor principalities, nor powers, nor things present, nor things to come, nor height, nor depth, nor any other creature, shall be able to separate us from the love of God, which is in Christ Jesus our Lord." (Romans 8:38-39)

"Know ye not that ye are the temple of God, and that the Spirit of God dwelleth in you?" (I Corinthians 3:16)

"Let no man glory in men, For ALL things are yours; whether Paul, or Apollos, or Cephas, or the world, or life, or death, or things present, or things to come; ALL are yours; And ye are Christ's, and Christ is God's." (I Corinthians 3:21-23)

"For by him were ALL things created, that are in heaven, and that are in earth, visible and invisible, whether they be thrones, or dominions, or principalities, or powers: ALL things were created by him, and for him: and he is before ALL things, and by him ALL things consist." (Colossians 1:16-17)

"And hath made of one blood ALL nations of men for to dwell on all the face of the earth, and hath determined the times before appointed, and the abounds of their habitation; that they should seek the Lord, if haply they might feel after him, and find him, though he be not far from every one of us: for in him we live, and move, and have our being; as certain also of your own poets have said, For we are also his offspring." (Acts 17:26-28)

"Therefore if any man be in Christ, he is a new creature: old things are passed away; behold ALL things are become new. And ALL things are of God, who hath reconciled us to himself by Jesus Christ, and hath given to us the ministry of reconciliation." (2 Corinthians 5:17-18)

"I am crucified with Christ: nevertheless I live; yet not I, but Christ liveth in me: and the life which I now live in the flesh I live by the faith of the Son of God, who loved me, and gave himself for me." (Galatians 2:20)

"And if ye be Christ's, then are ye Abraham's seed, and heirs according to the promise." (Galatians 3:29)

"And because ye are sons, God hath sent forth the Spirit of his Son into your hearts, crying Abba, Father." (Galatians 4:6)

"Verily, verily, I say unto you, if a man keeps my saying, he shall never see death." (John 8:51)

"Jesus answered them, 'Is not written in your law, I said ye are gods?'"

(John 10:34)

"Now is the judgment of this world: now shall the prince of this world be cast out. And I if I be lifted up from the earth will draw ALL men unto me. This he said, signifying what death he should die." (John 12:31-33)

"Therefore, leaving the principles of the doctrine of Christ, let us go on unto perfection; laying again the foundation of repentance from dead works, and of faith toward God, of the doctrine of baptisms, and of laying on of hands, and of resurrection of the dead, and of eternal judgment." (Hebrews 6:1-2)

"We know that we have passed from death unto life, because we love the brethren. He that loveth not his brother abideth in death." (1 John 3:14)

"Ye are of God, little children, and have overcome them: because greater is he that is in you, than he that is in the world." (1 John 4:4)

"Beloved, let us love one another: for love is of God; and every one that loveth is born of God, and knoweth God." (1 John 4:7)

"That which was from the beginning, which we have heard, which we have seen with our eyes, which we have looked upon, and our hands have handled, of the Word of life." (1 John 1:1)

"And these things write we unto you, that your joy may be full. This then is the message which we have heard of him, and declare unto you, that God is light, and in him is no darkness at ALL." (1 John 1:4-5)

"Then Jesus said unto them, 'Yet a little while is the light with you. Walk while ye have the light, lest darkness come upon you: for he that walketh in darkness knoweth not whither he goeth. While ye have light, believe in the light, that ye may be the children of light.'" (John 12:35-36)

"Ye have not chosen me, but I have chosen you, and ordained you, that ye should go and bring forth fruit, and that your fruit should remain: that whatsoever ye shall ask of the Father in my name, he may give it you."

(John 15:16)

"Ye are the light of the world. A city that is set on a hill cannot be hid. Let your light so shine before men, that they may see your good works, and glorify your Father which is in heaven." (Matthew 5:14, 16)

"Blessed are the pure in heart: for they shall see God. Blessed are the peacemakers: for they shall be called the children of God." (Matthew 5:8-9)

"Be careful for nothing, but in every thing by prayer and supplication with thanksgiving let your requests by made known unto God. And the peace of

God, which passeth all understanding, shall keep your hearts and minds through Christ Jesus. Finally, brethren, whatsoever things are true, whatsoever things are honest, whatsoever things are just, whatsoever things are pure, whatsoever things are lovely, whatsoever thing are of good report; if there be any virtue, and if there be any praise, think on these things." (Philippians 3:6-8)

"Rejoice in the Lord always; and again I say, Rejoice." (Philippians 3:4)

"As he is, so are we in this world." (1 John 4:17)

READING RESOURCES

Allen, J.H., *Judah's Sceptre and Joseph's Birthright*, (Destiny Publishers, Mass., 1917).

Arno, Richard and Phyllis, *Creation Therapy*, (Sarasota Academy of Christian Counseling, Florida, 2012).

Benner, Jeff A., *The Ancient Hebrew Language and Alphabet*, (Virtualbookworm Publishing, 2004).

Blosser, Don, Timothy J. Dailey, Randy Petersen, Dietrich Gruen, *Jesus His Life and Times*, (Publications International, Ltd, Illinois, 1999).

Connolly, Peter, *The Holy Land*, (Oxford University Press, Oxford, 1994).

Cooke, Graham, *Radical Perceptions*, (Brilliant BookHouse, California, 2011).

Daniels, Will, *Understanding the Oneness of God* (WestBow Press, Indiana 2014).

Drummonds, Bishop A., *Bringing Forth the Sons of God*, (Iuniverse, NE, 2004).

Drummonds, Bishop A., *God's Redemption for All*, (Iuniverse, NY, 2007).

Grunfeld, Dayan Dr., *The Sabbath*, (Feldheim Publishers, Jerusalem, 2014).

Huch, Larry, *The Torah Blessing*, (Whitaker House, PA, 2009).

Hurnard, Hannah, *Hinds' Feet on High Places Devotional*, (Destiny Image, PA., 2013).

Johnson, Bill, *When Heaven Invades Earth*, (Destiny Image, PA, 2003).

Johnston, Robert D., *Numbers in the Bible*, (Kregel Publications, Michigan, 1990).

Kenyon, E.W., *The Blood Covenant*, (Kenyon's Gospel Publishing Society, USA, 2012).

Mason, Phil, *Quantum Glory*, XPpublishing, Arizona, 2010).

Messer, Rabbi Ralph, *Torah: Law or Grace?* (Simchat Torah Beit Midrash, Colorado, 2012).

Nee, Watchman, *Song of Songs*, (CLC Publications, Penn. 2009).

Packer, J.I., Merrill Tenney, William White, *Nelson's Illustrated Encyclopedia of Bible Facts*, (Thomas Nelson Publishers, Nashville, 1995).

Russell, A.J., *God Calling*, (Barbour and Co., New Jersey, 1985).

Stern, David, *Complete Jewish Bible*, (Jewish New Testament Publications, Inc., Maryland, 1998).

Wootten, Batya Ruth, Redeemed Israel, (Keys of David Publishing, Florida, 2006).

Vallotton, Kris, *Developing a Supernatural Lifestyle*, (Destiny Image, PA., 2007).

Zucker, David J., *The Torah*, (Paulist Press, New Jersey, 2005).

Printed in the United States
by Baker & Taylor Publisher Services